The Dissolution of Character in Late Romanticism, 1820–1839

Edinburgh Critical Studies in Romanticism
Series Editors: Ian Duncan and Penny Fielding

Available Titles
A Feminine Enlightenment: British Women Writers and the Philosophy of Progress, 1759–1820
JoEllen DeLucia
Reinventing Liberty: Nation, Commerce and the Historical Novel from Walpole to Scott
Fiona Price
The Politics of Romanticism: The Social Contract and Literature
Zoe Beenstock
Radical Romantics: Prophets, Pirates, and the Space Beyond Nation
Talissa J. Ford
Literature and Medicine in the Nineteenth-Century Periodical Press: Blackwood's Edinburgh Magazine, *1817–1858*
Megan Coyer
Discovering the Footsteps of Time: Geological Travel Writing in Scotland, 1700–1820
Tom Furniss
The Dissolution of Character in Late Romanticism, 1820–1839
Jonas Cope

Forthcoming Titles
Peterloo and the Violence of Romanticism: Reflections on the Bicentenary of the 1819 Massacre of Reformers in Manchester
Michael Demson and Regina Hewitt
Dialectics of Improvement: Scottish Romanticism, 1786–1829
Gerard Lee McKeever

Visit our website at: www.edinburghuniversitypress.com/series/ecsr

The Dissolution of Character in Late Romanticism, 1820–1839

Jonas Cope

EDINBURGH
University Press

Edinburgh University Press is one of the leading university presses in the UK. We publish academic books and journals in our selected subject areas across the humanities and social sciences, combining cutting-edge scholarship with high editorial and production values to produce academic works of lasting importance. For more information visit our website: edinburghuniversitypress.com

© Jonas Cope, 2018

Edinburgh University Press Ltd
The Tun – Holyrood Road,
12(2f) Jackson's Entry,
Edinburgh EH8 8PJ

Typeset in 11/14 Adobe Sabon by
IDSUK (DataConnection) Ltd

A CIP record for this book is available from the British Library

ISBN 978 1 4744 2130 0 (hardback)
ISBN 978 1 4744 2131 7 (webready PDF)
ISBN 978 1 4744 2132 4 (epub)

The right of Jonas Cope to be identifiedastheauthorofthisworkhasbeen asserted in accordance with the Copyright, Designs and Patents Act 1988, and the Copyright and Related Rights Regulations 2003 (SI No. 2498).

Contents

Acknowledgements	vi
Introduction	1
1. The Reform Era: An Ethological Age	27
2. From Person to Text: Character and the Problem of Representation	56
3. Representing Representation: Walter Scott and Charles Lamb	73
4. The Politics of Unity: Hazlitt and Character Revisited	89
5. 'The Loved Abortion of a Thing Designed': Hartley Coleridge and the Drive for Dissolution	117
6. 'A Series of Small Inconstancies': Letitia Landon and the Politics of Consistency	143
7. Character and Paranoia in Beddoes' *Death's Jest-Book* and Peacock's *Crotchet Castle*	171
Afterword: Meta-characterisation – Dickens' *Sketches by Boz* and Carlyle's *Sartor Resartus*	193
Bibliography	213
Index	231

Acknowledgements

I would like to thank the faculty of the Department of English at the University of Missouri-Columbia for granting me several awards that enabled me to complete this project. I am also grateful to Stephen Behrendt, Devoney Looser, Ray Marks and Nancy West for generously providing me with advice and information. Ian Duncan and Penny Fielding, the Series Editors for the Edinburgh Critical Studies in Romanticism series at Edinburgh University Press, have been extremely helpful and encouraging throughout the entire editing process. Thanks as well to Michelle Houston and Adela Rauchova at EUP, who have made the production process as painless as possible. Finally, thanks to the anonymous readers of my manuscript, solicited by the Series Editors, who suggested a host of important critical studies with which to expand the theoretical foundations of this project.

I am grateful to the Trustees of Boston University for allowing me to reprint a version of Chapter 6 originally published in *Studies in Romanticism*. I am also grateful to the Trustees of the British Museum for permission to reprint the image in Chapter 6.

My greatest thanks goes to my colleague and friend, once my mentor, Noah Heringman. At every stage of my doctoral and postdoctoral education he has provided, and continues to provide, timely, invaluable advice and encouragement. I owe more to Noah than I am aware of, or can express.

To Noah Heringman,

Mentor of mentors

Introduction

> I often feel, and ever more deeply realize, that fate and character are the same conception.
>
> Novalis, *Heinrich von Ofterdingen* (1802)[1]

> Knowable man (soul, individuality, consciousness, conduct, whatever it is called) is the object-effect of . . . analytical investment.
>
> Michel Foucault, *Discipline and Punish* (1975)[2]

Character: Critical Contexts

In the first edition of his *Enquiry concerning Political Justice* (1793), William Godwin says the following about character:

> The idea correspondent to the term character inevitably includes in it the assumption of necessary connexion. The character of any man is the result of a long series of impressions communicated to his mind, and modifying it in a certain manner, so as to enable us, from a number of these modifications and impressions being given, to predict his conduct. Hence arise his temper and habits, respecting which we reasonably conclude, that they will not be abruptly superseded and reversed; and that, if they ever be reversed, it will not be accidentally, but in consequence of some strong reason persuading, or some extraordinary event modifying his mind. If there were not this original and essential connexion between motives and actions, and, which forms one particular branch of this principle, between men's past and future actions, there could be no such thing as character, or as a ground of inference enabling us to predict what men would be from what they have been.[3]

The sense of this passage is at once obvious and not so obvious. It is obvious if you believe that most people think and behave in predictable ways. I cannot always predict exactly what a given person will say or do under a particular set of circumstances, but I will usually approximate the truth if I have enough information about that person and the circumstances involved. David Hume (whose arguments about character Godwin seems to condense here) had maintained more or less the same position in his *Treatise of Human Nature* (1738–40), *Enquiry concerning Human Understanding* (1748) and other, minor essays in between, such as 'The Sceptic' (1742). And yet the passage above is not as perfect a piece of late Enlightenment confidence as it initially seems. Godwin doesn't begin by clarifying the actual 'idea correspondent to the term character', but by telling us about another idea – 'necessary connexion' – that the idea of character 'inevitably includes'. By 'necessary connexion', Godwin means that character is the end product or 'result of a long series of impressions communicated' to the 'mind' in a necessitarian chain. It is, of course, difficult to say precisely when character becomes an actual 'result' – when its formation or development is complete – but this probably happens, as was thought, at some point in childhood. After its maturation, character can begin to direct the very mind whose early impressions gave rise to it. From the matured character, in turn, come 'temper and habits', which never change in any lifetime except by extraordinary occurrences: not so much 'breaks' in the chain of Necessity, as one or more sudden and unpredictable series of links in that chain.

At first Godwin calls character a 'result'. Afterward he calls it a 'ground of inference'. The idea of character seems to exist like the idea of cause exists in the philosophy of Hume: as something we must posit but, per Hume, can't rationally justify or empirically verify. Godwin's claims about character may make intuitive and rational sense to modern readers, and perhaps they would have made sense to most late eighteenth-century British novelists and philosophers. But the fact is that Godwin identifies character only in its relation to other things: it is a 'result', a 'ground of inference'. What it is in and of itself is left opaque – perhaps because, like all such mental 'principle[s]', it has to be. The point is that, if on one level the passage seems quite sure of itself, on another it seems a little uncertain as to how or in what precise language to reveal the obvious. But *is* character obvious, and does this passage suggest as much? Does it make the most sense as a metaphysical or physiological or moral given? as a construct? as a principle, based on persons, fundamental to the structure of dramatic or narrative texts? as a principle, based on dramatic or narrative texts, fundamental to the structure of persons? Is everyone equally fortunate to 'possess' it under similar circumstances? Can its quite different meanings ever be manageably distinct in discourse? Might an investigation of character, and/or the concepts conventionally associated with it, preoccupy a given text even when they are not its nominal subjects? These are some of the important questions that I suggest drive a good deal of cultural production in Britain in the 1820s and 1830s – a period I will refer to from this point on as the 'reform era'.

This book synthesises two areas of recent scholarly interest: the study of dramatic/narrative character and the study of post-Waterloo literature and culture in Britain (*c.* 1815–40). Each of these fields has received increasing critical attention over the past twenty years, and I hope to show that this may not be a coincidence. Cultural production in the decades after Waterloo is deeply invested in character. Prose 'portraits' or 'sketches' of individuals (real or fictional, famous or obscure) that flourish in the 'magazine age' with the decline in the market value of poetry; 'ethological' debates in periodicals on the nature, formation and knowability of personal character that popularise philosophical enquiries written in the British empirical tradition; new human sciences like phrenology and sociology; conflicting accounts within scientific communities about the unity and 'organisation' of organisms: all such discourses attempting to document, regulate, totalise the concept of character create a space for a hermeneutic of suspicion that invites an openness to and interest in modes of 'characterlessness'. Operating within this space is a range of contemporary texts – familiar essays, auto/biographies, poems, 'poetical illustrations', engravings, annuals, novels of manners, fashionable novels, novels of ideas, closet dramas, 'sketches' of London life and unclassifiable hybrids like Thomas Carlyle's *Sartor Resartus* (1833–4) – that wrestle with character on a conceptual level. These texts tend to assume the truth of conventional, 'commonsensical' ideas about character even as they ironise these ideas: for instance, the idea that character is a reliable or knowable psychological determinant, that it is a commendable 'possession' (good reputation, proven integrity), that it is a thing representable in print, that it is an object of 'useful knowledge' and so on. Far from always granting character as a first principle (as Godwin's *Political Justice* does) or a stable frame of reference, these texts register its dialectical suspension somewhere between a powerful, psychosomatic reality (the epigraph from Novalis) and language (the epigraph from Foucault). Broadly speaking, the concept of character circulates prolifically in the literary-moral economy of the reform era until it is reified as something that writers, at one and the same time, both see and see through.

To make the argument as succinct as possible: the authors studied in this book tend to destabilise the concept of character within the moral, scientific and epistemological frameworks available to them (frameworks that sometimes seem similar to our own). In some cases, their time is spent defining and redefining the term, interpreting and reinterpreting it. In others, they explore, directly or indirectly, the often unsettling personal and literary implications of the concept however it is understood and used.

The major critical work done on character since the 1990s studies it as eighteenth- and nineteenth-century audiences imagined it to exist in print (primarily the novel) or on stage. David Brewer observes that the 'recent work in character . . . take[s] seriously the apparent desire of many readers to imagine characters in full possession of a deep interiority and a life which exists off-page'. Although he admits that 'this is still very much an emerging field' without a firm critical 'consensus', he also acknowledges that all the relevant scholarship 'focus[es] upon what characters allowed readers and viewers to do, rather than upon what those characters might mean in and of themselves'.[4] Catherine Gallagher, for instance, claims that early modern readers (largely women) were happy to appropriate the emotions of fictional characters precisely because fictional characters had no bodies, no 'referent[s] in the material world': assuming fictional emotions helped prepare women to operate in a culture of speculation.[5] Deidre Lynch traces changing modalities of characterisation across the eighteenth and nineteenth centuries in relation to contemporary reading practices. According to Lynch, eighteenth-century authors tended to 'link . . . person[s] "in" a text to the printed letters . . . that elaborated the text's surface'. The personhood of a fictional character was thus inseparable from the 'articulate surfaces and . . . verbal signs that made it public knowledge'. It was only in the Romantic era that a character, say, in a novel became 'more than the sum of its parts', 'exceed[ing] the requirements of the plot'.[6] The Romantic-era literary character started to live beyond the text, became round, autonomous, mysterious. For Lynch, this happened not because novels finally caught up with the 'rise of individualism' (Ian Watt's famous claim), but because a new literary market and mass readership inspired careful, more discriminating ways of reading. Round characters were now in demand by readers who wanted to refine, nuance, subtilise their reading practices and so distinguish themselves from an increasing population of readers with less cultivated 'sensibilities'. If a character like Elinor Dashwood seemed superficially polite, reticent, illegible, this was all the more reason for a discerning reader to study Elinor more closely, to read between the lines, to advance triumphantly toward the hidden depth beneath the textual surface: a depth ever receding and ultimately 'unsoundable', but worthy nonetheless of endless interpretations.

Lynch has set the stage for subsequent critics interested in the relationship between fictional characters and their audiences. Lisa Freeman and David Brewer both focus on eighteenth- and nineteenth-century audiences. Freeman contrasts two major 'paradigm[s] for representing identity' in the eighteenth century: novelistic and dramatic. Novels 'appear[ed] to render the inner depths, the conscious and even unconscious motives and thoughts of characters' under the guise of transparency. They 'produce[d] the illusion of continuity of self' and 'of access to other subjects', 'whose value could be assessed, authenticated, fixed, and appropriated ... as the property of readers'. Eighteenth-century drama, on the other hand, 'registered a kind of resistance to and critique of the illusion of transparency and plenitude that the novel offered in "the subject"'. Plays were events that were frequently interrupted. Rambunctious audience members distracted the rest of the playgoers. Actors were often celebrities whose personal notoriety interfered with their full absorption into their roles. All of this means, for Freeman, that plays had little interest in 'depth in characterization' or 'the persistence ... of individual consciousness across time'. Instead, dramas flaunted their mediation of the 'real', their 'technical virtuosity', whereas the realist novel did its best to hide the contrivances that made verisimilitude possible.[7] Brewer, like Gallagher, Lynch and Freeman, is also interested in how audiences interacted with and responded to fictional characters. He coins the term 'imaginative expansion' to refer to 'an array of reading practices in eighteenth-century Britain by which the characters in broadly successful texts were treated as if they were both fundamentally incomplete and the common property of all'.

Devoted readers, Brewer claims, went on to invent 'further adventures' for beloved characters beyond their originary texts. Appropriating the 'textual commons' in this way was a sort of community-building exercise: readers could 'imagine characters' as 'common object[s] to rally around', and 'themselves as part of a public, a virtual community interested in the same things'.[8]

In the past several years, critical examination of character has expanded its boundaries. It is not as firmly situated in a particular time period or culture, and its field of inquiry has increased beyond the confines of dramatic and narrative fiction. Susan Manning has recently argued that 'character was at the nexus of Enlightenment epistemology, ethics, pedagogy and understanding of social relations'. It functioned as an integrity to be 'owned', a 'style' performable in print, a device to elicit the sympathetic engagement of reading audiences, an ethical 'rationale for consistent conduct', a 'guarantor of "credit"' in the world of 'market exchange', a source of 'contagion' and, above all, a rhetorical figure that 'emerges in combinations and in relationships, rather than emanating from a unique locality, climate or moment in time'.[9] John Frow has also stressed the social and discursive functions of character, but with special emphasis on its 'interpellating' tendencies: character for Frow is 'not a substance but the literary or dramatic or filmic instance of an operation within a social assemblage, by means of which the reader is inscribed into the terms of a particular formation of personhood'.[10]

Although diverse, all these studies examine how eighteenth- and nineteenth-century audiences were affected by fictional characters emotionally and ideologically. But there is still no real consensus as to how or to what extent these audiences appreciated the radical instability of character as a concept, both within and apart from textual-dramatic representation. Freeman approaches this question. She observes that '[o]n both representational and etymological levels, character was too protean to hold a stable value', and that authors like Henry Fielding were all too conscious of this fact: in one of his essays, Fielding seems almost aware that character could not be 'enlist[ed] . . . as the conceptual basis for modeling *coherent* identities in the eighteenth century', since 'the concept of character raised the frightening possibility either that there was no true "inside" or that if there were, we have no "real" access to it'.[11] Lynch, aware herself that '[l]iterary character has no essence', ascribes no such awareness to nineteenth-century novel-readers. Indeed, if, as Lynch claims, Austen's readers spent so much time cultivating a 'refined receptiveness' to literary characters, it must be because they believed deeply in the 'individualized interiority' of these characters. Without an ostensible ontological object to interpret, that is, they would not bother to read painstakingly to find it. Changing reading practices, for Lynch, may have '*produc[ed]* the depth that needs explicating and with it the textual effects that signal the psychological real' – but how complicit in this process were the readers themselves who sought that 'real'?[12] To broaden the question and rephrase it in terms of texts: how and under what historical conditions did certain texts – fictional and nonfictional – register not only the slippery signification of 'character', but also the implications of that slipperiness within and beyond representative practices?

The answer to this question – the essential question of this book – requires some account of the salient historical conditions of reform-era Britain. For whatever reason, the *terminus ad quem* of recent character studies is around the early 1820s: Lynch and Freeman focus mainly on the eighteenth century (though Lynch devotes a long chapter to Austen); Gallagher and Brewer end their studies respectively in 1820 and 1825. Perhaps this has to do with the slow process of unlearning old stories told about post-Napoleonic British literature and culture. The scholarly consensus around the late twentieth century was more or less that 'the 1820s and 1830s seem an embarrassment to the historian of English literature'. Writers of the period, it was argued, produced what Virgil Nemoianu has termed a 'lower romanticism', relying on 'other sources and on rewriting'.[13] Several critics reinforced Nemoianu's position, including Herbert Tucker, Daniel Riess and Jerome McGann. But in labelling reform-era literature variously as vulgar, domesticated and commodified, they have run the risk (however unintentionally) of rationalising the neglect of the period in their very attempts to recover its literature.[14] This critical perspective, though now somewhat dated, is probably still responsible for why many of us continue to think of the period as an unspectacular transition between the Romantic and Victorian eras – if we think of it at all. Exclusive attention to the 1820s and 1830s, in fact, is a relatively recent phenomenon: only in the 'past twenty years' has there been a 'renewed interdisciplinary interest' in what one critic calls the 'post-Napoleonic period'.[15] Much of this interest has to do with the generic experiments and formal variety of reform-era writing, as well as with the dynamic role played by literary texts in the context of parliamentary reform.

Edward Copeland describes the period in Britain between 1820 and 1837 as the 'second half of the "long" Regency'. Victoria ascends the throne in 1837, and 1841 marks 'the defeat of Lord Melbourne's post-Reform Whig government'. It was a time 'in which Britain came closest to violent revolution since the seventeenth century'. Between 1815 and 1819 there was the institution of the Corn Laws, a resurgence of working-class radicalism (though of a kind different from that of the 1790s), a new wave of repressive legislation and the Peterloo Massacre. Afterwards came the 1825 market crash, the fracturing of the Tory party in 1827 over the Catholic question, the repeal of the Test and Corporation Acts in 1829 and the dissolution of the Wellington administration in 1830 after 'almost half a century' of Tory rule.[16] There were also the 1830 Swing Riots, precipitated by 'inadequate harvests', 'unemployment and low wages'.[17] The most important political event during these decades was the 1832 Reform Act, which increased 'the proportion of adult males entitled to vote in Parliamentary elections' from 'roughly 5 to roughly 10 per cent', 'produced intensive divisiveness at all levels of British politics' and led eventually to the Chartist movement.[18] The world of print was also in a state of flux. Richard Cronin identifies three features that 'dominated publishing in the post-war decade': the 'literary magazine', the 'extraordinary celebrity of Lord Byron' and the series of novels by 'the Author of Waverley that . . . outsold the work of all other novelists put together'.[19] Cronin's brief list suggests (by what it leaves out) a topic discussed in all analyses of postwar British literary culture: the abrupt decline in the market value of poetry.

The popular consumption of poetry underwent a sea-change in the 1820s and 1830s for a number of interrelated reasons. Lee Erickson has argued that the high cost of paper after the French Revolution and during the Coalition and Napoleonic Wars encouraged the production of verse manuscripts: bookmaking at that time was expensive, and relatively slim volumes of 'concentrated language' were preferred over 'diffusive' volumes of prose. For this reason, poetry experienced a 'boom during the first two decades of the nineteenth century'. But then by 1830 things had changed: 'almost all publishers refused to publish' manuscript volumes of poems. The Fourdrinier papermaking machine, stereotyping and the power press had increased the 'economic demand for discursive prose', such as Henry Colburn's 'energetically marketed' fashionable novels.[20] Verse manuscripts also had to start competing with the increasing popularity of periodicals. If poems were to make their way anywhere into print, it was probably into magazines.

In fact, literary culture in reform-era Britain was practically synonymous with the periodical. The founding of *Blackwood's Edinburgh Magazine* in 1817 seemed to usher in a 'new age', along with a host of important competitors: *The Literary Gazette* (1817), the *Westminster Review* (1824), *The Athenaeum* (1828), *Fraser's Magazine* (1832), *The Metropolitan* (1832), *Bentley's Miscellany* (1836) and others.[21] '[I]ncreasingly', as Mark Parker has observed, 'periodicals themselves were literature'. Original essays, 'such as those of Elia, the Opium-Eater, and the author of Table-Talk', enabled periodicals to 'dominat[e] the literary market . . . in the 1820s'.[22] As both 'arbiters of . . . taste' and 'purveyors of scientific, economic and social information', magazines formed a 'repository of "public opinion"', 'shap[ing] the ideological consciousness of their middle-class readers'.[23] Cronin even suggests that writers like Pierce Egan, Thomas Love Peacock and Lord Byron consciously aspired to produce magazine-like art, imitating the topical and structural miscellaneousness of magazines in their poems and prose.[24] Single-author contributions in periodicals were mostly written anonymously or under a pseudonym. Others were the work of multiple hands. *Blackwood's*, as is well known, regularly featured a heady variety of textual voices: correspondents (real or imaginary), alter egos of the editorial staff, 'corporate' identities like Christopher North, characters based on real persons – often authors (dead or alive) – characters pulled from fictional texts and so on: a wide cast, indeed, of 'slippery ontologies'.[25]

Character and Its Dissolution in the Reform Era

The first thing I want to note about my interest in character is that it is not the same as (though it is obviously related to) an interest in identity or subjectivity.[26] Although any attempt to differentiate these terms strictly is problematic and invokes centuries of debate, I have found a few definitions helpful. In his *Hume's Philosophy of the Self* (2002), A. E. Pitson distinguishes between 'personal identity' and 'character identity'. Personal identity is 'the identity I may ascribe to myself as a person over time notwithstanding the many changes I undergo'. Character identity is 'my sense of what makes me the person I am which arises from reflecting on the various traits which go to make up my character at different times'.[27] Marya Schechtman more or less agrees with this differential: she associates identity with 'what makes a person at time t_2 the same person at time t_1', and character with the 'beliefs, values, desires, and other psychological features [that] make someone the person she is'.[28] For the purposes of this book, I will (loosely) define identity in light of these formulations: as 'a consciousness of self as the being to whom sensation is referred'.[29] I will use 'character' in both its constitutive and its moral senses (each is described and historicised at more length in Chapter 1). In its constitutive sense, the term refers to 'traits', 'psychological features' and the like. In its moral sense, it refers to the extent to which a person maintains and/or regulates his or her desires, principles and responsibilities over time, resisting 'temptations to swerve and change' by means of sympathy and self-control.[30] A strong or 'decided' (a beloved reform-era word) moral character implies a lasting consciousness of and commitment to where one 'stands'.[31] One main reason I focus on 'character' and not 'identity' is that reform-era thinkers were focusing on it. According to Felicity Nussbaum, 'competing discourses of identity are redundantly in evidence from the end of the seventeenth century until they wear themselves out with repetition by the 1790s'.[32] In the 1820s and 1830s, on the other hand, metaphysical debates on identity merge with a burgeoning public discussion of textual/personal character, whose 'meaning ... and ... bearing on individual and social life preoccupied many people in the nineteenth century as it did in the eighteenth'.[33]

That the characters of persons, nations and 'types' could all be ascertained and their behaviours predicted were not truths universally acknowledged and acceptable in reform-era Britain. Nor was a nominalist scepticism about 'character' specific to this period. The word may be said to have acquired its peculiar semiological complexity in the eighteenth century. Freeman observes that in the seventeenth century 'character' 'carried primarily literal denotations'. It designated a 'preexisting', 'arbitrary', 'one-to-one correspondence between ... signifier and signified'. The Theophrastan 'characters' (character sketches) that flourished in the seventeenth century accordingly used concrete language that corresponded straightforwardly to the general 'types' evoked. It was not until the eighteenth century that the close relationship between signifier and signified, verbal portrait and designated type, began to be 'cleaved apart'. The 'outside of a "character" no longer bore any necessary or meaningful resemblance to its inside'. Eighteenth-century actors, according to Freeman, began to call attention to the fact that they were reproducing the signs of psychological realities that didn't exist.[34] Frow describes the etymological 'trajectory' of character as having moved from more to less concrete: from the instrument that makes an impression, like a letter on a page or an image on a coin; to the impression made; to a 'spoken or written style'; to 'a distinctive set of moral qualities'; and eventually to a distinct personality. All of these meanings were suddenly at play for the first time in the eighteenth century. The sense of character 'as a letter of the alphabet or as the repeatable and combinable unit of printer's type' also 'carrie[d] through' to its sense as 'something imprinted on the features ... suggesting the external, physiognomic traits of an inwardly figured personality'.[35]

The point is that 'character' was already 'too protean to hold a stable value' in the eighteenth century. But I would suggest that the conceptual instability of the term was more widely, variously and popularly registered in the 1820s and 1830s than beforehand. Some writers were increasingly sceptical about the concept as others took it more for granted. Character began to circulate as a concept whose ready appropriation in new print media and new scientific disciplines was strangely at odds with its unreliability as a holder of value. The familiar position that, for instance, 'personal' character was a single, inherent, active principle readable in bodies and directing individual behaviours (a 'bias') was defamiliarised, reimagined, reworked in a culture of 'unprecedented tendencies towards diversity and fragmentation'.[36]

One important effect of the period's 'unprecedented tendencies toward diversity and fragmentation' was the relatively arbitrary mode of organising knowledge promoted by encyclopaedias. The 'encyclopedic spirit' of the reform era insisted that it was 'possible to classify the world ... in discrete parts' without recourse to an organised, hierarchical system of knowledge as in the days of the *Encyclopédie*.[37] Coleridge, Peacock and Hazlitt all lamented at various points that Scottish encyclopaedists and intellectuals were cultivating 'centerless', encyclopaedic minds: minds comprised of miscellaneously arranged information, loose collections of facts, mental 'entries' liable to turn into 'crotchets' as if without rhyme or reason.

An 'encyclopedic' mind was thought to be 'fragmented' in that its sum of knowledge was not arranged according to a unifying, hierarchising principle. Around the same time, too, the phrenological head was being considered an amalgam of separately functioning parts. Phrenological science as popularised in Britain in the 1820s challenged the notion (to Hazlitt's dismay) that a 'common centre of communication' in the brain was responsible for regulating its various 'parts'.[38] In his *System of Phrenology* (1824), in fact, George Combe argues quite the opposite: that the mind is decidedly not a 'simple and indivisible substance' but 'an aggregate of separate powers'.[39] Phrenology 'quantified' 'human experience' and 'forced [it] into logical categories in the phrenological head' – a head whose 'interior' resembled a 'factory' operating according to a 'division of labor'. Even 'character itself' could be divided into mechanised units, 'reduced to digits on a graft'.[40] According to phrenologists (as one sceptical correspondent writes for *The Newcastle Magazine* [1824]), '[t]he present [that is, Lockean] mode of philosophizing is imperfect, because it pursues its investigations only through the medium of consciousness'. The phrenologists, this writer complains, disregard 'the office of the mind, "the monad"; all [its] labour is performed without her assistance, and the only use which she can be conceived of is, to appropriate and spiritualize the materials gained by the several organs'.[41] In the process of compartmentalising the mind, moreover, the phrenologists claim to have solved the mysteries of 'character':

> The very basis of this novel scheme is laid in the knowledge of human character ... the whole system supposes that it is easy to penetrate the secrets of the soul. Now this we can have no hesitation in denying ... even under the most favourable circumstances, to acquire a just acquaintance with the character of an individual is a task of no ordinary labour ... Is it by interrogating the individuals themselves that we can expect to gain a knowledge of their character? Is it by trusting to the inaccurate and prejudiced narratives of friends? Is it by one particular act, committed, it may be, under very peculiar circumstances, that we are to determine the nature of the general associations or the ruling disposition of the individual? Is it possible, in fine, for any man, let his industry be what it may, accurately to estimate motives, as it were, by wholesale, and, journeying from country to country, penetrate, as by a certain natural tact, the secret recesses of the human heart?[42]

It is, I think, somewhat difficult 'accurately to estimate [the] motives' of this writer. Does he or she mostly want to preserve or protect the 'secrets of the soul', the 'secret recesses of the human heart', from invasive new theories? Is he or she more concerned to prevent the spread of scientific inaccuracies? Are these two motives related? How? Such questions are hard to answer but important nonetheless. On the one hand, the author assumes that 'character' is quite real but will ultimately elude the phrenologists. Their ideas are simply too overreaching for so subtle and complicated a principle. Especially problematic is their unwillingness to start with 'consciousness' as a first (mind-unifying) principle. On the other hand, the passage hints at an anxiety that there may be no discoverable 'secrets' hidden away in the 'soul' after all, or in the 'character', or 'heart', or whatever else one calls it (does the monster in *Frankenstein* possess such secrets, or a character?). Perhaps the conventional notion of the 'ruling disposition', the veritable first principle of the Theophrastan tradition, is as elusive as it seems because, as an 'object-effect of . . . analytical investment', a ruling disposition has no verifiable or reliable existence outside discourse. Or if there is such a thing as a ruling disposition, as character (or if something exists that approximates what we imagine we know about either one), it may be in one's best interests to try to render it as unobservable, as inviolable, as ostensibly nonexistent as possible.

In light of the advent of phrenology, it may have been no coincidence that literary magazines like *Blackwood's*, *The London Magazine* and *The New Monthly Magazine* were sometimes 'distinguished from other periodicals by their miscellaneous character', their 'disunity of mind'. Cronin remarks that magazines 'had always been miscellaneous', but that by the 1820s they were positively 'volatile'.[43] Like contemporary encyclopaedias arranged alphabetically instead of according to a unified, hierarchical system of knowledge, magazines 'abandoned the notion that knowledge was contained within a single intellectual structure, for a notion that it was divided between a large number of distinct disciplines'.[44] Thomas De Quincey, in an article written for the December 1821 issue of *The London Magazine*, actually praises the *London* for its disunity: the magazine, he writes, seems to operate by disparate '[s]ingular faculties' as opposed to the 'one presiding mind' that governs great reviews like the *Edinburgh* and the *Quarterly*, 'studiously impressing its own stamp upon the whole body of the articles'.[45] Hazlitt has the opposite reaction to the *London*. In an 1823 article for the

Edinburgh Review, Hazlitt argues that, after the death of its editor John Scott in 1821, the *London* became less directed, regulated, focused: it

> wants a sufficient unity of direction and purpose . . . There is no particular bias or governing spirit, – which neutralizes the interest. The articles seem thrown into the letter-box, and to come up like blanks or prizes in the lottery – all is in a confused, unconcocted state.[46]

If De Quincey appreciates the play of 'singular faculties' in the *London*, Hazlitt suggests that its lack of any 'bias' or 'governing spirit' actually 'neutralizes' readers' 'interest' in the content. In fact, Hazlitt has the same problem with magazines like the *London* that he has with phrenology. Like the all too miscellaneous magazine, the phrenological head operates according to a division of labour, which Hazlitt finds anathema to the laws of association and common sense (many disparate contributors produce the one; many disparate faculties regulate the other). In several of his essays on 'character' he insists (as I describe in Chapter 4) on the inalienable and irreducible 'bias' of 'character' in persons and in art-objects, the concealment or apparent absence of which represents a kind of moral-aesthetic perversity. Most living and nonliving entities, for Hazlitt, need a 'bias': literary characters, personal characters, Elgin marbles, texts, minds, periodicals. He thinks that entities reach their full potential as all obstacles to the flourishing, the realisation of this bias are removed or surmounted. The larger point here is that the human mind began to be associated in a relatively short period of time with encyclopaedias, factories and magazines, so that it became increasingly possible to view both the mind, and the character that supposedly informs or directs it, as 'fragmented . . . arbitrary and decontextualized'.[47]

Yet the perceived threat or welcome pluralism of the fragmented mind/character is, I think, no more important than the general amount of energy invested during this period in hardening ethological categories and theories – to whatever end (character is simple and immutable, character is complex and adaptable, character is performative). Many articles in periodicals, drawing on emerging intellectual trends, emphasise that true moral freedom and civic responsibility are impossible without an informed, systematic knowledge of what character is and how it operates. And yet other texts challenge the grand narratives on which such popular ethologies, or sciences of character, are based. For instance, whether character was said to be situated mostly in the slow unfolding of some congenital bias (Hazlitt); in the interplay of external forces (Robert Owen); in the character of a nation (Harriet Martineau); in the material organisation of the organism (William Lawrence, John Elliotson and T. C. Morgan); in an immaterial vital principle (John Hunter, John Abernethy and Richard Saumarez); or in the product of some dialectic – such increasingly 'authoritative' accounts of character and its formation were seen by many writers as arbitrary, totalising or prescriptive.

As to the hardening of categories: the 1820s and 1830s were marked by a heightened and diffuse interest in taxonomy and codification, an interest with a strong impact on notions of character and characterisation. It was a 'great period of collecting, classifying, and arranging' on the part of professional and amateur naturalists (like John Clare).[48] Auguste Comte wanted to understand the classification of fauna and flora as part of an evolutionary trajectory culminating in the classification of social phenomena. In his *Positive Philosophy of Auguste Comte* (1830–42), Comte notes triumphantly that the 'comparative method, which discloses to us the gradual succession of the degrees of organization in life', applied first to nonliving, then to biological and finally to social phenomena: '[i]deas of order and harmony were originated by inorganic studies; but their highest manifestation, in the form of classification and a hierarchy, could issue only from biological science, whence it was to extend to social science'.[49] It was around this time, moreover, when Comte was writing his *Positive Philosophy of Auguste Comte*, that Romantic periodicals began experimenting with methods of ethological/social 'classification'. David Higgins has observed that '[b]y the 1820s, literary magazines were feeding the demand for information about the private lives of authors and other public figures with a variety of memoirs, literary portraits, ad hominem reviews, conversations, reminiscences and recollections'. Audiences became more interested in the 'psychological characteristics', personal 'appearance' and 'habits' of 'geniuses' through condensed, easily digestible 'literary portraits'.[50] Higgins especially highlights William Maginn's 'Gallery of Illustrious Literary Characters', published in *Fraser's* from 1830 to 1836, whose verbal portraits of famous men and women often had visual accompaniments in the form of drawings by the artist Daniel

Maclise. Such popular consumption of individual 'characters' was, in fact, implicated in a broader fascination with social documentation and categorisation. Marilyn Butler views the 'rage for ... literary *Lives*' during the reform era as 'part of a passion for documenting the natural world, including the human and social world'.[51]

Not just geniuses, or living or dead famous individuals, but all phenomena were subject to the reform-era compulsion to characterise, to taxonomise. *Blackwood's* in 1824 divided literary production into 'three different great veins of thought and sentiment' represented by Wordsworth, Scott and Byron. The 'irreducible heterogeneity' of these three 'great veins' meant that writers as different as Austen (sub-categorisable under Scott) and Shelley (sub-categorisable under Byron) could find their neat place.[52] Reviews and magazines also 'divided' their audiences 'into types that mirrored the genres of literature', 'carving out smaller audiences' within a broad middle-class readership and 'segment[ing] the reading public along existing political, religious and class lines'.[53] Appearing in the mid-1820s, the literary characters in fashionable novels often conformed to 'certain "types", such as the debutante, the manoeuvring mother and the rake'.[54] Gregory Dart observes, furthermore, that '[w]hat distinguished the 1830s in particular was ... a new interest ... in what we would call urban sociology, the identification and classification of various types of metropolitan man'.[55]

Thus whatever idea or object was theoretically characterisable could be put into some category or type. One profitable way to do this was to write a Theophrastan 'character' about one or another 'type' of thing or person, or a prose piece modelled on one. In fact, people were writing Theophrastan essays about practically everything: persons, poetic schools, social classes, streets, reading audiences, literary correspondents, heads, nations, poets, females, Christians, aborigines, sots, brewers, authors, fishes, God and so on. Scores of articles appeared in the 1820s and 1830s with titles beginning 'The Character of —'. The same decades witnessed a barrage of prose-fiction texts that, though differing in length and style, all shared a fundamental Theophrastan emphasis: John Russell's *Essays, and Sketches of Life and Character* (1820), Alaric Watts's *Scenes of Life and Shades of Character* (1831) and Dickens' *Sketches by Boz* (1833–6).

There were multidisciplinary reasons for this kind of output: for one, the Theophrastan trend was facilitated by new scientific (or quasi-scientific) disciplines. Spurzheim, in the appendix to his *Phrenology, in Connection with the Study of Physiognomy* (1826), compiled a list of basic character traits, subsuming under each trait whatever group of phrenological faculties he felt were responsible for its prevalence in an individual – admitting, as well, an endless possibility of combinations that could increase or decrease the prevalence of this or that trait. 'Characters', Spurzheim notes,

> are commonly divided into good and bad: that is to say, superior activity of the powers proper to man constitutes the good, whilst predominating energy of the merely animal nature composes the bad character ... I shall give the elements of a number of characters ... Those which I shall draw up may be strengthened or weakened by the addition or absence of certain faculties; and the reader must remember, that the combinations of thirty-five powers are numerous beyond conception; this, indeed, is a study which may be extended indefinitely.[56]

Hence the 'Affable' character possesses certain active phrenological powers including 'benevolence', 'acquisitiveness', 'courage' and 'self-esteem'. The 'Austere' character is marked by his or her powers of '[f]irmness, conscientiousness', 'destructiveness' and so on. The 'Tyrant' is full of 'self-esteem' but lacking in 'conscientiousness', 'veneration' and 'benevolence'.[57] One important point about phrenology is that in the 1820s it was viewed – depending on perspective – anywhere from hopelessly fatalistic to ethologically liberating. Gall and Spurzheim stressed the latter. Gall thought that his 'cerebral theory could be directly applied to the reform of character and thence to the reform of society: By withholding or providing stimuli to particular mental organs, he believed, specific forms of behavior could be encouraged or discouraged'. Spurzheim, too, 'laid stress on the meliorist implications of the doctrine while playing down the fatalistic preformationist aspects' (though of course these 'preformationist aspects' did not disappear).[58] Early sociologists placed greater emphasis than phrenologists on the environmental conditioning of character, albeit without discounting the importance of bodily constitution. In the 1830s, Harriet Martineau and Comte studied individual characters as calculable products of different social and national characters. In his *System of Logic* (1843) – which he began outlining in the 1820s – John Stuart Mill invented 'Ethology, or the Science of the Formation of Character', which he supposed was the dialectical product of certain psychological (universal) and empirical (time-and-place-specific) 'laws'. One could calculate the character of an individual based on the permanent, 'timeless' laws of the human psyche combined with careful observation of the environment into which that individual was born. Mill's ethology essentially takes the broad theorisation of Hume and Godwin to a positivistic extreme.

I want to suggest that the increasing interest in and theorisation of character in the 1820s and 1830s helped destabilise its already unreliable field of reference. Consider the onset of the 'personality' in post-Waterloo periodical culture. The term 'personality' was widely used to refer to a scathing ad hominem attack published in a review or magazine. Such attacks were often satirical, 'rancorous' and published anonymously (a few led to two famous duels fought in the 1820s, explored at length by Cronin and others). Periodical writers would exploit the minute bodily and biographical characteristics of targeted individuals (sometimes but not always based on fact) and subject these characteristics to public consumption and critique. The practice grew so widespread, in fact, that it became difficult to differentiate between the 'public' characters portrayed in print and the 'private' ones supposed to have been slandered or, as it were, misprisioned. Whatever 'strict boundaries' one imagined existed between public and private characters became 'fluid, rhetorical interventions in the social text'.[59] The 'calm but tenuous harmony between the public, abstract self, what people have of each other, and the reserve we think of as tied to our bodies, our actual selves', was disrupted.[60]

But I would add that not only the 'harmony between' the categories of 'public' and 'private' character was dissolving but also the integrity of the categories per se. Schoenfield observes that '[a]lthough [the concept of] character implied the potential of character assassination . . . it also provided a claim of legibility for individuals'.[61] Any 'attack on private character', in other words, seemed to presuppose 'a distinctive identity that exists prior to and independent of any particular example of behavior'.[62] And yet a major trend in reform-era literary culture was to resist or undermine this 'claim of legibility'. Authors experimented with and often valorised the idea or ideal of being unreadable. Hazlitt was fascinated with Sarah Walker in large part because she represented 'the ultimate negation of a great critic's powers of reading'. Walker remained 'liminal, shadowy' and 'powerful' precisely through her 'ability to remain elusive', her 'maddening illegibility', her 'resistance to being read'.⁶³ Another famous example of glorified unreadability evolved from the relationship between James Hogg and the editors of *Blackwood's*. The editors 'relegated' Hogg 'to [an] historical object', an immutable icon of his 'Scottish ancestry and shepherding origins', according to a 'theory of character' that stressed the 'unwavering consistency' of institutions and individuals across time.⁶⁴ Hogg, in turn, spent much of his career resisting the efforts of the Blackwoodsmen to, as it were, fix his character in formulated phrases.

This book reads the cases of Walker and Hogg as part of a network of reform-era texts that entertain the radical idea of textual/personal character as illegible or possibly nonexistent. Ahnert and Manning claim that in the eighteenth century the 'legibility of character' was a 'crucial issue' and an 'ai[d] to survival'.⁶⁵ Stronger character-readers simply had better chances of social and economic prosperity. By the 1820s, 'early psychological discourses on character traits', human 'typologies based on animal likenesses' and the popularity of 'physiognomy' and 'craneology [sic]' only intensified and popularised the interest in reading characters.⁶⁶ Further encouragement came from the new ways of reading novels that Lynch has traced. The point I want to emphasise is that this cultural fascination with the rhetorical and moral analysis of living and nonliving characters invited interest in and speculation about the possibility of being ethologically 'illegible'; and the possibility of being illegible, in turn, carried with it, as often as not, the further possibility that there was ultimately nothing substantial within or outside of bodies (textual and actual) to be read. If the 'private' character of an actual person could be disguised, performed, affected, assassinated, scandalised, textualised, how could it ever be truly 'possessed'? If it could be possessed, then by whom, or what, and to what extent, and for how long? These are questions (one could call them proto-poststructuralist questions) that several reform-era texts, I think, seriously entertain.

It follows that scanning surfaces to look for depths (the reading practice that Lynch historicises) is only one major interpretive practice in first four decades of the nineteenth century. Other ways of reading (akin to the ones Freeman discusses in the context of eighteenth-century drama) suggest an awareness, however incipient or unconscious, that much of what 'characterization does is memorialize a series of institutionally sanctioned versions of what "the self" is or should be'; that a novel may *not* contain secret clues to the deep souls of its characters; that all characterisation, literary and nonliterary, partakes of questionable typologies and practices of stratification; that personal character is subject to 'appropriation through representation'; that narratives and other texts create 'fictional taxonomies', 'character typologies', 'ready-made model[s] of personhood' useable for novels and real people.[67] John Bender has noted that as critics we often 'question what a character says or does but not the concept of character itself'.[68] I would say that cultural texts produced in post-Waterloo Britain did, in fact, question the reality and meaning of character and its customary qualifiers: literary, personal, public, private, moral, intellectual and so on. Literary discourse in the 1820s and 1830s can be read as a 'record of submerged, semiconscious structures', a 'borderlands where dissonance and incoherence are registered', a space of 'cognitive and affective discrepancies, which rarely find direct expression', a 'history of what hadn't quite been said'.[69] Hence 'character' may not have emerged in the public consciousness of the time as, say, a 'mere epiphenomen[on] of . . . dominant ideological structures', but neither was it exclusively recognised as an unproblematic and essential quality universally possessed and readable by discerning observers.[70] It occupied instead a middle ground: between noumenon and phenomenon, subject and actant, plenitude and surface, ontology and ideology. Examining the period closely 'disturbs what was previously considered immobile; it fragments what was thought unified; it shows the heterogeneity of what was imagined consistent with itself'.[71]

The first two chapters of this book describe a broad synthesis by which debates in several disciplines (philosophy, ethics, sociology, phrenology, medicine) are distilled into the concept of character associated with literary realism. I begin Chapter 1 by exploring how reform-era writers inherit character as a vexed philosophical problem and a vexed representational object through the philosophy of David Hume and the moral-rhetorical essays of seventeenth- and eighteenth-century authors writing in the Theophrastan tradition. In the rest of Chapter 1 and on into Chapter 2, I examine the emergence and development of ethological discourse across a range of texts: from the anonymous correspondent dashing off a paragraph about 'character' for a magazine; to multivolume treatises by John Stuart

Mill, August Comte, Harriet Martineau, Robert Owen and George Combe; to Letitia Landon's 'literary portraits' of Walter Scott's female heroines; to a few virtually unclassifiable and experimental texts by Lord John Russell, Theodore Hook and Charles Westmacott; and finally to Hegel's metaphysical analysis of 'character' in his *Philosophy of Fine Art*. Chapters 3 to 7 and the Afterword are largely case studies, based on the historical grounding of these first two chapters, of the literary production of one or two authors.

Chapter 3 takes a brief look at Walter Scott's early novel *Old Mortality* alongside a series of Charles Lamb's 'Elia' essays, exploring how and to what ends (rhetorical and metafictional) each author investigates character at the conceptual level, destabilising character as a concept and yet relying on it to produce meaningful texts. Both authors address the politics of literary realism and representation, interrogating, while nonetheless upholding, the reality of character not only as a psychosomatic principle presumed to be empirically observable and/or rationally justifiable in persons, but also as an object representable in print.

Chapter 4 examines William Hazlitt as an important contributor to a wide-scale cultural debate on the knowledge and formation of character. I am particularly interested in his commentaries on the subject that are creative, conflicting, self-conscious and tentative. In certain essays, for instance, he claims dogmatically that the inalienable root or 'bias' of character is fixed at birth and discernible through physiognomic observation of a person or his or her (well-executed) likeness. Nothing, least of all life-writing, can influence, hide or alter this bias, though dissimulation and wishful thinking can ignore its ruling existence for up to a lifetime. In other essays (beginning with his 1805 *Essay on the Principles of Human Action*), Hazlitt emphasises the mental autonomy of the individual whose future has no real relation to his or her present or past. It seems to follow that if the mind is autonomous (and the future a blank), it must be so within the limits of a fixed characterological bias. Hazlitt attempts to reconcile his views on human freedom to his views on human character in a variety of prose genres – the personal essay, the philosophical dialogue and the confessional novel *Liber Amoris*. It is in this sustained effort at reconciliation that he contributes to widespread anxieties over character and characterisation throughout the 'long Regency'.

The fifth chapter is an intensive study of the poetry of Hartley Coleridge, the subject of recent book-length criticisms by Andrew Keanie (2010) and Nicola Healey (2012). I emphasise the many poems in which Hartley fantasises about shedding the 'nature-boy' character fashioned for him by his father and Wordsworth. I read several of his poems as Lucretian/Swinburnian/Freudian fantasies about the pleasurable dissolution of body and character (but not quite consciousness) into inorganic matter after death: what it would 'feel like' to exist numbly and self-lessly as pure materiality, to be paradoxically conscious of unconsciousness, to experience what Keats famously called 'the feel of not to feel it'. Hartley writes a few poems flirting with Lucretian materialism, as well as several Christian/neo-Platonic poems that struggle against it. To me the spiritual poems only reinforce the tantalising appeal, to Hartley, of materialist discourses.

Letitia Landon is the subject of Chapter 6. Most students of Romanticism have at least heard of Landon by now. A few of her poems appear in Romantic-era anthologies published within the last twenty years, thanks to the surge of critical interest in Romantic women writers in the 1990s. One of her essays may occasionally show up in a companion to nineteenth-century culture. But I would hesitate to call her canonised. I would also argue that her work is now marginally anthologised but often misunderstood. A tiny fraction of her corpus serves to encapsulate her role as an artist wherever she appears in edited collections. Most of her prose stays out of the classroom and only her sentimental love-poetry tends to get read – which many critics continue to label as slavish or derivative. Examining Landon's Silver-Fork novels, essays, poems, letters and even footnotes, Chapter 6 argues that Landon was no mere slave to market forces and a popular taste she did not create. Instead, her work is important because it challenges the moral value and even the possibility of a 'decided' or 'principled' character in and outside of texts.

The seventh and final chapter reads Thomas Lovell Beddoes' drama, *Death's Jest-Book* (1829), and Thomas Love Peacock's 'novel of ideas', *Crotchet Castle* (1831), as texts that dramatise the pleasure, the bewilderment, the fear occasioned by the dissolution of character. The dramatis personae in *Death's Jest-Book* imagine existence without the centred structures of characters, bodies, souls. They envision or claim to experience instances of being invisible, characterless, unmade, reborn or recreated perpetually as new species. Neither body, nor character, nor soul, nor a combination of all three, is a sufficiently liberating medium of experience. All physical and metaphysical media are unpleasantly deterministic and confining. According to the men and women in *Death's Jest-Book*, consciousness that proceeds from a metaphysical centred structure (character, soul, ego, self) is no purer or freer than consciousness that proceeds from anatomical organisation. Both are structures with their respective limitations and constrictions. *Crotchet Castle* wrestles with the looming threat that personal character is solely a cultural product, a construct susceptible to being exposed, probed, discredited and then reinvented by the agents of the March of Mind. Its unquestionable existence as a metaphysical principle or as a reality grounded in physiological organisation has become – like every other 'crotchet' – subject to reexamination and reform.

The Afterword surveys the literary borderlands between reform-era fiction and the Victorian novel by comparing the treatment of literary character in two notably 'liminal' texts: Charles Dickens' *Sketches by Boz* and Thomas Carlyle's *Sartor Resartus*. Both were initially published in magazines or newspapers in the early 1830s and feature what may be called meta-characterisation. They describe and 'enflesh' and 'round' their textual characters with an ironic sense of confidence and authority, drawing attention to the arbitrary and political nature of characterisation even as their narrators try to convince readers that the fictional beings in their texts are possible or probable representations of living beings in the world. One main difference between these 'liminal' texts and Victorian novels proper is that Victorian writers – though writing 'with the awareness of the possibilities of indeterminate meaning' – nonetheless 'wrote *against* the very indeterminacy they tended to reveal', in the spirit of what George Levine has called the 'realistic imagination'.[72] Dickens and Carlyle – at least in these two early texts – write as much *with* as against the 'indeterminacy they tended to reveal'.

Notes

1. Novalis, *Heinrich von Ofterdingen*, 1802, qtd in Cavell, *Emerson's Transcendental Etudes*, p. 255. Novalis echoes Heraclitus (see Strawson, 'The Impossibility of Ultimate Moral Responsibility', p. 304).
2. Foucault, *Discipline and Punish*, p. 305.
3. Godwin, *Enquiry concerning Political Justice*, p. 158.

4. Brewer, *Afterlife of Character*, pp. 3, 6, 5.
5. Gallagher, *Nobody's Story*, p. xix.
6. Lynch, *Economy of Character*, pp. 6, 41, 124.
7. Freeman, *Character's Theater*, pp. 7, 16, 8, 7, 17.
8. Brewer, *Afterlife of Character*, pp. 2, 14. The 'imaginative expansion' of 'textual commons' is especially apparent among Jane Austen fans, who have been continuing and reimagining the characters in her novels since the early nineteenth century (see Lynch, 'Sharing with Our Neighbours', 'Cult of Jane Austen' and 'Sequels').
9. Manning, *Poetics of Character*, pp. 5, 13, 15, 20, 22, 60, 31. See also Ahnert and Manning, introduction to *Character, Self, and Sociability*.
10. Frow, *Character and Person*, p. ix.
11. Freeman, *Character's Theater*, pp. 24, 27.
12. Lynch, *Economy of Character*, pp. 133, 127, 131, 135. Italics in original.
13. Nemoianu, *The Taming of Romanticism*, pp. 41, 50.
14. See Tucker, 'House Arrest', pp, 521–48; Riess, 'Laetitia Landon and the Dawn of English Post-Romanticism'; and McGann and Riess, introduction to *Letitia Elizabeth Landon: Selected Writings*, pp. 11–31.
15. Hodgetts, 'William Hone and the Reading Public', p. 9.
16. Copeland, *The Silver Fork Novel*, pp. 1, 2, 66.
17. Garcha, *From Sketch to Novel*, p. 3.
18. Cronin, *Romantic Victorians*, p. 143; and Garcha, *From Sketch to Novel*, p. 3. The point of this list is not to reinforce a sense of history as a series of 'important' events, but to account for some of the material and cultural conditions that enabled a more critical investigation of character in print during the 1820s and 1830s.
19. Cronin, *Paper Pellets*, p. 11.
20. Erickson, *The Economy of Literary Form*, pp. 20, 21, 26, 11; and Cronin, *Romantic Victorians*, pp. 109–10.
21. Stewart, *Romantic Magazines*, p. 4.
22. Parker, *Literary Magazines and British Romanticism*, p. 110.
23. Schoenfield, *British Periodicals and Romantic Identity*, p. 1; and Higgins, *Romantic Culture and the Literary Magazine*, p. 1.
24. See Cronin, *Paper Pellets*, chapters 8 and 9.
25. Parker, *Literary Magazines and British Romanticism*, p. 111.
26. Critical work on the Romantic 'subject' since the 1980s has concentrated more precisely on the 'consciousness of self as the being to whom sensation is referred' than on 'character'. One of its major efforts has been to reassert the material (historical, political, social, economic) contingencies denied or displaced by the Romantic ideology of the self. See, for instance, Rzepka, *The Self as Mind* (1986); Cooper, *Doubt and Identity in Romantic Poetry* (1988); Richardson, *A Mental Theater*

(1988); De Bolla, *The Discourse of the Sublime* (1989); Nussbaum, *The Autobiographical Subject* (1989); Martin and Barresi, *Naturalization of the Soul* (2000); Yousef, *Isolated Cases* (2004); Khalip, *Anonymous Life* (2009); and Esterhammer, 'The Scandal of Sincerity' (2010).
27. Pitson, *Hume's Philosophy of the Self*, p. 85.
28. Schechtman, *The Constitution of Selves*, pp. 1–2.
29. Schoenfield, *British Periodicals and Romantic Identity*, p. 115.
30. Rorty, 'A Literary Postscript', p. 306.
31. Charles Taylor has associated the idea of 'where one stands as a person' more with the idea of 'identity' than with the idea of character. See his *Sources of the Self*, pp. 28–9.
32. Nussbaum, *The Autobiographical Subject*, p. 38.
33. Seigel, 'Necessity, Freedom, and Character Formation', p. 249.
34. Freeman, *Character's Theater*, pp. 22, 24.
35. Frow, *Character and Person*, p. 8.
36. McCalman, introduction to *An Oxford Companion to the Romantic Age*, p. 5.
37. Rauch, *Useful Knowledge*, p. 34.
38. Anon., 'Art. VIII. *Reflections on Gall and Spurzheim's System*', p. 557.
39. Combe, *A System of Phrenology*, pp. 110, 107.
40. Cooter, *The Cultural Meaning of Popular Science*, pp. 111–12.
41. J. R. B., 'On the System of Gall and Spurzheim', pp. 12, 17.
42. Ibid., pp. 14–15.
43. Cronin, *Paper Pellets*, pp. 154, 16.
44. Stewart, *Romantic Magazines*, p. 5.
45. De Quincey, qtd in Stewart, *Romantic Magazines*, pp. 29–30.
46. Hazlitt, qtd in Parker, *Literary Magazines and British Romanticism*, p. 73.
47. Hodgetts, 'William Hone and the Reading Public', pp. 17–18.
48. Grainger, introduction to *The Natural History Prose Writings of John Clare*, pp. xlii–xliii.
49. Comte, *The Positive Philosophy of Auguste Comte*, p. 453.
50. Higgins, *Romantic Culture and the Literary Magazine*, p. 60.
51. Butler, *Romantics, Rebels and Reactionaries*, p. 2.
52. Parker, *Literary Magazines and British Romanticism*, pp. 118–19, 128.
53. Schoenfield, *British Periodicals and Romantic Identity*, p. 2; Higgins, *Romantic Culture and the Literary Magazine*, p. 8; and Erickson, *The Economy of Literary Form*, p. 72.
54. Wilson, *Fashioning the Silver Fork Novel*, p. 14.
55. Dart, *Metropolitan Art and Literature*, p. 224.
56. Spurzheim, *Phrenology, in Connection with the Study of Physiognomy*, pp. 182–3.
57. Ibid., pp. 183–4, 189.

58. Cooter, *The Cultural Meaning of Popular Science*, p. 226.
59. Schoenfield, *British Periodicals and Romantic Identity*, p. 52.
60. Murphy, 'Impersonation and Authorship in Romantic Britain', p. 632.
61. Schoenfield, *British Periodicals and Romantic Identity*, pp. 201–2.
62. Cronin, *Paper Pellets*, p. 57.
63. Dart, *Metropolitan Art and Literature*, p. 100.
64. Schoenfield, *British Periodicals and Romantic Identity*, pp. 17, 203.
65. Ahnert and Manning, introduction to *Character, Self, and Sociability*, p. 14.
66. Hunter, 'Reading Character', p. 236.
67. Lynch, *Economy of Character*, p. 12; Manning, *Poetics of Character*, p. 235; and Frow, *Character and Person*, p. 119.
68. Bender, *Imagining the Penitentiary*, p. 212.
69. Gallagher, 'Counterhistory and Anecdote', p. 62.
70. Ibid., p. 66.
71. Foucault, 'Nietzsche, Genealogy, History', p. 147.
72. Levine, *The Realistic Imagination*, p. 4.

Chapter 1

The Reform Era: An Ethological Age

> A man's disposition is no further of any consequence than as his acts are the result of it . . . In truth it is only from a man's acts that his disposition can be judged of: or indeed to speak out: it is a man's actions only that exist: his disposition is but a fictitious entity.
> Jeremy Bentham, unpublished manuscript (c. 1775–6)[1]

> The ignorant and the giddy may embarrass such subjects with irrelevant fancies, and other absurdities that have no existence properly viewed – really no existence.
> Charles Dickens, *Hard Times*[2]

Inheritances: Hume and Theophrastus

All the literary texts discussed in this and in subsequent chapters are, in some important respect, driven by the problem of what Bentham calls 'disposition'. Bentham states in the epigraph that personal 'disposition' is a 'fictitious entity'.[3] We posit its existence based on the observation and analysis of human actions, but have no reliable (that is, empirically verifiable) way to account for that existence. In the increasingly utilitarian culture of the reform era, several writers struggle with this same basic problem. On one level, their texts entertain the possibility that character may have no existence except as the inferred product of biological and social forces; a product that may or may not be subject over time to the shaping power of an individual will (also a subject of dispute). On another level, these authors resist the idea that character is ultimately a 'fictitious entity', a term with no reliable referent in the real world. As a concept, therefore, character retains its firm hold on the nineteenth-century imagination despite that its throne, as I will argue, is somewhat shaken in the 1820s and 1830s. Character ultimately survives its own version of the 'philosophical scepticism about identity that persisted from eighteenth-century empiricism' onward.[4] Even the sceptical Hume had kept character intact (or tried to): he 'treats character realistically while maintaining the view that the self is a collection of perceptions'.[5] The rest of this book demonstrates how some reform-era texts began to do to 'character' and its associated concepts something like what Hume and others had done to 'identity' in the eighteenth century. Cultural production in the decades after Waterloo acknowledges and accepts the idea of character but not without a noticeable pattern of epistemological scepticism; not without traceable, intertextual reservations. Reform-era literature questions what it also assumes, deconstructs what it appropriates, parodies what it reifies.

Jerrold Seigel has distinguished between 'two common meanings of character' operative in the eighteenth century: 'the descriptive or classifying one we use when we speak of someone as possessed of, say, a calm or excitable, morose or cheery character and the emphatic or moral one we employ when we describe a person as admirable for "having character"'.[6] Kant maintained this distinction sharply in his treatises on ethics. He claimed that all individuals possess two 'characters': a 'natural' and a 'moral' one. The former is 'given ... by nature or experience' and lies beyond our control. The latter must be earned through the exercise of a good will in obedience to the categorical imperative: '[a]cting in accord with the behests of universal rationality frees us from determination by passions or inclinations, making the person who attains a genuinely moral character at once virtuous and autonomous'. This Kantian distinction did not go unchallenged, however, in the late eighteenth century. Seigel notes that Denis Diderot and other Enlightenment materialists challenged Kant's bipartite model of character. If, for Diderot,

> individual varieties of behavior were no more than the expression of different physical constitutions, then a disposition to act uprightly became merely one of a number of character types, not even necessarily admirable. In such a light, Kant's kind of distinction between having 'this or that' character and being 'a person of character' became very permeable indeed.[7]

According to the materialist view, our 'moral' character is no more under our control than our 'natural' character. If we are physiologically hardwired to have a good will, obey laws and treat others kindly, then we hardly deserve any praise for acting how we are constituted to act. Each individual simply lives out the moral programme wired into his or her constitution.

Although the rise of utilitarianism and positivism may have inspired a renewed interest in character in the 1820s and 1830s, the eighteenth century set the groundwork for the importance of the subject. Ahnert and Manning note that character was discussed 'widely in the Scottish Enlightenment across a range of intellectual disciplines and textual genres', including fiction, biography, 'historiography and moral argument'. It was considered from a variety of angles: as the rhetorical product of representation, as a measure of 'stoical self-control', as a readable essence and as a form of ethical and commercial 'currency'.[8] According to Alan Richardson, eighteenth-century novels (unlike, in his view, Romantic novels) emphasised the 'readable essence' aspect of character: they 'tended to . . . stress an inherited character or "disposition" over experience and training'.[9] In his 1742 essay 'The Sceptic', Hume refers to a 'predominant inclination' in all individuals that never goes away and 'to which . . . desires and affections submit'. No one can feel an emotion outside the mould of his or her character. If one could, he or she would have the resources to be permanently happy: 'PROTEUS-like, he would elude all attacks, by the continual alterations of his shape and form'.[10] As is well known, in *An Inquiry Concerning Human Understanding* Hume argues that a person cannot be held responsible for a crime of which he or she is accused unless it can be proven to derive from his or her character.[11] In this sense, character for Hume actually serves as 'a defence against scepticism in that it provide[s] a rationale for consistent conduct' and a measure of legal liability.[12]

Hume is vital to the present study because his extensive (and ambivalent) theories of character anticipate similar reform-era debates and ideas. Character for Hume may be stable and discernible but it also has no clear or traceable origins. He supposes that a certain disposition or temperament exists in everyone that is 'neither intrinsic nor causally formed'. It is not 'intrinsic' because one is not born with the character that one eventually comes to possess. It is not 'causally formed' because the habit and custom that Hume claims are responsible for the formation of character are not the same as causal forces. The growth of character is thus accretive, cumulating until it reaches a point of relative stability (as Godwin also argues). At this point of stability or maturity, habit and custom have effectively 'produced' an individual's character, and, from this point forward, they will also continue to 'sustai[n]' it.[13]

John Bricke argues that Hume holds a 'non-reductionist theory of dispositions' even if, as is often the case, he appears to hold a 'reductionist theory of dispositions'. What Bricke means is that, were Hume *actually* a 'reductionist', he would account for observable behaviours only hypothetically. He would explain human actions without acknowledging the existence of an occult power or faculty that produces them. For instance, as a reductionist, if Hume should say that '*x* is greedy', he would only mean that '*x* is greedy hypothetically under a certain set of conditions'. But since Hume is a 'non-reductionist', according to Bricke, he actually believes that behaviour stems from 'an enduring state of the individual which results from the conditioning process'.[14] Even though he cannot precisely say in what that state consists (as Godwin cannot), Hume still acknowledges its existence in an empiricist system that explains human action. In a later essay, Bricke argues that Hume defines character traits as 'relatively permanent mental properties' stemming from 'physiological states of the brain'.[15] It becomes clear, even from Bricke's account alone, that, '[o]f all the concepts of persons', character 'is the one in which psychological and physiological traits are most closely linked'. It is also an important subject to any writers interested in ethics, since 'various [character] traits' are thought to 'support different conceptions of responsibility'.[16]

Thus Hume seems to view character as stable yet flexible. It is 'typically known through action, but it is distinct from action; it is a cause of action, rather than constituted by action'. Perhaps, therefore, one could say that character simply amounts to how other people assume a given person will act based upon their experience of that person's behaviour. But according to Jane McIntyre, for Hume 'there must be some middle ground between character traits as occult qualities and character traits as spectators' expectations'.[17] For McIntyre, that middle ground is 'passion'. According to Hume, she argues, character is derived internally from the passions of an individual, not externally from the expectations that others have of that individual's behaviour.

Reform-era writers inherited not only the vexed question of character as debated in Scottish Enlightenment circles and theorised by

Hume, but also the tail end of the Theophrastan character sketch, which blossomed in the seventeenth and eighteenth centuries and continued into the nineteenth. Theophrastus produced his *Characters* in or around 319 BC. His teacher Aristotle had argued in *Nichomachean Ethics* that virtuous actions must proceed from 'a stable and unchangeable state of character'.[18] Theophrastus was inspired by Aristotle but arguably more interested in humour and style than in moral teaching. His character sketches were exaggerated and packed with vivid details supposedly associated with a perennial 'type' of humanity (the flatterer, the gossip, the grumbler, the coward and so on). They were meant to illustrate 'what happens when a particular quality is carried to an extreme, without making us disbelieve in the human being depicted'. The character sketch became hugely popular in the seventeenth century (J. W. Smeed observes that over twenty character-books were written between 1608 and 1700) and 'persisted, at least in England, throughout the nineteenth'.[19] Important seventeenth-century Theophrastan texts include Joseph Hall's *Characters of Virtues and Vices* (1608), Thomas Overbury's *Characters* (1614), John Earle's *Microcosmographie* (1628), Samuel Butler's *Characters* (c. 1650s–1660) and Jean de La Bruyère's *Caractères* (1688). The tradition was carried on in the eighteenth century largely through coffee house periodicals like *The Tatler, The Spectator, The Rambler* and *The Idler*, as well as in Pope's *Epistle to a Lady: Of the Characters of Women* (1735). Its more popular nineteenth-century practitioners included Thomas Hood, William Hazlitt, Leigh Hunt and Charles Lamb.

Eighteenth-century commentators sometimes invoked Theophrastan writers as models for contemporary novelists. The Scottish judge William Craig, in an article for the *Mirror* (1779), identifies Theophrastus as the best delineator of character among the ancients and La Bruyère as the best one among the moderns. Theophrastus, Craig notes, focuses on the 'external conduct' of a given type: its 'behaviour on this or that occasion', how it tends to be 'affected by this or that event'. La Bruyère, in contrast, describes 'the internal feelings of the mind', 'relating the qualities with which a person is endowed' rather than showing how that person acts under certain conditions. La Bruyère thus gives readers the 'general conclusion with regard to character', while Theophrastus invites readers to determine the character from a set of related behaviours. Both authors 'take for their object a character governed by some one passion, absorbing all others, and influencing the man in every thing'. Craig urges novelists to do the same: to 'illustrate some one distinguishing feature or passion' in their fictional characters, 'any one predominant or leading principle of the human heart': otherwise it is only their plots that sustain interest, and plot-driven novels, he claims, need only be read once.[20]

One of the ironies of Theophrastan sketches is that a lot of them urge readers to be free-thinking individuals at the same time that they reinforce the constraints of 'ruling passions'. Many 'characters', that is, emphasise the value of mental autonomy (Kant's 'moral character') while making its unattainability seem like a foregone conclusion. Hall, for instance, writes of 'The Unconstant' person that he or she is 'so transformable into all opinions, manners, qualities, that he ... is, in possibility, any thing or every thing; nothing, in present substance'.[21] Butler cries out against the 'opiniater' [sic] whose opinions and conceptions are 'Bastards ... unlawfully begotten'.[22] Among the principle vices that La Bruyère lists in one essay are 'inequality of Humour, inconstancy of Affection, and uncertainty of Conduct'. He claims that '[a]n unequal Man is several Men in one; he multiples himself as often as he changes his Taste and Manners'.[23] All these examples suggest the value of self-actualisation ('decision' of character) within a literary convention that tends to bury moral decisiveness under ruling passions. Although the Theophrastan sketch is supposed promote a 'balanced' character, or virtuous mean, by describing what can happen when a single harmful trait is taken to an extreme, its typological and determinist premises (this 'type' does this, that 'type' does that) weaken whatever moral philosophy it may seem to promote.

The philosophical interest in character à la Hume and the aesthetic interest in its typological representation à la Theophrastus and his imitators set the stage for what Coleridge famously called an 'Age of Personality'. By 'personality' Coleridge meant, of course, nasty gossip, the personality-driven feuds that circulated in periodicals during and after the Napoleonic Wars and resulted in several unfortunate deaths. But there is also good reason to call the reform era an 'Age of Character'. For one thing the reading public craved representations of character (not necessarily attacked) in two main forms: the biographical 'portrait' of an actual person – dead or alive – and the Theophrastan 'character' concerning a perennial 'type' (a third form, the hybridic 'portrait-character', is discussed in Chapter 4). The 'portrait' was part of a surge of interest in what Mark Schoenfield has called 'serial contemporary biography'.[24] By 1823, for instance, the *Public Characters of 1798* contained at least 3,000 items.[25] Hazlitt, to use a well-known example, wrote numerous 'portraits' in the years between his *Round Table* (1817) and *Plain Speaker* (1826) volumes, including ones on Rousseau, Pitt, Burke, Fox, Lord Chatham, Addison, Steele, Cobbett and others, as well as the famous 'Contemporary Portraits' collected in *The Spirit of the Age* (1825) and his long, controversial 'portrait' of Sarah Walker in *Liber Amoris* (1823). As to 'characters' – essays about 'types' – between 1825 and 1826 the *London Magazine*, 'in a series of five articles under the general head "Butleriana", printed, for the first time, some 582 lines of verse and 20 prose *characters* from the pen' of Samuel Butler.[26] The *London* was also the first print medium to feature several 'characters' by Hazlitt and Lamb that were subsequently collected in their respective *Table-Talk* and *Elia* volumes. Hazlitt, in fact, published numerous 'characters' during and after the Napoleonic Wars: 'Character of John Bull', 'On the Literary Character', 'On the Clerical Character', 'On the Regal Character', 'On Effeminacy of Character' and others. His two important essays, 'On Personal Character' (1821; 1826) and 'On the Knowledge of Character' (1821), may be read as theoretical rationales for his various biographical 'portraits'.

Hence the years after Waterloo may be said to have ushered in an ethological age. One writer for the *Oriental Herald* (1825) is quick to appreciate his or her culture's growing fascination with human 'types':

> In order to present a kind of frame to experience upon which it might spread out the various textures of humanity occurring in its way, philosophy has divided men into classes, – into the magnanimous, the poor-spirited, the phlegmatic, the irascible, the proud, the meek ... the whole utility of this division consists in the accurate enumeration of the signs of the classes.[27]

Philosophers have separated men and women into ethological 'classes' '[i]n order to present a kind of frame to experience'. Each class (at least ideally) corresponds to a set of external, legible 'signs' by which its constituents can be distinguished. It may come as no surprise that a conceptual 'frame' like the one described here, broad enough to encompass all human 'textures', can be put to any kind of ideological work. The author of 'Character of a Common Brewer' (1823), for instance, who indicates that he or she is also 'author of the character of a priest, of a soldier, &c., &c., &c.', writes in the *Republican* that the Brewer is a person of 'sordid avarice', 'cupidity' and 'gluttony ... actuated by a malignant passion'. In this article, representing a type to demonstrate the value of a virtuous mean or to dazzle with rhetorical finesse becomes less important than fomenting public awareness of 'a false, preternatural, and corrupt system of Government' resistant to change. '[C]an there be any hope of reform', the author asks (who signs the article 'Philanthropos'), 'while members of the legislative body unblushingly traffic in public poison?'[28] A piece in *Chambers's Edinburgh Magazine* (1832), a single paragraph entitled 'Aboriginal Character' excerpted from a Boston paper, explains the character of (all) indigenous peoples in a rapid anecdote about a Native American who begged a piece of tobacco from a 'gentleman' in Maine, only to return to the same gentleman about four months later with a 'beautiful miniature birch canoe'.[29] This anti-capitalistic, noble-savage-like gesture on the part of the Native American is quietly enlisted as one of the 'signs' of his – of the – 'Aboriginal Character'. In the case of the 'Common Brewer', the 'character' genre is used primarily as an excuse to talk about contemporary parliamentary reform. In the case of the 'Aboriginal Character', the boundaries between ethological and ethnic categories are effectively blurred.

An 'Ethological' Age

The writer for the *Oriental Herald* quoted above describes 'knowledge of character' as 'the only instrument of success upon which we can rely' – a 'science, which holds the golden keys of fortune and power'.[30] In the 1820s, character-reading was not only a prosperous but a relatively democratic 'science'. A novice writer could sell a short sketch of a 'type' or of contemporary 'manners' to a weekly magazine with little trouble. Cornelia Lambert has noted that '[t]he question of the ability of the human character to change ... was under scrutiny' in Britain after the Napoleonic Wars, to which I would add 'the basic question of in what human character actually consists'.[31] Character is unique in that it can be at once a truth universally acknowledged and what

Bentham calls a 'fictitious entity'. One can ultimately say whatever one wants about it since everyone acknowledges its 'truth' but no one seems to mind the absence of consensus on the nature or extent of its existence. And reform-era writers did say a lot about it. This is just a tiny fraction of the trove of articles on 'character' published between 1820 and 1839:

1820.	'The Character of an Honest Man' (*The Kaleidoscope: or, Literary and Scientific Mirror*)
1821.	'Character of the Stayed Man' (*The Imperial Magazine*)
1821.	'Character, – Principle, – with Other Grave Matters' (*Edinburgh Magazine and Literary Miscellany*)
1821.	'The Excellencies of a Manly Character' (*The Cambro-Briton*)
1822.	'The Character of a Happy Life' (*Christian Remembrancer*)
1822.	'On the Character of a True Poet' (*Imperial Magazine*)
1822.	'On the Moral Character of Authors' (*Literary Speculum*)
1823.	'Decision of Character' (*The Imperial Magazine*)
1823.	'Sketches of Character' (*The Lady's Monthly Museum*)
1824.	'On Keeping, or Costume in Character' (*New Monthly Magazine*)
1824.	'On the Formation of Character' (*Imperial Magazine*)
1825.	'The Character of Christianity' (*Imperial Magazine*)
1826.	'Character-Painting' (*Literary Chronicle*)
1832.	'On Refinement of Character' (*Monthly Repository*)
1832.	'Character of Fish' (*Chamber's Edinburgh Magazine*)
1835.	'Character of a Sot' (*Penny magazine of the Society for the Diffusion of Useful Knowledge*)

I omit here countless articles written on the 'female character' (the male character was never as popular a topic). As the list suggests, periodical essays on character involved more than historical 'portraits' of famous individuals, malicious gossip ('personalities') and Theophrastan 'characters' (essays on 'types'). Many of them were what I call popular ethologies: succinct essays on the nature and/or formation of personal character written in nonspecialised language for middle-class audiences, usually appearing in one but occasionally in two (consecutive) issues of a magazine during the reform era and culminating in what Mill in 1843 termed 'Ethology, or the Science of the Formation of Character'. Points of style and political allegiances aside, the ethologies vary mainly according to the emphasis placed on character as an 'original conformation' or as a work in progress subject to the ongoing influence of 'secondary or adventitious instances'. One writer for *The Athenaeum* insists that *'temper* or *disposition* is a radical ['original' or 'primary'] quality of mind, never entirely to be changed, but only modified in its agency by superinduced habits, or by principles of conduct'.[32] Another claims that 'the characters of men' are formed by a 'necessity imperious – irresistible – almighty – omnipresent'.[33] In these examples the stress is laid on character as a relatively fixed quality or principle with some but not much room for alteration. Other essays reinforce its dynamism and mutability. On certain 'great occasions', one author notes, 'the mind awakes to take an extended survey of her whole course', whereby 'she suffers the dictates of reason to impress a new bias upon her movements'.[34] For this writer the 'bias' or radical slant of character can be altered indefinitely provided the circumstances are sufficiently profound. The author of 'Character, – Principle, – with other Grave Matters' explains that the character of a genius emerges dialectically 'in the relation between individual genius and spectators'. It is the product of a 'reciprocal action and reaction' between a 'living principle in the consciousness of its possessor' and the attention given to that individual by his or her audiences.[35]

Some of these ethologies are more elaborate than others and read like miniature treatises on education. The author of 'Of the Influence of Early Impressions on the Future Character' (1825) identifies three sources of character: early impressions, hereditary disposition and education. Between birth and age six, an innate human 'instinct' develops in all individuals from an embryonic to a fully matured state. During this developmental period the instinct is shaped by early impressions: 'although it is innate, and under any circumstances would be manifest, yet it is so bent and moulded' by early impressions 'as to form the basis of character'. Once fully formed around age six, instinct is unalterable and permanent. As the 'impulse of our system', instinct 'gives tone to character'.[36] The second source of character, the hereditary disposition of a child, includes both the traits of his or her parents and the social situation into which he or she was born. Education (in the formal rather than in the general sense of 'moral education') happens to be the weakest influence on character. At best it provides an individual with 'an artificial, rather than an actual character'.[37] Education can affect the early impressions and hereditary dispositions of whole peoples over time, but can have no material effect on the character of any single person living at a particular moment. In other words, formal education tends to have its most important effects diachronically but not synchronically.

In some cases, the ideological allegiances of an author writing about 'character' are more prominent than in others.[38] Character could be enlisted in the service of laissez-faire capitalism as something that should be earned, amassed and re-circulated for the betterment of local community and nation. One writer compares it to capital: hard to acquire but, once acquired, easily accumulated. The only problem is that a 'great accumulation of character', as of capital, may 'bege[t] caution and timidity'. In such cases one has to be willing to spend freely what he or she has acquired in order to render it useful: 'securely hoarded' character is, after all, only a 'questionable sort of commodity'.[39] Another writer, according to view common since the mid-seventeenth century, advises the use of character as collateral in business transactions: a good deal of it often 'supplies the place of an additional portion of capital'.[40] Some popular ethologists treated character more as a political than as an economic concern. An article in the *Co-Operative Magazine* declares that the character of each and every British citizen should be an object of 'political regulation'.[41] The author of 'Decision of Character' in *The Imperial Magazine* (1823) associates regularity of character with political conservatism and irregularity of character with political radicalism. Among the worst traits a person can have are 'inordinate affections' and 'irregular appetites'; among the best are 'obedience' and 'steadiness', which are found in 'that mind only, which . . . scorns to be confined in the inglorious shackles of democratic clamour'.[42] For this author, a 'decided' character is a specifically nondemocratic possession.

Susan Manning has observed that character in the late eighteenth century was 'a possible solution to the puzzle of how to "read" others in a rhetorical world in which criteria of legibility based in local relations and physical presence no longer pertained'.[43] A running theme, accordingly, in several of these reform-era articles is character as a thing to be surveilled, discovered, rooted out of a person by investigative tactics. One ethologist insists at the outset that his or her 'office [is] not to prescribe, but to describe'. He or she claims that 'character remains essentially the same' from birth to death and is therefore detectable through careful investigation. The surest means to an accurate knowledge of character is an inductive study of the clothing, manners, domestic habits and handwriting of a given individual, since 'conduct in trifles leads to a discovery of the main attributes of individual character; and conversely ... an acquaintance with the main attributes will enable us to predict the conduct in trifles' (a position that anticipates Mill's science of ethology).[44] Handwriting was a particularly useful means of character analysis. Piper notes that seeing the handwriting of an author made nineteenth-century readers feel as if they had penetrated 'through the screen of the printed page and into the heart and mind of the author himself'.[45] The Blackwoodsmen describe the written hand of James Hogg, for instance, as a telltale sign of his socioeconomic class and general vulnerability in the world of print: 'Let Hogg publish a fac-simile of his hand-writing', says the Old Friend in *Blackwood's*, 'and the world will be thunderstruck by the utter helplessness of his hand'.[46]

The author of 'On the Knowledge of Character' (1825) – for whom character-reading is 'the science of great men' – offers a wealth of advice for the ethological student-surveillant. First, never trust the reports of family members, since most people are adept at hiding their characters from those they live with. Nor will the formal education a person has had tell us much about his or her character. More important than either of these (though difficult to access) is the '*virus*' or 'secret tinge' that families pass down through generations.[47] Personal conduct and facial features, as it happens, tell us far less about a character than is commonly thought. Conduct is unreliable because

> the character a man gains by his actions in society is never his real character; for what he does, flows from the fashions of the age, from his position, from the influence of others, and is no manner of rule by which to judge how he would conduct himself the next moment, were he removed to a new scene.

Nor will studying facial features always work, since

> [s]ome men's minds resemble a mirror, and reflect back exactly the character of him with whom they converse. Such persons, therefore, are not to be studied when their mental face is towards you, properly disposed to give you back your own image. They must be observed by a side view, when their mind's surface is receiving the impression of other objects

Because behaviour and appearance are both unreliable indices of character, all that is left to study are the 'passions' of a person. To this writer the passions are 'the keys of the soul', the restraint or excitement of which no one (not even actors) can successfully 'dissimulat[e]'.[48] Here the author seems to agree with what McIntyre claims about Hume's true view of character: that its real seat is in the passions.

John Stuart Mill aimed to establish perhaps the most strict and thorough science of character in the first half of the nineteenth century. In an 1838 essay he entertained the idea of a 'taxonomy that will explain the individual human beings who compose its categories'. By this date he had also written portions of *A System of Logic* calling for a 'systematic analysis of phenomena'.[49] *A System of Logic* was first published in 1843. In the fifth chapter of Book VI, Mill articulates his theory of 'Ethology, or the Science of the Formation of Character'. He calls ethological laws – the 'universal laws of the Formation of Character' – the *axiomata media* between empirical laws and psychological laws. Empirical laws are generalisations gleaned from observation and experiment that are only conditionally true. Psychological laws explain how all human minds operate across time and space and are always true. The first task of the ethologist is to come up with an empirical law: to 'deduc[e] theoretically the ethological consequences of particular circumstances of position' (for instance, persons born in the British Isles tend to be melancholy), 'comparing' these ethological consequences 'with the recognized results of common experience' (for instance, suicide rates are high in the United Kingdom).[50] In other words, the ethologist first deduces what character type an individual is likely to form under a given set of circumstances based on things like 'statistical studies and surveys'.[51] Once the type likely to form is determined, the ethologist 'reverse[s] [the] operation'. Now he or she considers 'the various types of human nature that are to be found in the world' – information provided by psychological laws – and 'account[s] for the characteristics of the type by the peculiarities of the circumstances': All melancholy persons think and behave according to x, y and z. This fact may have something to do with cold and rainy climates. Mill summarises the process as follows:

> The laws of the formation of character are, in short, derivative laws, resulting from . . . supposing any given set of circumstances, and then considering what, according to the laws of mind, will be the influence of those circumstances on the formation of character.[52]

Ethology was to have been at the heart of a great sociological treatise that Mill never wrote. Although he never developed ethology completely as a science, Terence Ball considers his four major texts – *On Liberty* (1859), *Considerations on Representative Government* (1861), *The Subjection of Women* (1869) and the *Autobiography* (1873) – as 'case studies in applied ethology'. The collective conclusion of these case studies, according to Ball, is that 'the causal formation of one's character does not mean that one is powerless to change one's character'. Although my character is entirely determined by causal antecedents (Godwin's Necessity), these antecedents are nonetheless subject in part to the shaping power of my desires and will. Said differently: wishes and desires for Mill may be 'among the antecedent circumstances that cause . . . character and conduct to be what they are'.[53] Mill's ethology was thus intended as a solution to hard determinism, however problematic its use of character types may seem to modern readers.[54]

Mill is somewhat less sceptical than Bentham as to the ontological reality of character. Bentham 'exposed . . . the fictional basis of character as accounted within jurisprudence (as well as its ideological dependence upon seemingly transparent concepts such as "nature" and the "social contract", which he also treated as fictional)'.[55] In the sixth chapter of his revised edition of *An Introduction to the Principles of Morals and Legislation* (1823), 'Of Circumstances Influencing Sensibility', Bentham introduces a thirty-two-part scheme that is supposed to account for the entire bodily and mental constitution of any given individual (see Table 1.1). The major divisions of this scheme include 'primary circumstances' (latent circumstances operating immediately of themselves and subdivided into 'connate' and 'adventitious') and 'secondary circumstances' (observable circumstances operating by means of the primary ones: sex, age, rank, education, climate, lineage, government and religious profession). Right before he explains each circumstantial item in turn, Bentham acknowledges in a note that 'words . . . are not . . . names of homogenous real entities, but names of various fictitious entities, for which no common genus is to be found'.[56] Words like 'character' and 'disposition' are special examples of the force of this claim. Mill may have shared Bentham's love of order and logic, but his views on character were different. He tended to give its ontological reality the benefit of the doubt and to view its moral aspect as the combination of freedom and compulsion. For Mill,

Table 1.1 Bentham's circumstances of sensibility. (Adapted from: Bentham, *An Introduction to the Principles of Morals and Legislation*, chapter 6.)

I.	primary (operate immediately of themselves / latent)

    a. connate
        i. radical frame of body (#23)
        ii. radical frame of mind (#24)
    b. adventitious
        i. personal
            1. dispositions
                a. body
                    i. health (#1) [negative circumstance]
                    ii. strength (#2) [positive circumstance / gift of nature]
                    iii. hardiness (#3) [negative circumstance / gift of education]
                    iv. bodily imperfection (#4)
                b. mind
                    i. understanding
                        1. quantity and quality of knowledge (#5)
                        2. strength of intellectual powers (#6)
                        3. insanity (#18)
                    ii. affections
                        1. firmness of mind (#7)
                        2. steadiness of mind (#8)
                        3. bent of inclination (#9)
                        4. moral sensibility (#10)
                        5. moral biases (#11)
                        6. religious sensibility (#12)
                        7. religious biases (#13)
                        8. sympathetic sensibility (#14)
                        9. sympathetic biases (#15)
                        10. antipathetic sensibility (#16)
                        11. antipathetic biases (#17)
            2. actions
                a. habitual occupations (#19)
                    i. exterior
                        1. things
                            a. pecuniary circumstances (#20)
                        2. persons
                            a. connexions in the way of sympathy (#21)
                            b. connexions in the way of antipathy (#22)

II.	secondary (operate by means of primary circumstances / observable)

    a. sex (#25)
    b. age (#26)
    c. rank (#27)
    d. education (#28)
    e. climate (#29)
    f. lineage (#30)
    g. government (#31)
    h. religious profession (#32)

individuals 'owned' or possessed moral character to the extent that their desires originated from within themselves and shaped the causal forces to which all individuals are ultimately subject. He called an individual 'characterless' in proportion as his or her impulses or motivating forces seemed to derive exclusively from external circumstances.

Both Mill and his contemporary Auguste Comte relied on systems involving taxonomies of human nature – although Mill considered ethology a far more libertarian system than Comtean positivism, which he thought urged individuals not to distrust but to venerate the idea of fatality. In his *Positive Philosophy of Auguste Comte* (1830–42), as noted in the Introduction to the present volume, Comte claims that inorganic and organic taxonomies have provided the groundwork for methods of social organisation. German and French naturalists 'have given us possession of this chief logical instrument' – the 'comparative method, which discloses to us the gradual succession of the degrees of organization in life'.[57] Hence any system that elevates the private idiosyncrasies or mysteries of individual character is the product of speculation or fancy. Comte saw what he called 'social physics' as the antidote to German metaphysics, which emphasised 'the ungovernable energy of the I'. At one point in *The Positive Philosophy of Auguste Comte*, he argues that 'the sense of personality' is 'more marked' in animals 'than in Man', since an animal, 'on account of [its] more isolated life', is less likely than a human to mistake itself for another one of its species.[58] Interestingly, it was also around this time that the rampant personalised attacks on individuals ('personalities') circulating in London and Edinburgh periodicals began to blur the boundaries between public and private character. Richard Cronin observes that in reform-era Britain, 'selfhood could no longer be regarded simply as an attribute of individuals', since it was increasingly being understood as a 'function of class and history'.[59] Even in what *Blackwood's* in 1823 called 'the age of confessions, – the era of individuality – the triumphant reign of the first person singular', the strictly social dimension of character was being charted and methodised by Utilitarians and early sociologists.[60] Character was at a unique crossroads.

Harriet Martineau (who translated *The Positive Philosophy of Auguste Comte* into English in 1853) was yet another social theorist in the 1830s interested in the 'science' of character. Her *How to Observe. Morals and Manners* (1838) was primarily concerned with the character of nations. The characters of individuals (whom Martineau calls 'agents') are mostly byproducts of social structures and therefore unimportant: '[i]n the workings of the social system, all the agents are known in the gross; all are determined. It is not their nature, but the proportions in which they are combined, which have to be ascertained'. Understanding these 'proportions' and 'combin[ations]', according to Martineau, is a matter of understanding 'what is fixed and essential' to a nation – its social institutions, its 'things': '[t]he grand secret of wise inquiry into Morals and Manners is to begin with the study of THINGS, using the DISCOURSE OF PERSONS as a commentary upon them'. The 'things' of a nation include its cemeteries, prison systems, national literature, popular idols and so on. An interview with a single citizen, on the other hand, tells the travelling observer nothing important in and of itself. Its only use is to validate or invalidate data gleaned from 'things'.[61]

How to Observe may dismiss the study of persons, but it ascribes to nations certain properties that seem intuitively to belong to persons. Nations may possess, for instance, 'moral qualities allied to physical or extrinsic power', like 'valour', 'glory' and 'pride', but not 'high spiritual qualities' like piety – these are 'matters of individual concern'. In other words, pious individuals may exist but not pious nations (though both proud individuals and proud nations are possible). Recall that, for Martineau, examining the characters of individuals tells us nothing inherently reliable about the character of the nation they inhabit. She holds true to this point, but does admit that the 'character . . . of the whole people [may] be, in certain respects, inferred' from the character of a single person, provided that that person is sufficiently and widely idolised. But she is careful to qualify this comment:

> The reveling of the French in Voltaire, of the Germans in Werter, and of the English in Byron, was, in each case, a highly important revelation of popular feeling; but it is not a circumstance from which to judge of the fixed national character of any of the three. It was a sign of the times, and not signs of nations.

A 'sign of the times', that is, must not be confused with national character. The latter is generally fixed, readable, substantial: nations per se possess studiable characters with actual 'physiognom[ies]' and 'mental and moral state[s]'.[62] A 'sign of the times' is a more like a wave of feeling or interest that occupies a nation for a time until it eventually disappears. Incidentally, in his 1815 travel narrative *England in 1815*, the Bostonian Joseph Ballard describes England in a manner of which Martineau herself might have approved. The 26-year-old Ballard was assigned to reestablish trade with Britain after the War of 1812 and travelled to England to document the state of the nation. In his account of wartime England, individual characters like Nelson are relegated to monuments and pictures hanging in veterans' hospitals; thrown into relief are detailed accounts of 'things': asylums, manufactories, theatres, hospitals, churches, graveyards, curiosity shops. Other important figures like Napoleon and the Prince Regent are mentioned briefly but more or less drowned in an examination of objects, institutions and customs.[63]

If Harriet Martineau wanted to calculate the characters of nations, Robert Owen wanted to recreate the characters of individuals – beginning with individual Britons and ending with everyone on earth. The full title of his first major publication is *A New View of Society; Or, Essays on the Principle of the Formation of the Human Character, and the Application of the Principle to Practice* (1813–16). The main premise of *A New View* is that no individual has any control over the 'causes of character'. Parents and educators 'create feelings' in children that will 'irresistibly lead' them in certain directions.[64] As a contributor to *The New British Lady's Magazine* noted a few years later in an article '[a]ddressed to all mothers' (1818), for example, a single instance of corporal punishment can permanently damage the (moral) character of a child: '[s]o easy can the first injustice which is suffered by a child, become the centre-point, round which the whole moral system turns and moves'.[65] Owen thought that it was the responsibility not only of parents and educators but of the state to produce a consistent environment conducive to 'a race of . . . superior beings'.[66] In an address to William IV in his *Book of the New Moral World* (1836), Owen claims that his utopian social arrangements at New Lanark and elsewhere have introduced a 'new foundation on which to re-construct society and re-create the character of the human race'.[67] Should this happen, 'the period of the supposed Millennium [would] commence, and universal love prevail'.[68] As Seigel points out, however, one of the logical inconsistencies of Owenism is that 'the character he wanted to form had to have an active and independent component' – despite that, as Owen himself repeatedly insisted, the production and development of character was an essentially passive process.[69]

Owen can talk about the character of the whole human race because ideally the character of all individuals should be identical. There must be an 'undeviating unity between all the thoughts, feelings, language, and actions of the human race', he claims, since, after all, '[i]nsanity is inconsistency'.[70] In 1826, a contributor to *The Mirror* argues less dramatically that inconsistency is not really 'insanity' so much as a result of 'the *ignorance* exhibited in custom and education': '[i]f any clear and positive inconsistency in man is pointed out, we find that custom has engrafted it, and education will not remove it'.[71] Owen's efforts at infant education culminated in the aptly named Institute for the Formation of Character in 1816, where dancing, singing and military tactics were systematically taught to young boys and girls. One of its many visitors was Robert Southey, who remarked disapprovingly that Owen was producing human machines.[72] Countless authors responded to Owenite utopianism in popular periodicals throughout the first half of the nineteenth century. Some praised his success at morally reforming the spinners and weavers in his manufacturing community at New Lanark. Others claimed that his ideas were centuries old and that his writing was vague. A few disagreed with his approach entirely – one author noting that true reform is not about remaking characters but remedying the 'depressed state of agriculture, manufactures, and trade' in England, circumstances which he or she thought Owen largely ignored.[73] One of Owen's supporters suggests that individual characters cannot be formed without outside interference until closed communistic organisations are firmly established.[74]

It is certainly hard to discuss Owenism without also mentioning the blossoming of phrenology in the mid-1810s, 1820s and 1830s that complemented Owenism and vied with it as an instrument of reform. Owenite socialism and phrenological 'science' were two momentous products of the ongoing tension between 'determinism and freedom' that – 'as an element in the problematic of character' – took a 'sharper form . . . in the nineteenth century'.[75] Popularised in Britain by J. G. Spurzheim and George Combe throughout the early nineteenth century and particularly in the era of reform, phrenology 'was to become in the English-speaking world an important vehicle of liberal ideology, helping to effect major reforms in penology, education, and the treatment of the insane'.[76] Its advocates argued that phrenological faculties could be selectively and harmoniously trained to produce better characters. (The phrenological geography of the mind was more or less a scientific endorsement of the moral anatomy promoted in 1823 by Bentham and could be put to similar legislative and social uses.) Texts on phrenology also advanced the circulation of new terms and methods of observation that were implicated in the broader study of 'character': pathognomy (the study of emotions expressed in faces), prosopology (the study of faces), craniology (the study of skulls), phreno-magnetism (communication between two sets of phrenological organs through an animal-magnetic medium), phreno-mesmerism ('touching the individual phrenological organs of a mesmerised person and having him or her perform the behavior associated with the mental faculty'), etc. The German phrenologist Franz Joseph Gall, in fact, 'promise[d] to provide at a stroke practical solutions to the mysteries of character'.[77]

As the 'most popular and popularized' nineteenth-century 'science', phrenology was a 'familiar part of medical education' by 1832 and produced about 200 active lecturers mostly between 1825 and 1845.[78] The Scottish solicitor and founder of the Edinburgh Phrenological Society (1820), George Combe, called it 'the greatest and most important discovery ever communicated to mankind'.[79] It was 'better known' in the early nineteenth century than its elder cousin physiognomy: 'more books were written about it, a journal was devoted to it, and polemics and public interest were aroused over it'.[80] An 1821 article in *Blackwood's* praised 'Gall, Spurzheim, and Combe' for their Promethean efforts to render the 'real character' of individuals knowable by virtue of cranial analysis: there was now 'little or nothing to discover' about character, it seemed, since the 'moral and intellectual geography of the head of man ... is laid down with a minuteness of accuracy'.[81] A few years later in 1823, however, the Blackwoodsmen qualified their initial endorsement: '[t]o prove that certain unvarying correspondences subsist between particular developments of the brain, and particular manifestations of human character, is one thing; to prove that the former indicate distinct corporeal organs, and the latter distinct mental faculties, is another'.[82] They also found it difficult to credit the existence of the faculty of 'covetousness' as '*a mere propensity to acquire*' – that is, an inherent desire to acquire anything, good or bad.[83] Other journalists were derisively sceptical: one writer for the *Eclectic Review* (1822) observes that the phrenologist who 'decide[s] on another's character ... from physical propensities ... would but discover a craniological deficiency ... in himself'.[84]

As any discipline, phrenology could be used to advance different ideological ends. It was not always clearly or exclusively applied as a 'vehicle of liberal ideology'. In the sphere of religion, for instance, it could be used either to reinforce or to invalidate basic Christian beliefs. In his highly influential *Constitution of Man* (1828), to take one example, Combe argues that minds sceptical or ignorant of divine laws are not functioning at optimum capacity – by which he means that their discrete phrenological faculties are not harmonised, their 'conflicting tendencies' not 'reconciled'.[85] In response to Owen (who, he claimed, paid too little attention to 'phrenological inequalities'), the radical agitator Richard Carlile advocated a plan of reform that would match prospective parents according their phrenological similarities.[86] Carlile felt that phrenology was '*essentially an Atheistical science*', not least because the character trait of 'faithfulness' was not traceable to God but to phrenological organisations that were generally more '*imitative and repetitive*' and less 'discriminating'.[87]

Though Owen considered men and women as members of a social collective, whose shared environment could be conditioned so as to make everyone in it uniformly happy and virtuous, while phrenologists like Gall applied 'cerebral theory ... to the reform of [individual] character[s]', 'withholding or providing stimuli to particular mental organs' so that 'specific forms of behavior could be encouraged or discouraged', the two perspectives were theoretically reconcilable.[88] The utopian socialist and women's rights advocate Catherine Barmby argues – in this powerful excerpt from an article in the *Co-Operative Magazine* (1826) – that phrenology agrees with her own, Owenite view

> that the human being is not, in any view, whether of his nature, or of his condition in the universe, free to choose, but that he is, *necessarily, what he is;* that his character is created for him by his conformation, as

much, or more than by the condition in which he is placed; that he has no self-directing power vested in himself to choose what he would be, or how he would act; that he is impelled to act by the force of those organs which nature has created and combined to form his brain, and by the influence of external circumstances acting upon, and in conjunction with those organs – that those organs are his nature or himself – that they will and must, *take their course*.[89]

Here, external circumstances cooperate perfectly with internal organs to produce completely determined beings. There is, of course, nothing profoundly new about this sentiment for 1826. Godwin and the French *philosophes* whose writings he scoured for *Political Justice* had made similar claims (albeit without the strong phrenological emphasis). Numerous nineteenth-century authors, too, would go on to worry about what Lionel Trilling has called 'the anxiety about the machine'. But there is something arresting and inexorable in the wording of this passage, I think, that gives new life to old ideas. For Barmby, there is almost no room for the Millian version of character that provides individuals with some chance to affect antecedent circumstances through personal will and desire. Whatever character an individual may be said to 'possess' is, in this case, part of a mechanism set to run according to an inevitable programme; and no 'active and daring character' from the future, fortunately, will ever be able to overthrow the utopian socialist order that Barmby has in mind, since everyone in it will be *necessarily* kind and good: unable even to 'desire evil'.[90]

Barmby claims that the 'character' of a 'human being ... is created for him by his conformation, as much, or more than by the condition in which he is placed'. So 'character' is mostly the result of one's brain organs ('conformation') but to a lesser extent also the result of one's 'condition in the universe'. This much is clear. But what happens at the end of the excerpt when Barmby refers to a person's 'organs' alone as 'his nature or himself'? What happened to 'condition'? Either its role as an ethological determinant has dwindled or the signifiers 'character' and '[s]elf' refer to different things. Maybe she means that 'character' equals brain organs plus condition, and that 'nature or himself' equals organs alone. The only thing we can be somewhat certain of is that '[s]elf' cannot mean anything like a will or 'self-directing principle' apart from phrenological organisation: Barmby is clear that no such thing has any real existence let alone influence on human action.

Barmby's article is important because it reveals just how vexed the term 'character' had become by the 1820s. Perhaps it was so hard to pin down because the very nature and origin of human life had just been hotly contested in the vitalism debate that spanned nearly the whole Regency period. Jon Klancher has described it as 'the great John Hunter debate of 1811–19', in which '"organicists" or "vitalists" struggled with "mechanists" or "materialists" in what actually became an elaborate dialogue about . . . "organization"':

> According to the debate that had been taking shape around John Hunter's physiological collections at the Royal College of Surgeons, bodies that organized themselves into life were coming to be defined as 'materialist' bodies; bodies generated into life by some prior force or principle were 'vital' or 'idealist' bodies. As a surgeon in the eighteenth century, Hunter had assiduously collected skeletons, heads, and organ specimens from animal and human bodies, partly from surgical practice and partly from voyages to the South Seas in the 1770s. By the time of his death in 1793, the size of Hunter's collection – some 14,000 specimens – had outgrown the square footage of his own house. Only after arranging these alcohol-preserved body parts in a certain order, as later displayed at the Royal College of Surgeons, was Hunter granted credit for transforming the period's natural-history collections from curious 'cabinets of rarities' to 'a systematic and illuminated record of the operations and products of life'.[91]

According to Klancher, the 1790s saw a 'proliferation of meanings about what it meant to "organize" or "be organized"' – a 'debate over the meaning of Hunter's physiological work'. The debate intensified in 1816 when 'the physiologist [William] Lawrence stood before the Royal College of Surgeons to interpret Hunter's great collection as a materialist legacy', attempting 'to locate the secret of living systems in the cellular action of tissue'. A shocked, pious Coleridge thought that Lawrence had 'failed to account for Hunter's most striking idea, that of a "life or vital principle, *independent of the organization*"'. Without such a 'motivating spark of vitality or divine prime mover', Coleridge worried, '[e]verything would take place in the complex interactivity of organisms with their environments' (an 'interactivity' that Barmby claimed 'created' character).[92] L. S. Jacyna describes the Hunter debate in terms of 'transcendentalists' and 'immanentists'. Transcendentalists (including the surgeons Richard Saumarez and John Abernethy) 'insisted that the order and power of the organism were not emergent properties of its constituent elements, but had to be imposed from above, by superior upon inferior beings'. Immanentists (including Lawrence and the physicians John Elliotson and T. C. Morgan) 'stressed that life and mind emerged . . . from below, by means of the elaboration of qualities inherent in matter'.[93]

Not that either view represented the pinnacle of imaginable human freedom. Transcendentalists and immanentists alike promoted 'alternative strategies of social control': '[b]oth sought some restriction upon human freedom; but while one found it in the power of a Deity omnipotent, the other discerned a sufficient check upon political innovation in the concept of man as a purely natural being'.[94] A being endowed with a vital principle by God, in other words, is restricted by the limits of that endowment and the laws of its Giver. A 'purely natural' being is a slave to its material (brute?) organisation and therefore – it could be argued – unqualified for the benefits of political reform.

Immanentists like T. C. Morgan believed that 'man's character' was 'dependent upon and determined by physical necessity'.[95] Further strengthening the materialist view, the article on 'Life' in Rees's *Cyclopædia* (1812) claimed that 'character' is 'the physiognomy of the passions'. This seems to mean that studying human passions as the physiognomist studies facial features will yield a reliable character portrait. Moreover, since passions cannot be altered by habit, exercise or education, neither can character:

> to attempt altering the character, [by] softening or exalting the passions, of which [character] is the habitual expression, or enlarging, or contracting their sphere, would be an enterprise analogous to that of permanently raising or diminishing the extraordinary force of the heart, or accelerating or retarding the motions of the arteries in the state of health. . . . . circulation and respiration are not under the influence of the will, and cannot therefore be modified by the individual, without the occurrence of disease. The same observation will apply to those who think they can change the character, and consequently the passions, since the latter are the produce of the actions of all the internal organs, or at least are especially seated in them.[96]

Passions are the 'produce of the actions of all the internal organs'. The human will has no power to manipulate the internal organs, and therefore no power to manipulate the passions whose 'habitual expression' is character. Willing the character to change is analogous to willing the 'circulation and respiration' to change; each, if possible, would initiate disease and the dissolution of the organism.

Other authors found it hard to believe that matter alone was the origin of things like sensation, intelligence and character. In an article 'On the Phenomena of Intelligence as Dependent upon Organization' (1831), Robert Willan Chapman writes that

> we have no evidence that the operations of matter, under any state or degree of organization, can give rise to sensation. This property necessarily implies a cause, and whether we designate it sentient, principle, a spirit, or a soul, it can in no wise affect the fact which is placed within the sphere of our comprehension, viz.: that sensation exists, and must be referable to an immaterial agent.[97]

The larger point here is that both cosmologies may be said to emphasise the ethological hold placed on individuals at the root of life. For immanentists, character is regulated by some mystery of material organisation (though Carlile, for his part, denies that organisation yields 'occult qualit[ies]').[98] For transcendentalists, on the other hand, character, if it exists, originates in the vital principle superadded to material beings by Providence. It may be interesting to recall that Gall himself was not a materialist: 'following Herder, Gall viewed material organs as essential instruments of natural forces or vital powers'.[99] That is, he treated vital powers or faculties as *dinge an sich* – unknowable except through their fleshy instruments.

The following chapter picks up immediately where the present one leaves off. I will explore how this broad, multidisciplinary interest in 'personal' character spanning the reform era becomes distilled into the concept of textual character, so that the increasing instability of the one necessarily promotes the instability of the other (and vice versa).

Notes

1. Qtd in Semple, *Bentham's Prison*, p. 93.
2. Dickens, *Hard Times*, p. 83.
3. Mark Canuel observes that the word 'disposition' is 'surely one of the oddest words in the English language', since it 'means both "control" and "getting rid of" control, a removal or displacement of property or power' (*The Shadow of Death*, p. 88). To 'dispose' of something, in other words, means both to manage it and to surrender the management of it.

4. Schoenfield, *British Periodicals and Romantic Identity*, p. 3.
5. McIntyre, 'Character: A Humean Account', p. 194.
6. Seigel, 'Necessity, Freedom, and Character Formation', p. 249.
7. Ibid., pp. 249–50.
8. Ahnert and Manning, introduction to *Character, Self, and Sociability*, pp. 23, 3, 11.
9. Richardson, *Literature, Education, and Romanticism*, p. 7.
10. Hume, 'The Sceptic', pp. 161, 169.
11. See Hume, *An Inquiry Concerning Human Understanding*, pp. 90–105.
12. Manning, *Poetics of Character*, p. 20.
13. Ibid.
14. Bricke, 'Hume's Theories of Dispositional Properties', p. 17.
15. Bricke, 'Hume's Conception of Character', pp. 108–9.
16. Rorty, 'A Literary Postscript', pp. 321–2.
17. McIntyre, 'Character: A Humean Account', pp. 194, 196, 200.
18. Aristotle, *Nicomachean Ethics*, p. 7.
19. Smeed, *The Theophrastan 'Character'*, pp. 2, 114.
20. Craig, '*The Mirror*, No. 31', pp. 195–7.
21. Hall, *Characters of Virtues and Vices*, p. 105.
22. Butler, *Characters and Passages from Note-Books*, p. 167.
23. La Bruyère, *The Works of Monsieur De La Bruyere*, p. 211.
24. Schoenfield, *British Periodicals and Romantic Identity*, p. 2.
25. Story, 'Emblems of Identity', p. 81.
26. Bauer, 'Some Verse Fragments and Prose "Characters"', p. 160.
27. Anon., 'On the Knowledge of Character', p. 230.
28. Philanthropos, 'The Character of a Common Brewer', pp. 504, 506.
29. Anon., 'Aboriginal Character', p. 39.
30. Anon., 'On the Knowledge of Character', p. 225.
31. Lambert, '"Living Machines"', p. 420.
32. N. N., 'Further Thoughts on the Formation of Character', p. 97.
33. Chas., 'On the Formation of Moral Character', p. 69.
34. Hall, 'Effects of Infidelity on Character and Conduct', p. 151.
35. Anon., 'Character, – Principle, – with Other Grave Matters', p. 210.
36. Jarrold, 'Of the Influence of Early Impressions on the Future Character', pp. 193–5.
37. Jarrold, 'Of the Influence of Early Impressions on the Future Character [cont.]', p. 305.
38. This fact contradicts one of James Wilson's main points in *On Character* (1995), at least as far as the 1820s and 1830s are concerned: '[t]o investigate character and to seek ways of improving it are not tantamount to taking ideological sides' (*On Character*, p. 6).

39. Anon., 'Character, – Principle, – with Other Grave Matters', pp. 209, 211.
40. Anon., 'Value of a Good Character', p. 280. Freeman likewise acknowledges the value of character in the eighteenth century as 'credibility in social and economic transactions' (*Character's Theater*, p. 24).
41. Chas., 'On the Formation of Moral Character', p. 62.
42. T. W. B., 'Decision of Character', p. 412.
43. Manning, *Poetics of Character*, p. 22.
44. H., 'On Keeping, or Costume in Character', pp. 162, 167.
45. Piper, *Dreaming in Books*, p. 61.
46. Qtd in Schoenfield, *British Periodicals and Romantic Identity*, p. 44. Hogg himself ironically reinforces the notion of handwriting as a window to the 'heart and mind' by providing a facsimile of Wringhim's hand in the *Private Memoirs and Confessions*.
47. Anon., 'On the Knowledge of Character', pp. 225, 227, 229, 231.
48. Ibid., pp. 227, 232–3.
49. Carlisle, *John Stuart Mill and the Writing of Character*, pp. 131, 134.
50. Mill, *A System of Logic*, pp. 540, 546.
51. Feuer, 'John Stuart Mill as a Sociologist', p. 87.
52. Mill, *A System of Logic*, pp. 546, 543.
53. Ball, 'The Formation of Character', pp. 25, 29, 32.
54. David Leary has noted that 'the development of a science of character demanded a more systematic, more biological, more emotionally oriented, and more empirical psychology' than was available to Mill ('The Fate and Influence', pp. 155–6). Typologies, too, are inherently limiting because their 'dimensions represent concepts rather than empirical cases. The dimensions are based on the notion of an ideal type, a mental construct that deliberately accentuates certain characteristics and not necessarily something that is found in empirical reality'. Typologies are 'categories that are neither exhaustive nor mutually exclusive, are often based on arbitrary or ad hoc criteria, are descriptive rather than explanatory or predictive, and are frequently subject to the problem of reification' (Smith, 'Typologies, Taxonomies, and the Benefits of Policy Classification', p. 381).
55. Bender, *Imagining the Penitentiary*, p. 213.
56. Bentham, *An Introduction to the Principles of Morals and Legislation*, p. 45.
57. Comte, *The Positive Philosophy of Auguste Comte*, pp. 452–3. The proto-sociological view of individual character in the nineteenth century parallels the biological view of character that emerged around the same time. Lindley Darden has noted that according to 'an important shift in

nineteenth-century biology', organisms were no longer 'viewed as having "essences"' so much as 'being composed of independently variable characters... whose *variations* within a population [became] important objects of study' ('Character: Historical Perspectives', p. 41).
58. Comte, *The Positive Philosophy of Auguste Comte*, pp. 390, 384.
59. Cronin, *Paper Pellets*, p. 49.
60. Qtd in Cronin, *Paper Pellets*, p. 50.
61. Martineau, *How to Observe*, pp. 14, 20–1, 63.
62. Ibid., pp. 93–4, 106–7, 123–34.
63. See Ballard, *England in 1815*.
64. Owen, 'A New View of Society', p. 65.
65. H., R., 'On the Dangerous Influence of Injustice', p. 261.
66. Owen, 'A New View of Society', p. 65.
67. Owen, *The Book of the New Moral World*, p. 3.
68. Owen, 'Address Delivered to the Inhabitants of New Lanark', p. 130.
69. Seigel, 'Necessity, Freedom, and Character Formation', p. 258.
70. Owen, *The Book of the New Moral World*, p. 16; and Owen, 'Address Delivered to the Inhabitants of New Lanark', p. 138. See Chapter 6 in the present volume for an analysis of the literary career of Letitia Landon, which I argue repeatedly defies Owen's claim that '[i]nsanity is inconsistency'.
71. C., A. B., 'The Character, Nature, and Power of Man', p. 84.
72. Lambert, '"Living Machines"', p. 427.
73. Anon., 'Art. XI. 1. *A New View of Society*', p. 454.
74. See Tucker, 'On the Formation of Character', pp. 44–5.
75. Seigel, 'Necessity, Freedom, and Character Formation', p. 259. Both Owenism and phrenology were often viewed as fatalistic doctrines. According to Cooter, however,

a truer basis of accord between the doctrines was in the mutual effort of their exponents to *rid* them of gloomy associations with determinism. What Owen and Combe both required, though for different reasons and extending from different determinisms, was to show that in spite of basic nonresponsibility, people were morally accountable. Without some degree of 'self-directing power' there would be no reason for people to strive for new moral codes'. (*The Cultural Meaning of Popular Science*, p. 229)

76. Cooter, *The Cultural Meaning of Popular Science*, pp. 6–7.
77. Ibid., pp. 150, 6.
78. Ibid., pp. 2, 29, 151.
79. Combe, *A System of Phrenology*, p. iv.

80. Fahenstock, 'The Heroine of Irregular Features', p. 335.
81. Anon., 'I. – Essays on Phrenology', p. 690.
82. Anon., 'Anti-Phrenologica', Sec. I, p. 101.
83. Anon., 'Anti-Phrenologica', Sec. II, p. 199.
84. Anon., 'Art. VIII. *Reflections on Gall and Spurzheim's System*', p. 552.
85. Combe, *Constitution of Man*, p. 2.
86. Cooter, *The Cultural Meaning of Popular Science*, p. 213.
87. Carlile, 'Dr. Spurzheim and Phrenology', p. 498.
88. Cooter, *The Cultural Meaning of Popular Science*, p. 226.
89. Barmby, 'Phrenology', p. 280.
90. Trilling, *Sincerity and Authenticity*, p. 126; Barmby, 'Phrenology', pp. 280–1.
91. Klancher, *Transfiguring the Arts and Sciences*, pp. 133–4.
92. Ibid., pp. 134–6.
93. Jacyna, 'Immanence or Transcendence', pp. 314–15.
94. Ibid., p. 328.
95. Ibid.
96. Qtd in Thomas Rennell, *Remarks on Scepticism*, pp. 56–7. An anonymous writer in *The Quarterly Review* claims that William Lawrence wrote the article on 'Life' for Rees's *Cyclopædia*, and that Thomas Rennell had made the discovery: 'he [Lawrence] is understood to be the writer of several articles on life … in the interminable Encyclopædia of Dr. Rees … in which Mr. Rennell has discovered, that he has translated whole sections from M. Bichat, without the slightest acknowledgement' (Anon., 'Art. I. 1. *An Enquiry into the Probability and Rationality of Mr. Hunter's Theory of Life*', p. 4).
97. Chapman, 'On the Phenomena of Intelligence', p. 59.
98. Carlile, 'Organization-Intellect', p. 83.
99. Van Whye, 'The Authority of Human Nature', p. 26.

Chapter 2

From Person to Text: Character and the Problem of Representation

The Spatialisation of Character

Ethology, phrenology, sociology, Owenism, immanentism, transcendentalism: all became important topics around the same time and all tried to explain the nature and formation of personal character more or less scientifically. Character thus became a vital object of multidisciplinary knowledge in postwar Britain. It was anatomised, taxonomised, naturalised in new ways. Its temporal dimension, of course, could never be realised in these new discourses as it was in certain kinds of narrative fiction. Realistic novels examined networks of individual characters that seemed to live, move and change over time. The new disciplines, at best, could infer how passing time influenced character in an abstract sense but could not so easily represent that influence. What is interesting is that other discourses coinciding with these new knowledges – multigeneric mixtures of narrative fiction, cultural commentary and journalism – were also interested in character in a more abstract sense (in a less concrete or 'living' sense of the sort we find in novels). I view these discourses as part of a general diversion from the tendency of realistic novels to dramatise character 'development'. Realist fiction 'flourishes in narrative amplitude, where character has "space" to be presented as unfolding over time'.[1] It fetishises the concept of ethological 'development', a concept that Clifford Siskin argues was invented – or least elevated and consolidated – by the aesthetic experiments of early Romantic authors.[2]

A lot of reform-era writing tends to minimise or even ignore character's temporal dimension. From one perspective, such writing 'dissolves the tensions between plot and character ... that are the mandatory signs of personal depth; it circumvents the reconciliations of the individual and the social that signal character development'.[3] Both real and fictional characters become spatialised in postwar British literary culture. As to the real ones, the 'new sub-genre' of the 'literary portrait' began to flourish in the 1820s. Higgins observes that '[m]ost of the literary magazines of the early nineteenth century contained series of portraits of authors': 'articles' that discussed 'their subject's intellectual characteristics', 'life history, personal character and appearance (some included actual portraits)'.[4] A prime example is William Maginn's 'Gallery of Illustrious Literary Characters', published in *Fraser's Magazine* in the early 1830s. As to fictional characters, in the late 1830s Letitia Landon began writing a series of texts (sketches? essays? portraits?) on select female characters from Walter Scott's novels, called 'The Female Portrait Gallery'. Landon died before she could finish it, but Laman Blanchard included the portraits she did complete in his *Life and Literary Remains of L. E. L.* (1841), published in two duodecimo volumes by Colburn. The 'Gallery' consists of 'portraits' of twenty-two female characters drawn or adapted from Scott's novels. Julie Watt observes that Landon 'began writing the essays from memory', until 'luckily, and improbably, she was sent a set of Scott's novels by one of the merchants on the Gold Coast'. It was clear that Landon had also 'read Lockhart's very recently published *Life of Sir Walter Scott* before she began'. One of Landon's observations is that Scott tended to base his important male characters on persons he knew, but that his female ones were usually idealised constructions. Her own 'portraits' of these females, therefore, 'added a dimension and breathed some life into them, for few of the originals have a life of their own'. For Watt, Landon describes the female characters 'as she wanted them to be, rather than as Scott portrayed them'.[5] Cronin claims that the 'Female Portrait Gallery' was meant to 'appropriate for women . . . Scott's . . . robustly masculine novels'.[6] One could also say that Landon's 'Gallery' helped increase what Brewer calls the 'social canonicity' of Scott's female characters: the thinking of them as 'common object[s]' whose 'felt value' readers could 'rally around' and appreciate as a community.[7]

It is interesting to consider Maginn's 'Gallery of Illustrious Literary Characters' and Landon's 'Female Portrait Gallery' as a pair. Both appeared in the 1830s. Landon supposedly tries to add what Watt calls 'life' and 'dimension' to beings that never existed. She extracts them from fictional universes that ostensibly enabled the characters inside them to 'unfol[d] over time' through dynamic interactions with social and cultural forces. Maginn writes short articles on real people: 'always a page in length'; 'based on Daniel Maclise's accompanying drawings, which often depicted the subject in a state of private, domestic relaxation'; and 'not always . . . avoiding gossip and scandal' (Maginn being a 'notorious scandalmonger').[8] In both kinds of writing, the elusive object 'character' emerges as a thing that is manifestly nowhere: neither in the original nor in its hypothetical representation. Landon seems to have a problem with Scott's female characters because they are not as interesting, 'round', true-to-life as his male ones. This fact raises the question: do her 'portraits' represent something 'contained in' the novels better than the novels themselves did? Is she adding lights, shades and colours to a bare outline – as when the eponymous protagonist in Mary Wollstonecraft's *The Wrongs of Woman, Or Maria* observes of Henry Darnfield that his 'steady, bold step, and the whole air of his person . . . gave an outline to the imagination to sketch the individual form she wished to recognize'?[9] And what about the 'illustrious' characters of Maginn? Does the 'actual' or 'true' character of any one of his real-life subjects exist somewhere between an idealised Maclise portrait, contemporary gossip and the available accumulated facts of his or her life? Is it significant that the 'Literary Characters' in his title is easily mistaken for textual characters instead of professional authors? Does either 'Gallery' reinforce or even suggest a fundamental difference between the textual characters Landon 'revitalizes' and the 'real' ones Maginn condenses in his one-page summaries?

The 'portraits' of Landon and Maginn coincide with and relate to another contemporary genre that Amanpal Garcha has called the 'sketch'. All three kinds of writing emphasise the spatial at the expense of the temporal. Garcha argues that novelists like Thackeray, Dickens and Gaskell all started out small, 'gravitat[ing] toward short forms' in the 1820s and 1830s that she calls 'sketches'. Including texts like Mary Mitford's *Our Village* (1824–32), Dickens' *Sketches by Boz* (1833–6) and Thackeray's *Paris Sketchbook* (1840), reform-era 'sketches' were deliberately 'incomplete, fragmented, and hurried, like modern time itself'. They offered readers a desired 'sense of atemporal stability' – an 'escape from time's movement' – in an 'increasingly fast-paced, crowded literary market'.[10] Eventually, however, the 'fragmented forms and more-or-less synchronic temporality' of the 'sketch' ceded power to the 'narrative diachrony' of the novel.[11] Why? Why were reform-era readers rapidly enchanted and then rapidly disenchanted with 'sketches' in the short span of two decades? According to Garcha:

> The fact that fictional sketches grew in popularity – and novels declined – through the 1820s and 1830s suggests that readers began to find plot less appealing and fragmentation and stasis more so. At the same time, they desired *fictional* descriptions and essayistic accounts of people and places rather than the more realistic, objective travel sketches published in previous decades. Readers wished, in other words, for an explicitly *aestheticized* sense of fragmented temporality and stasis.[12]

No doubt, too, the forms and modes of publication suitable to the periodical format contributed to the rise and fall of what Garcha calls the 'sketch'.

Garcha focuses on reform-era 'sketches' written in early in the careers of authors who went on to become famous novelists; other collections of sketch-like texts appearing around the same time were composed by individuals who have since remained relatively obscure as literary artists. In 1820, the young reformist politician Lord John Russell published his little-known *Essays, and Sketches of Life and Character. By a Gentleman Who Has Left His Lodgings* (London: Longman *et al.*). The preface – signed 'Joseph Skillett' – reports that the content of *Essays, and Sketches* derives from 'a large number of manuscripts' left by a brooding 'gentleman' of irregular habits who rented the first floor of the London apartment building where Skillett also lived. One February, at midnight, the gentleman simply disappeared and never returned. Skillett (the preface continues) goes through the former lodger's things to see what he can sell for rent money. He notes that the manuscripts left behind were written in 'all kinds of languages, ancient and modern', and that he hoped to recover a part of [his] rent by their means'.[13] *Essays, and Sketches* consists of seventeen short prose pieces of social and cultural commentary. Some of them read more like personal anecdotes with slight narrative arcs, while others resemble didactic essays. Many move in and out of the Theophrastan mode. The 'real John Bull', according to a piece called 'English and French Pride and

Vanity', 'take[s] no pleasure in society', considers conversation 'an involuntary obligation' and 'likes to have a mutton-chop in his own parlour' at minimal expense.[14] He also prefers to stay in dim, cramped rooms and to dress like everyone else. In another sketch Russell describes 'men of letters' – particularly poets – as sensitive, irritable, quarrelsome, envious and servile.[15]

Essays, and Sketches is followed over the next few decades by several publications with similar formal and rhetorical patterns. In the preface to his three-volume collection *Sayings and Doings, a Series of Sketches from Life* (1824–8) – thought to have influenced Dickens' *Sketches by Boz* – Theodore Hook tells readers that he has 'not[ed] down what [he] saw passing in society, in order to judge, by the events of real life, the truth or fallacy' of ancient 'axioms'. He compares a series of modern 'characters' whose 'lives and conduct' – their 'doings' – 'unconsciously exemplified' certain 'sayings' of the ancients.[16] The individual texts are about the length of short stories, have relatively wide narrative arcs and are drawn from Hook's personal experience (with the names of real people and places omitted). Of all these multigeneric, reform-era experiments, however, the most relevant to this study is the two-volume collection published in 1831 by Alaric Watts, editor of the *Literary Souvenir*, called *Scenes of Life and Shades of Character*. Watts notes in the advertisement to *Scenes* that '[t]he following pages'

> are the production of several hands. A portion of the papers contained in them was printed several years ago in a periodical Work of limited circulation, which has since been continued. These, however, have undergone so much alteration, as to give them a title to be regarded almost as novelties; and, with the addition of several original sketches, may fairly be said to constitute a new work.[17]

Scenes contains more explicitly, more dramatically Theophrastan texts than can be found in the collections by Russell and Hook. Its two volumes feature titles like 'Sensible People', 'The Female Splenetic', 'The Squire of Dames', 'Particular People', 'Book Borrowers', 'Book Beggars', 'The Maiden Aunt', 'The Magazine Publisher', 'Nobody', 'The Child of Impulse' and 'The Awkward Man'. Many of these demonstrate the reform-era penchant for interpreting a social landscape of 'characters' through typological/taxonomic lenses. The author of 'Sensible People' observes that 'there are three kinds of sense, – fine sense, common sense, and nonsense. The first constitutes a man of genius, the second a man of business, and the last . . . a sensible man'. For this writer the 'sensible' man is the reverse of agreeable. He administers unsolicited lectures about the 'indiscretions of his friends' at happy social gatherings. '[E]ntirely made up of negatives', he is 'a dealer in truism' and 'the very prince of commonplace'.[18] Another piece entitled 'The Squire of Dames' describes a man of this 'type' as 'commonly a pert, pragmatical coxcomb, of from twenty to thirty years of age, who is not wholly unacquainted with fashionable society, but who has scarcely seen enough of it to acquire the polish of a perfect gentleman'. Such 'squires' – humorously taxonomised like animals or plants – are small and smooth, and can be found in their natural habitat of drawing rooms:

> he is rather diminutive, never exceeding the height of five feet eight inches, and seldom attaining to more than five feet five. If he have a smooth chin, light hair, and blue eyes, he is the more likely to be a genuine specimen; although we confess we have occasionally met with animals of this genus with beards as black, and mustachios as luxuriant, as those of the celebrated Baron Geramb.

Additional traits of the 'true Squire of Dames' include Werther-like facial expressions, a 'profusion of rings', the need to 'unburthen' himself to ladies of scandalous secrets, the ability to dissect fowl with 'geometrical precision', hands of 'almost feminine whiteness' and an 'Anglo-Italian' name with a 'mellifluous' sound drawn from Minerva Press novels. Traits are piled upon traits upon traits in this article until even the author seems exhausted: '[a]nother characteristic or two, and we have done'.[19] Using Linnaean language to describe human 'types' is a staple of the Theophrastan sketches in *Scenes*. The author of 'Book Borrowers' claims that 'various are the tribes, or orders, into which these destructive animals are divided and subdivided; but however they may differ in their minor characteristics, they are all beasts of prey, whose appetites are as unsatiable [*sic*] as the grave'.[20] Book borrowers, as it happens, dress in black and wear shovel hats, and are not to be confused with 'another species of the same genus, namely, professed Book Beggars'.[21] In another piece from *Scenes*, a 'maiden aunt' is said to be 'classed under the *genus*, old women, or at best, specified as old maids – rarely, if ever, individualized'. Fortunately for the ethologist, the characteristics of 'old maids' are perfectly distinguishable from the 'various foibles peculiarly characterizing certain individuals, who form component parts of the class called *maiden ladies*'.[22]

Such generically unclassifiable prose pieces circulating in the 1820s and 1830s tend to destabilise whatever it is in which 'character' may be said to consist. It is provocatively unclear in much of reform-era discourse where character belongs or how it is situated in space and time. The 'Female Portrait Gallery' is particularly interesting because it denies a set of narrativised characters the opportunity to demonstrate their 'moral' characters: to actualise themselves over time against the pressure of external circumstances. In other contexts (see Chapter 6 in the present volume) Landon depreciates the idea of ethological 'conservation' in fiction and ethological 'constancy' in life.

Character and Its Discontents

In an 1823 article published in the *London Magazine*, Thomas De Quincey observes that 'every man and woman was a most interesting book, if one knew how to read them. Here opened up a new world of misery. For if books and works of art existed by millions, men existed by hundreds of millions'.[23] The mania for ethological speculation and observation could be unsettling to reform-era readers and writers. Part of what was unsettling has already been discussed: fear of gossip or the invasion of privacy. Any reasonably well-known person could find the details of his or her private life – private 'character' – available for public consumption in the next weekly or monthly magazine. In the 'new prose', notes Cronin, 'no aspect of a subject's life was safe from biographical scrutiny'.[24] The Scottish solicitor Macvey Napier was one of countless others to complain that monthlies like *Blackwood's* 'ransacked' '[a]ll the privacies of life', 'explored and violated' 'all the sanctuaries of . . . nature'.[25] Napier is referring to the nonfictional world of actual people, but a ruthless penetration into constitutive-moral character could be a praiseworthy trait in a novelist. In 1826, J. G. Lockhart praised the novel form for its 'exhibition of human character under every light and shade which could result from the conflicting influence of principle and passion on every possible variety of temperament and constitution'.[26] The language here – meant as admiration – is almost panoptically invasive: the novelist 'exhibit[s]' and anatomises 'every possible variety of temperament and constitution' 'under every light and shade'. The same praise, too, might have been given by an enthusiast to the new phrenological science. Phrenology (to requote the *Newcastle Magazine* in 1824) claimed to 'penetrate the secrets of the soul', to 'penetrate ... the secret recesses of the human heart' in order to 'acquire a just acquaintance with the character of an individual' (one wonders what an 'unjust' acquaintance would look like). According to Combe, phrenology now made it 'possible ... to discover the true dispositions which individuals possess' – a possibility that enabled phrenologists to indulge their 'urge to dominate others, obscured in the urge to know and control ... human nature'.[27] Thus character as public reputation, character as private habits and character as the secret principle of thought and action were concepts reinvented and remarketed, in new disciplines and media, as knowledge – and all at approximately the same time.

A few literary professionals during and after the Napoleonic wars wrote as self-professed 'spies': experts at reading the characters of others but relatively 'illegible' themselves. The culture of espionage prevalent in the 1790s seems to have survived that tumultuous decade in the form of professional character-readers, or, to use the name that Percy Bysshe Shelley gives his Gothic villain Ginotti in 1810, 'mysterious scrutineer[s]'.[28] Schoenfield notes that '[a]lthough character implied the potential of character assassination, of exposing ... the vested interests of petty individuals, it also provided a claim of legibility for the individuals that, as an aggregate, amount[ed] to historical force'.[29] In the first number of his short-lived weekly paper *The Spy* (1 September 1810), James Hogg has his Hogg-like persona the 'Spy' – frustrated in his efforts as a preacher, farmer and poet – go 'to the Devil' and 'commenc[e] a Spy upon the manners, customs, and particular characters of all ranks of people', 'travell[ing] over the greatest part of Britain in various characters' for 'twenty years'.[30] Eventually the Spy becomes

> an observer so accurate, that by contemplating a person's features minutely, modelling my own after the same manner as nearly as possible, and putting my body into the same posture which seems most familiar to them, I can ascertain the compass of their minds and thoughts ... not precisely what they are thinking of at the time, but the way that they would think about any thing.[31]

The Spy turns the act of sympathising – which Burke and Hume claimed could be aided by 'physica[l] mimicry' – into the 'professional practice' of character-reading.[32] The same skill would be used fourteen years later by the demonic suborner Gil-Martin in Hogg's *Private Memoirs and Confessions of a Justified Sinner* (1824). Gil-Martin shadows the self-righteous Calvinist Robert Wringhim, convincing Wringhim to commit a series of heinous acts (though the novel makes it unclear whether Robert himself is the perpetrator, or Gil-Martin in the person of Robert). One of Gil-Martin's 'rare qualification[s]' is the ability to shapeshift:

> My countenance changes with my studies and sensations . . . If I contemplate a man's features seriously, mine own gradually assume the very same appearance and character. And what is more, by contemplating a face minutely, I not only attain the same likeness, but, with the likeness, I attain the very same ideas as well as the same mode of arranging them, so that, you see, by looking at a person attentively, I by degrees assume his likeness, and by assuming his likeness I attain to the possession of his most secret thoughts.[33]

Ian Duncan associates this strange ability with the voluntary and involuntary powers of sympathy discussed respectively by Smith and Hume: the 'Smithian imaginative discipline has become a technique that harnesses the involuntary, contagious force of sympathy [the sort discussed by Hume] for a diabolical will to power'.[34] Duncan also compares Gil-Martin to Tommaso Companella, the 'celebrated physiognomist' whom Edmund Burke mentions in his *Philosophical Enquiry into the Origin of Our Ideas of the Sublime and the Beautiful*. Burke notes that Companella

> had not only made very accurate observations on human faces, but was very expert in mimicking such, as were in any way remarkable. When he had a mind to penetrate into the inclinations of those he had to deal with, he composed his face, his gesture, and his whole body, as nearly as he could into the exact similitude of the person he intended to examine; and then carefully observed what turn of mind he seemed to acquire by this change. So that . . . he was able to enter into the dispositions and thoughts of people, as effectually as if he had been changed into the very men.[35]

According to Duncan, this sort of physiognomic practice is 'flagrantly invasive – a colonization of the other that erases the properties of his interiority'.[36] Both Gil-Martin and Companella appropriate the appearances and interiorities of others through manipulative acts. Several critics have interpreted this power in light of Hogg's relationship with the periodical industry (mostly his relationship with *Blackwood's*). Schoenfield observes that this professional/diabolical ability enables Hogg to 'write himself from one position into the other, within the frame of the periodical industry in which identity is sold, imitated, appropriated, and contested'.[37] Cronin argues that Gil-Martin 'has his origins ... in a relationship with *Blackwood's Magazine* that had demonstrated to Hogg so powerfully that in the new world of print no one could command his own identity'.[38] Fang likewise calls the *Confessions* an 'allegorical novel about Hogg's relations with *Blackwood's*'.[39] I agree with these claims, though I also think that Gil-Martin's sinisterly 'sympathetic' power can be viewed both in light of Hogg's career and as a reflex of a broader cultural fixation with the 'properties of ... interiority': character being portrayed in a variety of media at the time (within and beyond periodicals) and by a variety of authors as an interiority that is also an exteriority, a thing 'owned' and not owned, irreducible and reducible, inalienable and appropriable by social agencies in and through characterising acts.

Apropos of spies, in 1825 Charles Westmacott released the first volume of his book *The English Spy* (London: Sherwood Jones). A second volume followed in 1826. *The English Spy* is a gossipy miscellany written in the tradition of *Life in London* by the younger Pierce Egan. Most of the text – including paratextual pieces like a note to reviewers, an introduction and a preface in the form of a satirical dialogue – is narrated through one Bernard Blackmantle, an '"eccentric in every respect"' who '"must not be judged of by the acquaintance of an hour"'.[40] In one of the opening sections, entitled 'A Few Thoughts on Myself', Blackmantle offers readers his 'character' as credential – an 'invariable custom' featured also in the first number of *The Spy* – though without revealing much about himself.[41] He says that he is '[u]nwilling to speak of himself, lest he should incur the charge of vanity or egotism', leaving it to his cousin Horatio Heartly to provide the 'character' that the chapter designated for that task proved unable to do.[42] Two chapters go by and then 'Horatio Heartly' finally begins to narrate a section called 'Character of Bernard Blackmantle'. (We are meant to understand that Blackmantle, as author-editor of this strange collection, whose own penned stories form a good part of it, interpolates in it scenes spoken by others that he has either made up or recorded with or without their permission.) Heartly (or Blackmantle under the guise of Heartly) seems to account for the reticence of 'A Few Thoughts on Myself' by suggesting that Blackmantle is sensitive about the 'ambiguity of [his] birth' and would not want to talk about it.[43] He then proceeds to give his own version of Blackmantle's 'character' rather as an editor than as a cousin. Heartly removes from his own personal 'portfolio' a miscellaneous set of papers he claims were written by Blackmantle himself:

> scraps of Bernard's that will best speak his character; prose and poetry, descriptive and colloquial, Hudibrastic and pastoral, trifles in every costume of literary fancy, according with the peculiar humour of the author at the time of their inditing, from these you [Heartly is speaking to his aunt Lady Mary Oldcastle] shall judge my eccentric friend better than by any commendation of mine.[44]

Heartly goes on to say that, at Eton, Blackmantle was 'surrounded' by 'mystery' and possibly 'watched over' by 'some protecting spirit'.[45] The first revelatory 'scrap' he pulls from his portfolio is not, in fact, written by Blackmantle himself but by one of their mutual Eton friends – a short lyric poem entitled 'A Portrait'. The second scrap Heartly discloses is Blackmantle's own 'first poetical essay', a 'school-boy tribute to friendship'. These two documents being a bit inconclusive, Heartly moves on with his 'Character', recalling that one morning, after two years at Eton, he stumbled upon the elusive Blackmantle writing in his room, frantically 'endeavor[ing] to conceal his papers' upon the entrance of his cousin. Heartly immediately demands that Blackmantle reveal what he is working on – gaining his end, but forced to take an '"oath of secrecy"' beforehand. It turns out that the 'lucubrations' Blackmantle has been so anxious to conceal for two years are textual 'portraits of the group, with whom we were in daily association' – 'colloquial scenes' of Eton life in which Blackmantle has given their mutual 'friends' 'assigned' 'parts', a veritable 'key to the characters'.[46] The next chapters consist of some of these 'scenes'. So *The English Spy* from then on is made up of the 'secret' papers written by Blackmantle, supposedly pocketed by Heartly and then inserted into the collection as chapters by Blackmantle (who, we are meant to believe, has reacquired them from his cousin for this purpose).

The point is that Blackmantle himself (perhaps a persona for Westmacott) cultivates a fantastic kind of 'illegibility' while presuming that all the objects of his pen are readily legible – thanks to his 'mastery of the great secret in his power' of 'appreciating the characters of the age'.[47] To 'appreciate' during this time could mean to 'set a price on', to 'recognize as valuable' and 'to apprehend . . . clearly or correctly'.[48] Blackmantle apprehends/appraises the characters of his friends in a neat 'key' while diffusing his own across a pile of literary 'scraps' (which anticipate the zodiacal packages concealing the 'character' of Thomas Carlyle's Teufelsdröckh – see the Afterword in the present volume). As in the case of Egan's novels, which read like magazines, *The English Spy* is 'willfully heterogeneous'.[49] Its first and second volumes – perhaps not coincidentally – were published in the exact two years that William Hone released his *Every-Day Book; or, Everlasting Calendar of Popular Amusements, Sports, Pastimes, Ceremonies, Manners, Customs and Events* (1825–6). The *Every-Day Book* was 'structured according to the calendar and documented historical events, feast days, literary extracts, street cries, buildings, hagiography, natural history, pagan customs, fairs, local traditions, urban sports, peculiar new items' and so on. Hone would solicit his audiences to supply their own 'personal reminiscences and factual snippets to create a collaboratively authored record of popular culture'. The *Every-Day Book* appeared weekly and was collected monthly at the price of a shilling. This miscellany – made up of the 'eclectic and fragmented accumulation of memories from various sources' – is an important index of the general miscellaneousness of the new world of print and sheds light on alternative modes of imagining, packaging and marketing character.[50] Recall that phrenology claimed that the human mind worked by a division of labour as factories did. The mind was a composite of several distinct craniological faculties working simultaneously, though producing, for many, the false impression that it was a unified organ governed by a single principle, like consciousness. It would seem, at this time, that superintending principles in general were loosening their grips on minds, books, characters. I would argue that a predictably 'conserved' character in a text or a predictably 'constant' one in a life was increasingly felt to afford less room for radical spontaneity, reinvention, the thrill of disorganisation.

'Having' a character involves being determined in some sense or to some extent, no matter what kind of language is used to conceive and delineate character as a concept. In *Phenomenology of Spirit* (1807), Hegel assumes that everyone 'has . . . an *intrinsic* being or has an *original* determinate being of his own – a determinateness which is in principle the same as what psychology [that is, physiognomy and phrenology] thought to find outside of him'.⁵¹ Hegel makes a similar point in his *Philosophy of Fine Art* (1835) – a text in which, Joel Haefner says, the 'Romantic conception of character . . . received its most philosophical formulation'.⁵² *Philosophy of Fine Art* distinguishes between two 'formal' aspects of character: the 'executive' and the 'personal'. The executive aspect stabilises a character and 'restricts its line of action to specific aims'. A strongly executive character acts according to 'its own specific nature' and with minimal 'reflection'. Hence someone of a powerfully executive character does essentially what his or her character bids. The 'personal' aspect of character, on the other hand, is what gives someone a sense of his or her 'totality': a sense of completeness, of being one thing. Yet one can never arrive at an accurate estimate of what that totality actually is or in what it consists. This is because the totality per se is never 'wholly articulated throughout the content of that inward life and in the unsounded depths of the soul', 'unable to unravel itself wholly, or express itself with absolute clarity'. Totality is a thing 'undisclosed and formless', and with a 'defect of expression and expository power'.⁵³ Hegel's executive and personal aspects of character correspond to the two kinds of character that Kant respectively called 'moral' and 'natural', whose essential distinction Diderot and other materialists collapsed. Vital to the literary case studies that follow this chapter is the fact that a 'totality' that cannot 'unravel' or 'express' itself on its own becomes all the more poised to be unravelled or expressed by other agencies. What the *Edinburgh Review* said about paper money after the 1797 bank crisis, in fact, applies in an important sense to the conundrum of character: '[t]he *Edinburgh* suggests that the debate regarding paper money is not about discovering an inevitable meaning' of it. In the nineteenth century paper money was no longer a 'fixed signifier'. It ceased to 'mean' or represent or correspond to precious metals but instead became subject to 'the cultural need for its continual definition'.⁵⁴

The 'cultural need' to redefine, to reconceptualise 'character' so many times and in so short a span of time, I suggest, could only draw attention to character's instability as a holder of value. Maybe 'character' didn't point to any necessarily or coherently existing thing after all. An article published in *Chamber's Edinburgh Journal* entitled 'The Pleasure of Being without a Character' (1836) declares that it is a 'blessing . . . to be without a character'. Those with a 'character and reputation and station to sustain' miss out on the pleasures of life. They know and feel little of what is beautiful in the world. Their 'natural tastes are curbed . . . impulses are restrained . . . real feelings are concealed. Their whole life is a mask. They are "star"-actors on the world's stage, while we poor, unwashed, unvaccinated gentlemen are the "supernumeraries"'.[55] This Theophrastan essay combines 'character' with 'reputation' and station' in a single rhetorical unit. All three are said to 'cur[b] natural tastes', 'restrai[n]' 'impulses' and 'concea[l] 'real feelings'. Character is presented as an artificial dress that covers up an inner real: a pernicious affectation similar to aristocratic titles, which Tom Paine in *Rights of Man* calls 'circles drawn by the magician's wand, to contract the sphere of man's felicity' so that any titled person 'lives immured within the Bastille of a word, and surveys at a distance the envied life of a man'.[56] It follows that one way to read the passage is to take 'character', 'reputation' and 'station' as a rhetorically consolidated group of 'mask[s]' that repress the otherwise 'natural', raw, Painite character of unadulterated 'man'. At the same time, however, it is difficult to separate entirely the sense of character as adventitious circumstance from the sense of character as inner real. Both senses are at play in this article, and both are prominent and often conflated in reform-era discourse. If the article had been called 'The Pleasure of Being without a Reputation', or without a 'Rank', 'Position', 'Status' or 'Role', it could have made more immediate sense to some readers but its important anti-foundationalist implications would have been less obvious. As it is, the title is catchy because it suggests both persons without social roles to play and – far more provocatively – persons without clear-cut self-directing principles whose laws resemble the laws of the physical world. The ambiguity in the title steers readers toward more radical implications that could otherwise have been missed.

How does all of this square with familiar stories about the fate of Romanticism in the 1820s and 1830s? One advantage of reading late

Romantic writings in the context of character discourse is that one can avoid an undue emphasis on the anxiety of influence. When, say, Keats claims that 'Men of Genius are great as certain ethereal Chemicals operating on the Mass of neutral intellect – by [*for* but] they have not any ... determined Character', or that the 'poetical Character ... has no character', he may have been influenced by contemporary ethological discussions as well as by Shakespeare and Hazlitt's essay 'On Gusto'.[57] Another advantage is that one comes to notice a network of (often valorised) 'characterless' characters cropping up in more and more texts. Consider John William Polidori's horror tale *The Vampyre* (1819). The narrator of *The Vampyre* asserts 'the very impossibility of forming an idea of the character of a man [the vampyre Lord Ruthven/Strongmore] entirely absorbed in himself, of one who gave few other signs of his observation of external objects, than the tacit assent to their existence'.[58] Recall the periodical article that advises studying the character of men with all-too-mirror-like faces 'by a side view, when their mind's surface is receiving the impression of other objects'. Here and elsewhere in *The Vampyre*, Lord Ruthven avoids being an object of ethological surveillance despite the existence of plenty of practical advice (popular ethologies) on the subject. At one point, the young gentleman Aubrey realises that he 'had had no opportunity of studying Lord Strongmore's character, and he now found that, though many of his actions were exposed to his view, the results offered different conclusions from the apparent motives to his conduct'.[59] Another vampiric and illegible villain with whom De Quincey happened to be obsessed in the 1820s and 1830s is the famous murderer John Williams, whose 'corpse-like face', according to De Quincey, 'wore at all times a bloodless ghastly pallor' dotted with eyes that 'seemed frozen and glazed'. No one 'could avail to unmask' such a person, who 'most flexibly adapt[ed] himself to all varieties of social life'.[60] A less sinister but no less unreadable figure is Junius (fl. 1768–73), the pseudonymous author (or authors) of letters published in the *Public Advertiser* in the mid-eighteenth century, whom Lord Byron seems to heroise in his *Vision of Judgment* (1820). Byron describes Junius as an alluring 'Shadow' with indistinguishable features that '[c]hanged every instant'. Others swear they 'knew him perfectly', but 'the wight/ Mysterious changed his countenance at least/ As oft they their minds'. Sometimes 'you might deem/ That he was not even *one*': '[n]ow Burke, now Tooke, he grew to people's fancies,/ And certes often like Sir Philip Francis'. The speaker imagines that 'what Junius we are wont to call,/ Was *really, truly*, nobody at all'.⁶¹ Is this just a banal acknowledgement that 'Junius' was probably several authors writing under one name, or is there more to it? Perhaps there is something appealing to Byron not just about how corporate entities publish in periodicals under single names but about the idea of a living '[s]hadow' that can change its features by the second: a characterless character that defies the limitations inherent in bodiliness, organisation, the 'properties of . . . interiority'.

Notes

1. Manning, *Poetics of Character*, p. 45.
2. See Siskin, 'Historicity of Romantic Discourse'.
3. Lynch, *Economy of Character*, p. 18.
4. Higgins, *Romantic Culture and the Literary Magazine*, pp. 60–1.
5. Watt, 'We Did Not Think That He Could Die', pp. 127, 122.
6. Cronin, *Romantic Victorians*, p. 83.
7. Brewer, *Afterlife of Character*, p. 14.
8. Higgins, *Romantic Culture and the Literary Magazine*, pp. 66, 72.
9. Wollstonecraft, *The Wrongs of Woman, Or Maria*, p. 177.
10. Garcha, *From Sketch to Novel*, p. 4.
11. Ibid., p. 8.
12. Ibid., p 10.
13. Russell, preface to *Essays, and Sketches*, pp. v–vi.
14. Russell, 'English and French Pride and Vanity', in *Essays, and Sketches*, pp. 3–4.
15. See Russell, 'Men of Letters', in *Essays, and Sketches*, pp. 9–13.
16. Hook, advertisement to *Sayings and Doings*, pp. iv–v. For the influence of *Sayings and Doings* on *Sketches by Boz*, see Dart, *Metropolitan Art and Literature*, p. 223.
17. Watts, advertisement to *Scenes of Life*, n.p.
18. Anon., 'Sensible People', in Watts, *Scenes of Life*, vol. 1, pp. 19–20.
19. Anon., 'The Squire of Dames', in Watts, *Scenes of Life*, vol. 1, pp. 53–4, 56, 62.
20. Anon., 'Book Borrowers', in Watts, *Scenes of Life*, vol. 1, p. 91.
21. Anon., 'Book Beggars', in Watts, *Scenes of Life*, vol. 1, p. 117.
22. Anon., 'The Maiden Aunt', in Watts, *Scenes of Life*, vol. 2, pp. 63, 66.
23. De Quincey, 'Letters to a Young Man', p. 328.
24. Cronin, *Paper Pellets*, pp. 54, 43.

25. Qtd in Higgins, *Romantic Culture and the Literary Magazine*, p. 58.
26. Qtd in Richardson, 'Character and Craft', p. 52.
27. Combe, *A System of Phrenology*, p. 70; and Cooter, *The Cultural Meaning of Popular Science*, p. 126.
28. Shelley, *St. Irvyne*, p. 130.
29. Schoenfield, *British Periodicals and Romantic Identity*, pp. 201–2.
30. Hogg, *The Spy*, pp. 3–4.
31. Ibid., p. 4.
32. Schoenfield, *British Periodicals and Romantic Identity*, p. 210.
33. Hogg, *The Private Memoirs and Confessions of a Justified Sinner*, p. 95.
34. Duncan, 'Fanaticism and Civil Society', p. 346.
35. Burke, *A Philosophical Enquiry*, p. 120.
36. Duncan, 'Fanaticism and Civil Society', p. 346.
37. Schoenfield, *British Periodicals and Romantic Identity*, p. 211.
38. Cronin, *Paper Pellets*, p. 113.
39. Fang, *Romantic Writing and the Empire of Signs*, p. 19.
40. Westmacott, *The English Spy*, p. 21.
41. Schoenfield, *British Periodicals and Romantic Identity*, p. 208.
42. Westmacott, *The English Spy*, p. 14.
43. Ibid., p. 27.
44. Ibid., p. 25.
45. Ibid., p. 26.
46. Ibid., pp. 30–1.
47. Ibid., p. 14.
48. 'appreciate, adj.'. Defs 1a, 2a and 3a. *OED Online*. Oxford English Dictionary, February 2017, <http://www.oed.com> (last accessed 13 February 2017).
49. Cronin, *Paper Pellets*, p. 162.
50. Hodgetts, 'William Hone and the Reading Public', pp. 8, 17–18.
51. Hegel, *Phenomenology of Spirit*, p. 185.
52. Haefner, '"The Soul Speaking in the Face"', p. 663.
53. Hegel, *Philosophy of Fine Art*, pp. 155–6, 160.
54. Schoenfield, *British Periodicals and Romantic Identity*, p. 69.
55. Anon., 'The Pleasure of Being without a Character', p. 391.
56. Paine, *Rights of Man*, p. 320.
57. Keats, *Letters of John Keats*, pp. 36, 157.
58. Polidori, *The Vampyre: A Tale*, p. 41.
59. Ibid.
60. De Quincey, 'Postscript', pp. 100–1.
61. Byron, 'The Vision of Judgment', in *Lord Byron: The Complete Poetical Works*, 6: 335–7, lines 585, 600, 606, 611–13, 627–8, 631–2, 639–40.

Chapter 3

Representing Representation: Walter Scott and Charles Lamb

Walter Scott and Charles Lamb are two authors whose prose experiments respond incisively to the politics of character and characterisation in reform-era literature and culture. By 1820, Scott was 'widely identified as "the Great Unknown", "the author of *Waverley*"', and although it was not until 1827 that financial pressures forced him to reveal his identity, an August 1814 review of *Waverley* had already supposed that Scott had written it.[1] Anyone who has read the introductory sections to, say, *Old Mortality* (1816) can safely conclude with Duncan that 'Scott's prose resists the dynamics of transparency and identification we have come to associate with nineteenth-century realism'.[2] The 1830 Magnum Opus edition of *Old Mortality* opens with an introduction to the to the *Tales of My Landlord* series (*Old Mortality* being the second novel of the First Series of *Tales*), narrated by Jedediah Cleishbotham, parish clerk of Gandercleugh. Cleishbotham informs us that he has collected and edited certain tales written by a local schoolmaster, Peter Pattieson. This initial introduction by Cleishbotham is followed by the introduction to *Old Morality* written by Scott for the 1830 edition. After that we have a sort of third introduction, which is actually chapter 1, in which Pattieson tells readers how he once met Robert Paterson, aka Old Mortality, and '"embod[ied] into one compressed narrative many of the anecdotes which I had the advantage of deriving from Old Mortality"'.[3] Meanwhile, according to the general framework of *Tales*, *Old Mortality* and the other novels in each series belong somehow to the 'Landlord' of Wallace Inn in Gandercleugh. After Pattieson's account of having met Paterson (whose names seem to blend into one another) in 'chapter one', the story of *Old Mortality* proper begins. This use of fictional compilers/editors to tell stories was obviously not new with Scott. It was part of 'a long and illustrious novelistic tradition' dating from Cervantes and including authors as diverse as Swift, Walpole, Mackenzie and Goethe.[4] But the sheer, unapologetic fictionality of the prolegomena in *Old Mortality* operates dynamically alongside the novel's historicity – for instance, Scott's scholarly notes appended to the Magnum Opus edition – in such a way as to make an old convention seem fresh. For one critic, the novel can seem quite unrealistic and quite realistic at the same time: *Old Mortality* both 'suspen[ds] . . . referentiality (through its fictiveness)' and 'affirm[s] . . . referentiality through "realist" narrative techniques'.[5]

In 1817, Scott persisted in refusing to admit to his London publisher Murray and others that he was the author of *Waverley* and the *Tales of My Landlord* series by reviewing *Tales* himself in the *Quarterly Review*. In that review the speaker wonders why whoever authored these *Tales* 'should industriously endeavour to elude observation by taking leave of us in one character, and then suddenly popping out upon us in another'.[6] In this single comment Scott accomplishes several things: he maintains his anonymity as the author of *Tales*, reinforces his culture's broad interest in 'elud[ing] observation' and exploits the instability of the term 'character'. Scott's own life was also strangely implicated in his metafictional experiments. Prior to the mid-1820s bank crash, his publishers Constable and Ballantyne had given Scott several advances, so that after the crash he found himself in considerable debt and forced to publish furiously to make ends meet. After this point in his life, according to Alex Dick, Scott was 'no longer mystified as a singular presence through the serial publication of individual novels'. He and his persona, 'the Author of *Waverley*',

> were systematically and serially 'unbound' . . . spread through a myriad of genres and venues, from the shortest note to the complete works that never quite measure up to the totality they are meant to comprise. Rather than a mysterious presence on which the reading public could speculate as it absorbed each successive work in turn, Scott, his pseudonyms and personae, his editors and his publishers, became pieces in a puzzle that never produced a coherent image.[7]

Dick, of course, assumes that, as the mere 'author of Waverley', a 'mysterious presence on which the reading public could speculate', Scott once was or once approximated some kind of 'coherent image'.

But in any case Scott's interest in – as he himself put it in the *Quarterly Review* – 'industriously elud[ing] observation' seems to amount to more than just a complicated game or marketing strategy (although it may be both of these). It is to some degree a playfully postmodern response to a culture obsessed with ethological 'apprehension' and classification – with human sciences like phrenology that promised to 'provide at a stroke practical solutions to the mysteries of character'. In this sense the postmodern experiments of Scott, of Hogg and of many others are reactions to forces operating within and yet far beyond their own lives.

It is well known that Scott tries both to '*antiquate* the psychology of his characters' and to acknowledge what 'his characters and readers have in common'.[8] Thus the characters in his novels are products of the past but also share a certain universal human nature. To antiquate the psychology of characters is to view past interiorities as products of what Lukács has called a single 'social-historical ensemble'. This can have positive and negative effects. One the one hand, it can give readers 'a heightened awareness of what made [a particular] period different'. On the other, it can reduce characters to the representatives of crude sociographic types that supposedly inhabited a bygone age. Stuart Ferguson observes that

> Dugald Stewart, one of Scott's most influential teachers, coined the term, theoretical or conjectural history, to describe the way in which historians, when 'unable to ascertain how men have actually conducted themselves upon particular occasions', find it necessary to consider 'in what manner they are likely to have proceeded, from the principles of their inner nature, and the circumstances of their external situation'. Certain 'detached facts' may 'serve as landmarks to our speculations', while our abstract speculations may on occasion 'tend to confirm the credibility of facts, which on a superficial view, appeared to be doubtful or incredible'. Underpinning this approach is the assumption that people in a similar social environment will act in similar ways and will demonstrate similar psychologies.[9]

Stewart was writing in 1793, though he certainly seems to anticipate the 'ethological laws' that interested Mill a half a century later. Both methodologies advise historians/ethologists to make informed generalisations based on recorded facts or empirical observation and then to cross-check these generalisations against certain 'truths' of human nature – what Stewart calls 'principles of . . . inner nature' and what Mill calls 'psychological laws'.

Thus one can view Scott's historical characters as essentially products of their 'social-historical ensemble' garnished with a bit of 'human nature' to suit the tastes of modern audiences. As one critic puts it, his 'characters are explained both psychologically, culturally and historically, but history is the most important causal factor'.[10] Manning observes that Scott tried to 'articulate [his] own versions of national character with a universalist understanding of human nature'.[11] Some of his contemporary readers, including Scott himself, worried that the 'moral characters' of his fictional characters were too often sacrificed in the process of sociohistorical reconstruction. By 'moral characters' I mean Mill's definition in *On Liberty* (1859): '[a] person whose desires and impulses are his own – are the expression of his own nature, as it has been developed and modified by his own culture – is said to have a character'.[12] The same definition is still being used well over a century later:

> to have a character is to act in such a way that the person one is plays a major role in any explanation of one's behavior. To have no character is to act in such a way that one's behavior might be viewed as (at least approximately) the product of forces acting on one. Thus, the person who always yields to temptation quickly, without a struggle, would be spoken of as having no character, as would the extreme conformist who always does what is expected of him or her.[13]

This definition presumes three things: 1) that there is such a thing as a subject or 'person' distinct from contextual 'forces'; 2) that there is more moral worth or freedom in actions that seem to proceed from within a person as opposed to actions that seem to proceed from without; and 3) that – in the case of the second point – one can tell the difference. Scott, I suggest, troubles this longstanding definition of character. I would not say that he simply reverses the terms of its binary opposition – applauding characters who yield to every temptation or who conform to the expectations of others – but I would say that his novels question basic assumptions about 'character' that enable this definition to make sense in the first place: first, that character really exists in persons either as a constitutive 'bias' or as a moral possession; and second, that lay and scientific efforts to understand it and artistic efforts to represent it are more or less truth-seeking enterprises with the same basic object in view.

Scott admits that his own 'chief characters are never actors, but always acted upon by the spur of circumstances'; that they had to be somewhat uninformed or passive – sometimes 'represented . . . as foreigners to whom everything in Scotland is strange' – in order that nineteenth-century readers could receive historical 'explanations and details' through them. A hero or heroine also had to be a little 'inconsistent or flexible in . . . principles' in order to be carried along with the historical 'twists and turns' of the plot.[14] One critic notes that Edward Waverley lacks 'coherence' because of the 'bad effects . . . of a haphazard and hazy education on an indolent and romantic mind'.[15] Cronin observes that the 'historical distance, the lapse of years that separates the reader from the characters who inhabit the fiction, reinforces . . . an effect that [Scott's] contemporaries prized': when '[a]t moments of high emotional intensity in Scott's novels the characters are . . . frozen into tableaux, and the reader invited to regard them as if they composed a genre painting, or as if they were characters disposed on a stage'.[16] Landon complicates this 'effect' – which recalls the spatialising aim of the 'sketch' according to Garcha – when she (re)produces Scott's female characters within so many frames of her own prose 'Portrait Gallery', characters she may have thought a bit *too* 'frozen into tableaux'. The Gallery itself is a genre almost hard to describe: short prose sketches of fictional characters meant to be the verbal equivalent of visual portraits, the characters thus 'sketched' having originally appeared in novels in which they sometimes, perhaps too often, resembled figures in paintings or on stage.

I want to call attention to a point in *Old Mortality* at which representation itself seems to be represented. General Claverhouse and his prisoner Henry Morton are riding along together after the defeat of the Covenanters at Bothwell Bridge, while Claverhouse 'take[s] pleasure . . . in . . . attempt[ing] to appreciate [Morton's] real character'.[17] Recall that Bernard Blackmantle possessed 'the great secret' of 'appreciating' Eton characters in the sense of both apprehending and appraising them. It turns out that, for Claverhouse, to 'appreciate' the 'real character' of Morton is to construct or assemble it based upon a document of questionable (politically slanted) evidence. During their ride, Claverhouse produces what he calls his '"black book"' – an 'ominous record of . . . disaffected' Covenanters and their suspected sympathisers 'arranged in alphabetical order' like an encyclopaedia.[18] Jane Stevenson and Peter Davidson observe that Claverhouse's 'black book' 'corresponds to' the 'porteous (portable) rolls put together after Bothwell Bridge' described by Robert Wodrow in his *History of the Sufferings of the Church of Scotland from the Restauration to the Revolution* (1721).[19] At one point we find the General turning over the leaves of his book, reading aloud and searching for the entry on the faithful ploughman Cuddie Headrigg:

'Gumblegumption, a minister, aged 50, indulged, close, sly, and so forth . . . I have him here – Heathercat; outlawed – a preacher – a zealous Cameronian – keeps a conventicle among the Campsie hills – Tush! – O, here is Headrigg – Cuthbert; his mother a bitter puritan – himself a simple fellow – likes to be forward in action, but of no genius for plots – more for the hand than the head'.[20]

The 'black book' is a list of individuals and their supposed characteristics/allegiances – not a collection of Theophrastan 'types'. Yet one can read its entries as so many 'portrait-characters': evocations of 'types' through descriptions of particular individuals (see Chapter 4 in the present volume). Morton responds that it seems a bit menial for someone as important as Claverhouse '"to follow a system which is to be supported by such minute enquiries after obscure individuals"'. Claverhouse, in turn, replies that not he but parish curates '"collect all these materials for their own regulation"', since they '"know best the black sheep of the flock"'. He adds that he has had Morton's '"picture for three years"', from which he then reads:

'Henry Morton, son of Silas Morton, Colonel of horse for the Scottish Parliament, nephew and apparent heir of Morton of Milnwood – imperfectly educated, but with spirit beyond his years – excellent at all exercises – indifferent to forms of religion, but seems to incline to the Presbyterian – has high-flown and dangerous notions about liberty of thought and speech, and hovers between a latitudinarian and an enthusiast. Much admired and followed by the youth of his own age – modest, quiet, and unassuming in manner, but his heart peculiarly bold and intractable. He is – Here follow three red crosses, Mr Morton, which signify triply dangerous. You see how important a person you are'.[21]

One immediately notices that the 'picture' of Morton is executed with more polish than that of the others. Either the parish curates decided to compose the entry on Morton with more care, or Claverhouse has decided to slow down his reading of it to get every word; or perhaps Morton's latitudinarian 'character' is so anachronistic and idiosyncratic that it could not possibly be reduced to a crude type. In any case, the General tells Morton that '"my construction of the information has not been unfavourable to you"' – that, in other words, he has interpreted the contents of the black book so as to rescue Morton from his supposed Presbyterian inclinations, and to make himself and Morton seem more similar than different: '"we are both fanatics"', Claverhouse tells his prisoner, only '"there is some distinction between the fanaticism of honour and that of dark and sullen superstition"'.[22]

I would suggest that the black book in *Old Mortality* is more than another marker of historical realism drawn possibly from Wodrow. It is also a device that calls attention to the liabilities of the historical novelist as well as to all acts of characterisation inside or outside of print. Scott admitted his self-consciousness about creating characters who seemed to have no (moral) character: who, 'like all other commodities, had been flattened and regularized by the mechanical systems that produced them'.[23] The 'black book' segment partly registers this self-consciousness. The parish curates who amass questionable 'picture[s]' of suspected religious fanatics in an international atmosphere of paranoia can serve as doubles for the historical novelist, self-conscious to the extent that his textualised Covenanters – with names like Kettledrummle, Poundtext, Gumblegumption and Heathercat – can seem like 'laughable . . . stage fanatics', 'bloodthirsty, cruel . . . bigoted' and 'ignorant mechanicals unfitted to make decisions about spiritual or political matters'.[24] Even more important is that the episode after Bothwell Bridge intimates that all characterisation, whether accomplished through realist narrative techniques, the examination of phrenological heads or other philosophical, scientific, folkloric or 'commonsensical' methods, is inevitably a selective and constructive process, organised according to a specific set of prejudices circulating within a specific literary-moral economy.

I have suggested that, aside from acknowledging the artificiality or literariness of his historical fictions in elaborate paratextual material,

Scott invites readers to consider what it means to characterise both within and beyond narrative texts. He shows us how Claverhouse has collected specific, polarising data from local curates to construct a tendentious catalogue of names and traits. This scene after Bothwell Bridge echoes, if not parodies, the efforts of a variety of contemporary writers and scientific thinkers (phrenologists, for instance) to force the epistemological validity of character. Charles Lamb goes even further than Scott to suggest that extratextual character is no less a historically contingent construct than what we find in fiction. The one is not necessarily an authentic model – a ground of being – and the other is not necessarily a copy of that model. For Lamb, the extralinguistic reality of character is deconstructed in the discursive practices that refurnish and reinvent it over time.

All of the following examples are from the *Elia* essays. Some of these essays are loosely Theophrastan, enumerating the traits and behaviours of a certain 'type' but meandering frequently via personal anecdote and reflection. Others are written as relatively strict 'characters' minus much of the didactic emphasis. Lamb is certainly no Bishop Hall, who claims to have written his *Character of Virtue and Vices* (1608) primarily so that the reader would 'abjure those vices, which before thou thoughtest not ill-favoured, or fall in love with any of these goodly faces of virtue'.[25] His Elia-spawned 'characters' read more like pageants of wit in which each act of description, each flourish of characterisation, is immediately ironised by its own relentlessly stylised form. Consider the opening paragraph of 'Poor Relations' (published in the *London Magazine* in 1823):

> A poor Relation – is the most irrelevant thing in nature, – a piece of impertinent correspondency, – an odious approximation, – a haunting conscience, – a preposterous shadow, lengthening in the noontide of your prosperity, – an unwelcome remembrancer, – a perpetually recurring mortification, – a drain on your purse, – a more intolerable dun upon your pride, – a drawback upon success, – a rebuke to your rising, – a stain in your blood, – a blot on your scutcheon, – a rent in your garment, – a death's head at your banquet, – Agathocles' pot, – a Mordecai in your gate, – a Lazarus at your door, – a lion in your path, – a frog in your chamber, – a fly in your ointment, – a mote in your eye, – a triumph to your enemy, an apology to your friends, – the one thing not needful, – the hail in harvest, – the ounce of sour in a pound of sweet.[26]

The paragraph is worth quoting in full if only to show the accumulation of epithets in which Elia instantly drowns his subject. Even before the copula in the first sentence he seems overwhelmed with the imminent explosion of labels drawn from a host of pagan and Christian sources. The paragraph that follows this one contains no fewer than eighteen sentences beginning with 'He' and loading the Poor Relation with additional idiosyncrasies recorded in fastidious detail. By the end of it we have been told how the Poor Relation knocks, how he shakes hands, what he eats, his preferred method of travel and so on. If we feel we know a specific individual or individuals who fit this description, it is not in the same way, of course, that we feel we know a Mr Micawber – that famous Dickensian instantiation of the 'Poor Relation'. Micawber develops, lives in narrative time: he returns again and again, repeats old behaviours, wears the same shabby-genteel clothes, speaks in the same idiom and occasionally adds new flourishes to his unique 'art' of insolvency. The Poor Relation, on the other hand, is some combination of an economic, social and psychological type, one that does not develop in time, and at least one of whose epithets or habits is likely to resonate with readers, recalling some such penniless friend or relative caught repeatedly in financial scrapes.

The *Elia* essays simultaneously enact and critique the Theophrastan characterising practices they inherit, and in so doing suggest the arbitrariness of characterisation itself. 'The Two Races of Men' is an essay written much like 'Poor Relations'. In that essay Elia divides up the 'human species' into 'two distinct races, *the men who borrow* and *the men who lend*. To these two original diversities may be traced all those impertinent classifications of Gothic and Celtic tribes, white men, black men, red men'. The men who borrow are the '*great race* ... discernible in their figure, port, and a certain instinctive sovereignty', 'trusting', 'generous', 'careless', 'rosy'. The ones who lend are 'born degraded', 'lean and suspicious'.[27] In a similar essay (originally entitled 'Jews, Quakers, Scotchmen, and other Imperfect Sympathies' but published as 'Imperfect Sympathies' in 1823), Elia admits that he 'feel[s] the differences of mankind, natural or individual, to an unhealthy excess'. He is 'a bundle of prejudices ... the veriest thrall to sympathies, apathies, antipathies'.[28] At one point in a note, however, he seems to excuse his personal prejudices by blaming the stars: '[t]here may be individuals born and constelled so opposite to another individual nature, that the same sphere cannot hold them'.[29] Perhaps stellar influence is responsible for the 'imperfect sympathies' he has observed between English and Scottish, 'Jew and Christian'.[30] What else could explain the divergent conformations of English and Scottish minds? Elia observes that the Scottish intellectual seems to possess only ready-made ideas. One can 'never catch his mind in an undress. He never hints or suggests any thing, but unlades his stock of ideas in perfect order and completeness': '[s]urmises, guesses, misgivings, half-intuitions, semi-consciousnesses, partial illuminations, dim instincts, embryo conceptions, have no place in his brain'.[31] The English mind, on the other hand, is more or less the exact opposite. Its 'intellectual wardrobe . . . has few whole pieces in it'. It is 'content with fragments and scattered pieces of Truth', '[h]ints and glimpses, germs and crude essays at a system'. 'The light that lights [it]', Elia claims, 'is not steady and polar, but mutable and shifting: waxing, and again waning'.[32]

Lamb is fond of speculating on the nature of character both as an object representable in print, and as an object that may or may not be possessed and maintained outside of print. In his unexpectedly morbid essay 'New Year's Eve', Elia declares that there is virtually no continuity between his character as a child (at least, as he remembers it) and his character as an adult. The 'child Elia – that "other me", there, in the back-ground' – is nothing like Elia the man – 'this stupid changeling of five-and-forty'. 'From what have I not fallen', Elia reasons, 'if the child I remember was indeed myself, – and not some dissembling guardian, presenting a false identity, to give the rule to my unpractised steps, and regulate the tone of my moral being!'[33] Like Blake, Elia sees the transition from childhood to adulthood in terms of a fall, but unlike Blake he holds no hope in personal redemption through the synthesis of innocence and experience. Nor does the adult Elia comfort himself with Wordsworthian stoicism or salvation through memory. In this strange, powerful sentence, he claims that if the character of the child Elia as he remembers it – 'honest', 'courageous', 'religious', 'imaginative', 'hopeful' – was, in fact, the same as that of the man writing the essay – 'shy', 'light', 'vain', 'stammering', 'buffoon[ish]' – then the man has, indeed, fallen from a great height, fallen from childhood. Perhaps, however, Elia wonders, the child self he recollects was only a beautiful mirage, a glittering facade, a 'false identity' concocted by some 'dissembling guardian' to help his 'real' childhood self along. If this were the case, then that 'false identity' has effectively seduced the adult Elia into believing that he once possessed the virtuous qualities he remembers, when in fact he never had these character traits as a child; they were more like correctives, administered from an external source (the 'dissembling guardian'), to strengthen and regulate what was in fact (and still in a sense is) a weak and helpless boy.

This is an incredible burst of the imagination in a single sentence. The statement first depicts the child Elia as a summit from which to fall, a being of purity susceptible to corruption. Then it imagines the child Elia as a sort of Spenserian spirit, summoned by an Archimago-like 'dissembling guardian', who on a literal level teaches the 'real' child Elia to walk ('rul[ing]' his 'unpractised steps') and on a figurative level guides his character along the straight and narrow path ('regulat[ing] the tone of [his] moral being'). The fact that 'moral being' is said to have a 'tone' immediately registers the problematics of character. A 'tone' can refer to the 'quality' of a 'musical or vocal sound', 'the degree of luminosity of a colour' or a 'particular style in discourse or writing', among other things.[34] How is the word functioning here? How, moreover, does the essay understand 'character'? Is it as a 'moral being' whose 'tone' a 'false identity' can 'regulate'? Recall that the author of 'Early Impressions on the Future Character' referred to a certain mental phenomenon, 'instinct', which, as the 'impulse of our system', begins to 'giv[e] tone to character' once it (instinct) is fully formed around age six. A comparison between the terms of the two essays seems apropos here: 'instinct' is to 'character' in 'Early Impressions' as 'false identity' is to 'moral being' in 'New Year's Eve'. The one 'gives tone to character'; the other 'regulate[s] the tone of . . . moral being'. However the meanings of the respective terms may be related, the two essays participate in a broad cultural interest concerning the early formation and development of personal character, and, by extension, the politics of 'representing' such a thing in print. Unlike the article in the *Monthly Magazine*, though, the *Elia* essay seems to problematise the concept of character even as it takes that concept for granted. If, on the one hand, the child Elia was as glorious as the adult Elia remembers, then the latter did indeed fall from grace. If, on the other hand, the magnificent, recollected child Elia was no more than a 'false identity' imposed by an external agent, then the 'real' Elia has never changed: he is quite as weak, insecure, 'stammering' and unhappy as an adult as he was when he was a child.

Elia seems content to go with the lesser of two evils: adulthood as a fall from something wonderfully separate rather than an embarrassing continuity obscured by self-delusion. In another essay, 'A Bachelor's Complaint of the Behaviour of Married People', he claims that

> children have a real character and an essential being of themselves: they are amiable or unamiable *per se*; I must love or hate them as I see cause for either in their qualities. A child's nature is too serious a thing to admit of its being regarded as a mere appendage to another being.[35]

The 'another being' is presumably the adult into which the child grows (or falls). Elia is so convinced here of the absolute 'character' and 'essential being' of the child that he cannot possibly imagine the child as the 'mere appendage' of an adult. The child must exist on its own and as its own being. This conception of childhood – the child is one character and the adult is another – was common in Romantic literature and culture, and in this instance it is relatively disheartening. The idea that the child is a separate, glorious being forces Elia to come to terms with an ontological height from which he has fallen. The adult character into which he has fallen, as it happens, is decidedly worse than what he once was. In his preface to *The Last Essays of Elia* (1833) – which Lamb had originally written in 1823 as 'A Character of the late Elia. By a Friend', leaving it out of the press for ten years – Lamb finally kills off his alter ego. The title page of the first edition of *The Last Essays of Elia* reads: 'Preface, By a Friend of the Late Elia'. Lamb is writing as a 'Friend' of his own famous persona and announcing that persona's death to the public. The 1833 Preface, unsurprisingly considering its 1823 title, is written like a traditional 'character', but with two exceptions: it analyses not a 'type' but a specific persona, and it is written mostly in the past tense (since 'Elia' is now declared to be dead). The accumulation of ethological detail, however, remains as a driving force of the essay, as Charles Lamb talks about Charles Lamb in the capacity of a 'Friend' of his persona Elia talking about Elia: Elia 'gave himself too little concern what he uttered'; 'He observed neither time nor place'; 'he would pass for a free-thinker'; 'He too much affected that dangerous figure – irony'; 'He sowed doubtful speeches'; 'He would interrupt the gravest discussion with some light jest'; 'He was *petit* and ordinary in his person and appearance'; 'He has been accused of trying to be witty'; 'He never greatly cared for the society of what are called good people'; 'He was temperate in his meals and diversions'; 'He did not conform to the march of time'; 'His manners lagged behind his years'; 'He was too much of the boy-man'.[36] Lamb seems to alienate himself from his character as an adult (he has, after all, lost forever his character as a child) by concentrating that character under the name of 'Elia' and then murdering that name.

It may come as little surprise that one of his essays, 'Sanity of True Genius', almost romanticises the idea of being without a character. 'Sanity' appeared originally in the *New Monthly Magazine* in May 1826. Its main point is to challenge the 'popular fallacy' that literary genius 'has a necessary alliance with insanity'. Elia argues that great geniuses like Shakespeare and Spenser are actually among the 'sanest' of English writers.[37] If any authors deserve to be called 'mad' it is the ones who published Gothic and sentimental novels for the Minerva Press around the turn of the century. Only insane authors, Elia claims, would create such insubstantial characters as can be found in titles put out by the Minerva Press. The 'common run of [William] Lane's novels' featured 'inconsistent characters, or no-characters', 'neither of this world nor of any other conceivable one; an endless string of activities without purposes, of purposes destitute of motive', 'innutritious phantoms', '*fantasques* [whims] only christened'. It must not be said, he goes on, that these whims-with-a-name were 'create[d]', 'call[ed] . . . into act and form', since creation 'implies shaping and consistency' and these quasi-beings show evidence of neither. They are more like 'mental hallucinations' that strike suffering minds in 'sick dreams' – not so much 'super-natural, or something super-added to what we know of nature', but 'plainly non-natural'. All of this, Elia claims, would be somewhat tolerable if only these 'non-natural' characters inhabited plainly imaginary worlds. But the problem is that a lot of the Minerva Press writers place their 'phantoms' – 'a Lord Glendamour and a Miss Rivers', for instance, caught in 'some third-rate love intrigue' – in real, recognisable locations like 'Bath and Bond-street'. Hence London becomes full of structureless whims with Christian names masquerading as sentient, intelligent beings.

Someone like Spenser, on the other hand, may place his characters in vague, fantastic landscapes – Elia gives the example of Mammon in his infernal cave – but the characters themselves are never 'unnaturally' drawn. They never absorb the 'unnaturalness' of their environments, and so resemble actual Londoners more than the lords and ladies in Minerva Press novels. As Shakespeare 'subjugates' his dramatis personae 'to the law of [Nature's] consistency', 'loyal to that sovereign directress, even when he appears most to betray and desert her', so Spenser gives his fictional characters an 'inner nature', a 'law of their speech and actions'.[38]

In light of the above, it seems logical to conclude that Elia applauds the characters who he feels, in spite of what is extravagant about them or their environments, resemble actual persons in the real world. If a fictional character appears to have an 'inner nature' that legislates its 'speech and actions' then that character is well (because 'naturally') drawn. This appears to be the gist of the essay. But I think that we can also read 'Sanity of True Genius' as a text that contains the materials of its own deconstruction. Elia may also romanticise the 'plainly non-natural' characters in Gothic and sentimental novels even as he compares them unflatteringly to the 'natural' ones in Elizabethan plays and poems. The Minerva characters can 'tur[n] life into a dream'. The Elizabethan ones make 'the wildest dreams' seem like 'the sobrieties of every day occurrences'. The Minerva characters, additionally, follow no ethological 'laws' promulgated by a 'sovereign directress'. They are not the 'seeming-aberrations' of the Elizabethans – 'so shifting, and yet so coherent' – but *actual* aberrations, shifting without coherence, Proteuses unbound.[39] They are appealingly radical in their very indifference to the tradition of 'conservation' and other ostensible 'law[s]' of character. The qualities Elia associates with these 'innutritious phantoms' appear even quintessentially Romantic, liberating, alongside the qualities he associates with their Elizabethan counterparts: the latter are marked by 'balance', 'consistency', 'policy', 'sobriet[y]', 'san[ity]', 'tame[ness], 'law'; the former are 'disproportionate', 'inconsistent', 'intoxicated', 'insan[e]', 'excess[ive]', 'lawless'.[40]

There is additional evidence for this claim in an essay that Lamb writes seven years later for the *Athenaeum* – 'Barrenness of the Imaginative Faculty in the Productions of Modern Art' (1833). In 'Barrenness', Elia complains that modern artists can no longer 'trea[t] a story *imaginatively*'. There is hardly a contemporary artist, he explains, 'upon whom his subject has so acted, that it has seemed to direct *him* – not to be arranged by him'; upon whom the 'leading or collateral points' of the subject 'have impressed themselves ... tyrannically', as in divine 'revelation', so that the very 'senses' of the artist seem to have been 'upturned from their proprieties, when sight and hearing are a feeling only'.[41] Here, Elia depicts the imaginative artist (all too rare in the 1830s) as a vassal/vessel to the Muse. The imaginative artist is 'direct[ed]'; 'tyrannically' 'impressed'; reduced, before a 'revelation', to a state in which sense impressions are more like vague feelings than conscious experiences. And yet, in 'Sanity of True Genius', Elia had described Shakespeare and Spenser in nearly opposing terms. He called them the 'sanest' of writers because of their staunch loyalty to that 'sovereign directress' Nature. Their filial obedience to Nature enabled them to produce characters that were sober, balanced, consistent, tame, licit. As artists they were sobered, obedient and in control of their art. My point is not, of course, that Lamb secretly venerated the general stock of Minerva Press characters and would have filled the pages of Shakespeare and Spenser with them if he could. It is rather that his essays register a certain fascination with what Elia calls the 'non-natural': with characterlessness, consciousness without inflexible 'laws', consciousness – in real life and on the page – without even stable rhythms or patterns discernible across time.

Notes

1. Cronin, *Paper Pellets*, p. 24.
2. Duncan, introduction to *Approaches to Teaching Scott's Waverley Novels*, p. 20.
3. Scott, *Old Mortality*, p. 34.
4. Piper, *Dreaming in Books*, p. 109.
5. Ibid.
6. Scott, '*Tales of My Landlord*, 1817', p. 238.
7. Dick, 'Walter Scott and the Financial Crash', para 8.
8. Ferguson, 'The Imaginative Construction of Historical Character', pp. 35, 37. Italics in original.
9. Ibid., pp. 34, 40.
10. Daiches, 'Scott's *Waverley*: The Presence of the Author', p. 10.

11. Manning, *Poetics of Character*, p. 29.
12. Mill, *On Liberty*, p. 108.
13. Kupperman, *Character*, p. 7.
14. Scott, 'Tales of My Landlord, 1817', p. 240.
15. Raleigh, '"Waverley" as History', p. 21.
16. Cronin, *Paper Pellets*, p. 192.
17. Scott, *Old Mortality*, p. 355.
18. Ibid., p. 357.
19. Stevenson and Davidson (eds), *Old Mortality*, p. 535.
20. Scott, *Old Mortality*, pp. 357–8.
21. Ibid., p. 358.
22. Ibid., pp. 355–6.
23. Cronin, *Paper Pellets*, p. 103.
24. Stevenson and Davidson, introduction to *Old Mortality*, p. xxv.
25. Hall, *Characters of Virtues and Vices*, p. 84.
26. Lamb, *Elia and the Last Essays of Elia*, pp. 157–8.
27. Ibid., pp. 22–3.
28. Ibid., p. 58.
29. Ibid., pp. 58–9.
30. Ibid., p. 62.
31. Ibid., p. 60.
32. Ibid., p. 59.
33. Ibid., p. 28.
34. 'tone, n.'. Defs 1a, 10b and 5d. *OED Online*. Oxford English Dictionary, February 2017, <http://www.oed.com> (last accessed 13 February 2017).
35. Lamb, *Elia and the Last Essays of Elia*, p. 129.
36. Ibid., pp. 152–3.
37. Ibid., p. 187.
38. Ibid., pp. 188–9.
39. Ibid., p. 189.
40. Ibid., pp. 187–9.
41. Ibid., pp. 226, 230–1.

Chapter 4

The Politics of Unity: Hazlitt and Character Revisited

God has stamped certain characters upon men's minds, which, like their shapes, may perhaps be a little mended but can hardly be totally altered and transformed into the contrary.
John Locke, *Some Thoughts concerning Education*[1]

[L]et the germ of his character reveal itself freely; constrain it in no way whatsoever in order better to see the whole of it.
Jean-Jacques Rousseau, *Émile*[2]

[C]haracter is not cut in marble – it is not something solid and unalterable. It is something living and changing.
George Eliot, *Middlemarch*[3]

Hazlitt's Ethological Essentialism

The epigraph from *Middlemarch* views character as an organism. Like an organism, character grows and develops, while nonetheless retaining its individuation (presumably Eliot means that character may grow and develop beyond its hypothetical point of maturation in childhood). Contra Eliot, in several of his essays William Hazlitt emphasises not the organic qualities of character but its fixedness: its permanent conformation at birth – not, say, at age six, as Thomas Jarrold argued in 1825 – and its role thereafter as a determinant of all individual feeling and action. Yet in other contexts Hazlitt suggests, like Eliot, that character is fluid, changeable. In still others he implies that the substantial existence of character itself is questionable: that the concept may have no knowable or reliable basis in reality other than one we find it convenient or desirable to invent. This chronic struggle on the part of Hazlitt to know and define the limits of character – despite periodic waves of scepticism regarding its existence – shapes a large portion (perhaps the majority) of his essays and the arc of his literary career.

While several critics[4] have conducted article-length studies of Hazlitt centred on his view of character, none of them has reached beyond a handful (if more than one) of his texts. The recent work on literary character by Manning and Frow makes a systematic and comprehensive study of Hazlitt and character all the more urgent. The fact is that Hazlitt wrote about character broadly and deeply and in response to an intellectually vibrant age determined to define it. I view him primarily as a critical ethologist whose efforts to understand and explain character lie at the heart of his metaphysical and familiar essays, as well as his autobiographical *Liber Amoris*. In this respect, the span of his career resembles John Stuart Mill's, all of whose major texts (including, like Hazlitt, an autobiographical text) are preoccupied with an ideology of character. Both authors rely on empirical observation and on general psychological 'laws' to understand character. Both betray similar anxieties over the limitations imposed by their respective ethologies. Mill can never quite rescue his faith in individual freedom from the looming threat of determinism.[5] Hazlitt struggles to resolve the tension between a mind that is unified and autonomous, but also strictly regulated by a congenital 'bias'. Though he usually argues that an essential and readable character exists in persons, texts and objects, his prose occasionally registers an unfreedom implied in his own doctrine. The human mind may be unified, free and spontaneously formative, but the bias said to condition mental behaviour from birth tragically compromises that freedom.

Hazlitt discusses character directly and indirectly in the majority of his essays, no matter what the topic. Whether he writes of the characters inherent in poems, paintings, sculptures or human beings, he usually treats the concept as an absolute: as a non-negotiable first principle on the basis of which persons, ideas and things can be reliably read and judged. In his view all individuals are born with an 'internal, original bias' that 'remains always the same, true to itself to the very last'. By 'bias' he means temperament, the balance of biological elements: '[t]he greater or lesser degree of animal spirits, – of nervous irritability, – the complexion of the blood, – the proportion of "hot, cold, moist, and dry"'. Though circumstances may lead us to change our conduct, how and what we are able to 'feel' in any given situation is no less alterable than our bodies are (the article on 'Life' in Rees's *Cyclopædia*, ascribed to William Lawrence, makes a similar point).[6] The drunk always feels and thinks like a drunk; the criminal like a criminal; the radical like a radical (even the ultra-turncoat Robert Southey). In his writings on art, Hazlitt claims that the characterological bias of any given artist is present in his or her creations. He calls a painting, for instance, 'an emanation from [the painter's] character, transferred to the canvass'. What distinguishes an original artist from a hack is that the former 'attract[s]' that in nature which 'harmonize[s] with' his or her bias, while 'softening and moulding' that in nature which 'repel[s] it'.[7] In other words, the original artist selects only those materials drawn from the natural world that either harmonise with his or her native temperament or can be softened into a state of harmony with it.

Hazlitt differentiates sharply between identity and character – a vital, though somewhat overlooked, distinction. With a few exceptions (most notably his 1828 essay 'On Self-Love and Benevolence'), he confines his sustained, critical interest in identity mostly to *Essay on the Principles of Human Action* (1805), while character preoccupies him throughout his career. His overall claim concerning the two is that identity is a metaphysical fiction and character is a physiological fact. Identity is erroneously thought to include our past, present and future selves. This is a mistake, because our future selves are as little known to us as other people are. We have no access to our future selves as immediate or reliable as the access we have to our present and our past selves. A future self cannot form part of our conscious being. As Hazlitt claims in *An Essay on the Principles of Human Action*, the fact that '[e]very human being is distinguished from every other human being, both numerically, and characteristically', is the result of individual characters established congenitally in human bodies. But as to 'the continued identity of the whole being, that is the continued resemblance of my thoughts to my previous thoughts, of my sensations to my previous sensations and so on', that is only a reassuring construct. The 'absolute, metaphysical identity of my individual being', which 'must be strictly and logically true of it at all times', exists nowhere but in the imagination (*Essay on the Principles of Human Action*, *SWWH*, 1:30, 33, 5). Hazlitt thus relegates identity to the realm of metaphysics but makes character an object of empirical observation – not to mention the ground of aesthetic, forensic and moral judgement.⁸

Hazlitt attacks modes of thought that seem to undermine the unity and authority of character. He is especially sensitive to his culture's 'unprecedented tendencies towards diversity and fragmentation'. In *The Spirit of the Age* (1818), for instance, he observes that

> in Scotland generally, the display of personal character . . . is not much encouraged – every one there is looked upon in the light of a machine or a collection of topics. They . . . drag you into a dispute with as little ceremony as they would drag out an article from an Encyclopedia. They criticise every thing, analyse every thing, argue upon every thing, dogmatise upon every thing; and the bundle of your habits, feelings, humours, follies and pursuits is regarded by them no more than a bundle of old clothes. (*The Spirit of the Age*, *SWWH*, 7:198)

Scottish intellectuals treat dialogue between persons as dialogue between encyclopaedias (Lamb, we recall, makes a similar point in his essay 'Imperfect Sympathies'). Each conversationalist wants to extract a select portion of information from the other as efficiently as possible – as one would find that information by browsing an alphabetised list of encyclopedic entries. Scottish characters seem arranged, for this purpose, as searchable factual compendia. S. T. Coleridge was similarly disenchanted with new sources and arrangements of knowledge. He complained that certain Presbyterian encyclopaedists of his day had abandoned the principled method of arranging knowledge current in the eighteenth century: the method of organising all 'gradation[s] of ideas' and 'partial forms' of knowledge, like 'ranks in a well ordered state' or 'commands in a well regulated army', under the supreme authority of 'one universal form of good and fair'.⁹ In a broad sense, both he and Hazlitt saw the new encyclopaedia as an emblem of disorganisation. For Hazlitt it encouraged, in a sense, the fragmentation of personal characters. For Coleridge it disarranged the sum of human knowledge. The former believed (or wanted to believe) that personal character was a unified and unifying principle that one could either resist or accept, and that to defy it was to rebel against the laws of human thought and action: '[i]t is well not to *go out of* ourselves', advises Hazlitt, since '[s]ome views and modes of thinking suit certain minds, as certain colours suit certain complexions' ('On Consistency of Opinion', *CWH*, 17:33, emphasis mine). Presumably Hazlitt did not think that one could actually 'go out of' oneself – or at least his theory of the congenital bias suggests as much. Yet in other moments he argues that an actor can find or spontaneously invent a new personal character precisely because he or she has 'left' the original in the process of acting. It is as if Hazlitt wants to leave open the possibility of 'go[ing] out of' one's character, and even allow it to be part of a natural process. Perhaps his ultimate aim is to minimise the determining power of the bias under special conditions.

Hazlitt imagines the French (unlike the English) as perennially in danger of 'go[ing] out of' their characters. In one essay he writes that French 'feelings and ideas are so slight and discontinuous that they can be changed for others' on a whim ('Madame Pasta and Mademoiselle Mars', *SWWH*, 8:307). His *Essay on the Principles of Human Action* contains a footnote several pages long that explains how the French cannot retain sense-impressions: before one impression can fully materialise in the French mind another has arrived and taken its place (*Essay on the Principles of Human Action*, *SWWH*, 1:22–6). Reading French faces through physiognomy is also difficult, if not impossible. In an essay on portraiture Hazlitt notes that 'a real English lady of the seventeenth century . . . looks like one, because she cannot look otherwise'. But a portrait of a French woman painted in the same century always looks affected, since the 'French physiognomy . . . is often spoiled by a consciousness of what it is, and a restless desire to be something more' ('On a Portrait of a Lady by Vandyke', *SWWH*, 8:262). In other words, a typical portrait of a French face reveals a character in the act of trying to escape itself. Consider the following anecdote:

> I once knew a French lady who said all manner of good things and forgot them the next moment; who maintained an argument with great wit and eloquence, and presently after changed sides, without knowing that she had done so; who invented a story and believed it on the spot; who wept herself and made you weep with the force of her descriptions, and suddenly drying her eyes, laughed at you for looking grave. Is this not like acting? Yet it was not affected in her, but natural, involuntary,

incorrigible. The hurry and excitement of her natural spirits was like a species of intoxication, or she resembled a child in thoughtlessness and incoherence. She was a Frenchwoman. It was nature, but nature that had nothing to do with truth or consistency. ('Madame Pasta and Mademoiselle Mars', *SWWH*, 8:307)

The mademoiselle here is not blamed for her 'incoherence' because she is not play-acting. She just naturally happens – as Hazlitt says of the French in another essay – to '"have no . . . real character"' ('Character of John Bull', *SWWH*, 2:99). It is difficult to determine precisely what Hazlitt means here. Is this woman in some sense characterless (a metaphysical valuation) or is she simply unprincipled (a moral valuation)? The constitutive and moral meanings of character enable both possibilities and each is at play in this and in similar statements.

Hazlitt criticises the sensuous Della Cruscan poetry of Thomas Moore on the similar grounds that – like the encyclopaedia or the mademoiselle – it features and seems to promote disunified characters. It either misrepresents (denaturalises) personal character as a set of heterogeneous images, or it distorts the natural act of perception. In the first case, Moore tends to represent characters as miscellaneous inventories of qualities. He

> makes out an inventory of beauty – the smile on the lips, the dimple on the cheeks, *item*, golden locks, *item*, a pair of blue wings, *item*, a silver sound, with breathing fragrance and radiant light, and thinks it a character. (*The Spirit of the Age*, *SWWH*, 7:222)

Moore presumes that some Frankensteinian collage of body parts, sounds, scents and shades can somehow cohere in the mind of the reader as an agent. For Hazlitt, this carelessness involves more than a just frustrating reading experience. Moore actually 'stunts and enfeebles equally the growth of the imagination and the affections' (*The Spirit of the Age*, *SWWH*, 7:222). His readers cannot possibly imagine the characters he depicts, let alone feel for them, and so they are trained to imagine and feel badly. It is because he 'indulges in every sentiment' that Moore is unable to give 'full force to the masses of things', to 'connec[t] them into a whole' ('On the Living Poets', *SWWH*, 2:305). Dart claims that Hazlitt has a similar problem with how the cockney character 'conceive[s]' the world: 'entirely in terms of a free-floating and arbitrary juxtaposition of objects'.[10]

At other points in his poetry, Moore garbles the natural act of human perception by describing the world in such a way as no mind could possibly experience it. He 'creates a false standard of reference' in his poetry, 'invert[ing] or decompound[ing] the natural order of association, in which objects strike the thoughts and feelings' (*The Spirit of the Age*, *SWWH*, 7:222). This is a fascinating literary-critical objection. Hazlitt is not faulting Moore on aesthetic, or even on moral, but on phenomenological grounds. Moore describes phenomena as accumulating out of order: there is no hint of a mind, or consciousness, or 'standard of reference' present that is actually or correctly processing what it perceives. These 'false standard[s] of reference' resemble what Rorty calls 'presences': 'modes of . . . being present to . . . experiences' 'without dominating or controlling' those experiences. To such modes of being, Rorty claims, 'psychological and physical characters' are at best 'incidental'.[11] Moore's Della Cruscan 'presences' serve only as catalysts for accumulations of perceptions. They cannot contain or process those perceptions. Jon Mee has observed that another Della Cruscan poet, Robert Merry, cultivates an '[un]bounded subjectivity' in his verse that is 'infinitely open to sensation'.[12] Such poetry, Mee claims, threatened individual stability and traditional forms of sociability in the late eighteenth century. Moore, likewise, threatens the unity of character by reducing it to a set of miscellaneous images or random sense-perceptions.

It is unsurprising that Hazlitt faults Moore for not giving 'full force to the masses of things', since he has the same problem with phrenologists that he has with Moore: phrenologists divided the mind into localised faculties seated in discrete brain organs. They were fragmenting personal characters at the same time that Moore was fragmenting textual characters. Phrenology was at least partly supposed to be an empirical science: the bumps or knobs felt on human skulls were thought to mark the presence of various brain organs and the faculties for which these organs were responsible. Knowing how the brain organs cooperated in any one mind could maximise human potential. Spurzheim, in fact, argues that most people fall short of their destinies precisely because 'the unity of faculties is believed'.[13] The masses are simply unaware of how to stimulate the productivity of some brain organs and curtail that of others. Hazlitt rejects the notion of brain organs operating independently, arguing instead that 'a certain . . . disposition of the mind, a 'bias or scope' of 'sensibility', a unifying power, controls all mental faculties at once. The phrenologists denied the existence of any such power. They also, according to Hazlitt, cared only about the relative size of brain organs, paying no comparable attention to the 'texture, irritability' or 'tenacity' of these organs ('On Dr Spurzheim's Theory', SWWH, 8:140, 133). Nor could phrenologists account for the 'general characters of sprightliness, of gravity, of voluptuousness, of severity, of artfulness, of fickleness, of gloom, of indifference, of impulse, of calculation, &c.'. '[S]hall we say that these go for nothing', Hazlitt asks, 'because there is no room for them in the geographical chart of the human understanding?' ('Phrenological Fallacies', CWH, 20:253).

Phrenology, for Hazlitt, was too theoretical and deductive (not to mention immoral) to be a proper measure of character. It lacked the force of common sense. At one point he observes that

> women have more *tact* and insight into character than men, that they find out a pedant, a pretender, a blockhead, sooner. The explanation is, that they trust more to the first impressions and natural indications of things, without troubling themselves with a learned theory of them. . . . Women are naturally physiognomists, and men phrenologists. The first judge by sensations; the last by rules. ('Paragraphs on Prejudice', CWH, 20:327)

Here Hazlitt assumes a binary between impressions and rules. Sensations and first impressions are natural and therefore reliable evidence of character. Reading character is an intuitive science that benefits from 'tact and insight' more than from reason and judgement. In his own career as an ethologist, Hazlitt prefers 'slight physiognomical observations taken at random' over strict phrenological rules ('On Dr Spurzheim's Theory', SWWH, 8:144). He assumes the role of Mr Spectator, or a Scottish or English Spy, or Boz: a hypothetically undogmatic and impartial flâneur-figure who pieces together the truth of character bit by empirical bit. But the more of Hazlitt's essays one reads, the more it becomes clear that his 'observations' are not as 'slight' or 'taken at random' as he would like to think. They are actually carried out with some pretence to a system.[14] Hazlitt casts phrenologists as God-playing villains animated by the 'spirit of dogmatism' to inquire into 'unknown causes', the 'mysteries of nature', when in fact the 'nature and faculties of the human mind are . . . an inextricable labyrinth' ('Burke and the Edinburgh Phrenologists', *CWH*, 20:201). Only 'daring anatomists of morals' would reduce the mind to 'the skeleton' and, 'in their own eager, unfeeling pursuit of scientific truth and elementary principles . . . "murder to dissect"'.[15] His own theory of character may indeed be much less 'scientific' than that of the phrenologists, but it is arguably no less dogmatic (and possibly no less 'murder[ous]'). He simply prefers to generalise rather than particularise; to typologise rather than 'dissect'. In so doing, he can be quite a bit more 'unfeeling' than his more 'theoretical' rivals.

One of the most elaborate accounts of Hazlitt's *method* of character analysis – similar to that in Mill's *System of Logic* – is found in his essay 'On Genius and Common Sense'. Hazlitt notes that a

> certain look has been remarked strongly indicative of a certain passion or trait of character, and we attach the same meaning to it or are affected in the same pleasurable or painful manner by it, where it exists in a less degree, though we can define neither the look itself nor the modification of it. Having got the general clue, the exact result may be left to the imagination to vary, to extenuate, or aggravate it according to circumstances. ('On Genius and Common Sense', *SWWH*, 6:32–3)

The reader of character begins by observing some 'modification' of a 'certain look' (perhaps a look that belongs to a physiognomical type) in a countenance. He or she has an intuitive awareness of the general 'look', if not of all its various modifications. While he or she cannot quite 'define . . . the look itself nor its modification' on this particular occasion, he or she can *estimate* the nature of the modification based upon the amount of pain or pleasure it arouses. It remains only for his or her imagination to fine-tune that estimation to an 'exact result' (a practice that presumably improves with experience). As a practical example, Hazlitt refers to portrait of Oliver Cromwell by the seventeenth-century miniaturist Samuel Cooper. The portrait

> denote[s] the character of the man for high-reaching policy and deep designs as plainly as they can be written. How is it that we decypher this expression in the face? First, by feeling it: and how is it that we feel it? Not by pre-established rules, but by the instinct of analogy, by the principle of association, which is subtle and sure in proportion as it is

variable and indefinite. A circumstance, apparently of no value, shall alter the whole interpretation to be put upon an expression or action; and it shall alter it thus powerfully because in proportion to its very insignificance it shews a strong general principle at work that extends in its ramifications to the smallest things. ('On Genius and Common Sense', *SWWH*, 6:33)

The viewer relies on a lifetime of stored associations in order to 'decypher' the character of Cromwell in the painting. The more 'variable and indefinite' the associations he or she has, the more 'sure' his or her discernment will be. A person of wide physiognomic experience will detect the most 'insignificant' nuance in the portrait and assimilate it automatically into his or her judgement. He or she knows that one subtle circumstance added to an artistically rendered expression can make it a new expression altogether – and therefore the seat of a different character – since there is a 'strong general principle at work' in a good portrait that incorporates all details into itself. The physiognomically experienced person is attuned to this principle.

All of this reinforces the idea that the automatic process of association preconditions perception of character. Association works in and through the perceiving mind without its conscious participation. Hazlitt refers elsewhere to 'the well-known principle of the *association of ideas*; by which certain impressions, from frequent recurrence, coalesce and act in unison truly and mechanically – that is, without our being conscious of anything but the general and settled result' ('Paragraphs on Prejudice', *CWH*, 20:326; italics in original). The principle of association causes the mind to learn to separate human character into types. Awareness of and sensitivity to these types is essential to the discerning critic. In his essays, Hazlitt is 'anxious to establish criticism of all types on a firm and observable base'.[16]

Not only association, but 'abstraction' seems to naturalise, and therefore justify, the tendency of the mind to separate human character into types. According to Hazlitt, all ideas are necessarily 'general and abstract'. We can have no 'perfectly distinct idea of any one individual object or concrete existence, either as to the parts of which it is composed, or the differences belonging to it, or the circumstances connected with it'. This is because the mind works by abstraction, which Hazlitt calls a 'necessary consequence of the limitation of the comprehensive faculty' ('Madame de Staël's Account of German

Philosophy and Literature', *CWH*, 20:33).[17] Take our concept of a square. The term 'square' refers to a 'collective idea' that we falsely imagine is 'one thing'. But any given square is in fact many things. It consists of 'lines, their direction, equality, connection, &c. all which must be combined together in the mind, before it can possibly form any idea of the object'. If for some reason 'we think to exclude all generality from our ideas of things, as implying a want of perfect truth and clearness, it will be impossible for the mind to form an idea of any one object whatever' ('Madame de Staël's Account of German Philosophy and Literature', *CWH*, 20:24, 34). The point seems to be that words are efficient but delimiting symbols that allow the mind to conceptualise vast sets of otherwise inconceivable particulars. Without them we could not turn sense data into manageable ideas.

Some seventy years later, Friedrich Nietzsche uses the same habit of mind to draw important, anti-moral conclusions. He observes that

> [e]very word instantly becomes a concept precisely insofar as it is not supposed to serve as a reminder of the unique and entirely individual original experience to which it owes its origin; but rather, a word becomes a concept insofar as it simultaneously has to fit countless more or less similar cases – which means, purely and simply, cases which are never equal and thus altogether unequal. Every concept arises from the equation of unequal things. Just as it is certain that one leaf is never totally the same as another, so it is certain that the concept 'leaf' is formed by arbitrarily discarding these individual differences and by forgetting the distinguishing aspects. This awakens the idea that, in addition to the leaves, there exists in nature the 'leaf': the original model according to which all the leaves were perhaps woven, sketched, measured, colored, curled, and painted – but by incompetent hands, so that no specimen has turned out to be a correct, trustworthy, and faithful likeness of the original model.

Nietzsche goes on to apply this phenomenological account to the practice of character trait attribution. We may call a person honest because we perceive that he or she acts honestly. But the fact is that there exists no 'essential quality called "honesty"'. All we have to go by are 'countless individualized and consequently unequal actions which we equate by omitting the aspects in which they are unequal and which we now designate as "honest" actions'. Then we 'formulate from them a *qualitas occulta* which has the name "honesty"'.

The broad implication of Nietzsche's point is that not only character traits but truth itself consists of

> [a] moveable host of metaphors, metonymies, and anthropomorphisms: in short, a sum of human relations which have been poetically and rhetorically intensified, transferred, and embellished, and which, after long usage, seem to a people to be fixed, canonical, and binding.

Truth, in a word, is 'the duty to lie according to a fixed convention'.[18] Hazlitt, of course, undertakes no such drastic revaluation of all moral values. Yet some of his essays register a related, if relatively tentative, scepticism concerning the reality of character as active principle or *qualitas occulta*. In the rest of this chapter I will show how this guarded scepticism reveals itself in subtle ways.

Most of Hazlitt's essays seem to assume that character is real and exists in persons and objects. Hazlitt presupposes the validity of the Theophrastan type as a necessary consequence of mental processes like abstraction. A few critics have acknowledged his debt to the Theophrastan tradition and its revitalisation in the seventeenth and eighteenth centuries.[19] Knight claims that Hazlitt reverses the 'normal pattern' of the Theophrastan 'character' in *The Spirit of the Age* by describing 'specific, contemporary figures' instead of nonspecific types. For Knight, the 'characters of *The Spirit of the Age* are explicitly individuals and implicitly types, while the character essay proper presents an explicit type that could be, and frequently was, a particular individual'.[20] Story likewise acknowledges that Hazlitt is concerned with real-life figures but emphasises his interest in 'discovering the ostensibly timeless, universal type underlying the complexity of individual behavior'.[21]

Knight and Story are primarily interested in what Benjamin Boyce has called 'portrait-characters', or word-portraits of actual, living individuals that simultaneously suggest a type to which they seem to conform.[22] Most students of Hazlitt focus on his portrait-characters because they fill his enduring *The Spirit of the Age*. But Hazlitt also wrote several essays of the opposite sort that critics have neglected: Theophrastan 'characters' like 'Character of John Bull', 'On Effeminacy of Character', 'On the Clerical Character', 'On the Literary Character', 'On the Regal Character' and so on. These examine a type – at least on the surface – and the less Hazlitt writes *directly* about contemporary figures in such essays, the more slanted, and occasionally vitriolic, his prose can afford to be. He calls the 'effeminate character' a 'disease' or 'infirmity' (one 'branch' of which he denotes the 'trifling' or 'dilatory' character). Effeminate poetry (the examples he gives are Della Cruscan verse and Keats's *Endymion*) lacks decidedness and energy and in a general sense is without character altogether ('On Effeminacy of Character', *SWWH*, 6:224–5). The character of a priest is 'something positive and disagreeable', while the Quaker has 'a negative character' ('On the Clerical Character', *SWWH*, 4:230). The literary character tends to be selfish, bookish and myopic ('On the Literary Character', *SWWH* 2:131–5).

Perhaps these and similar judgements can be overlooked as unremarkable products of popular prejudice. But consider the following invective on what Hazlitt would have called the 'rural character', from an essay in *The Round Table* (1817) on Wordsworth's *Excursion*:

> All country people hate each other . . . There is nothing good to be had in the country, or, if there is, they will not let you have it . . . Their common mode of life is a system of wretchedness and self-denial, like what we read of among barbarous tribes . . . rustic ignorance is intolerable . . . Their selfishness and insensibility are perhaps less owing to the hardships and privations, which make them, like people out at sea in a boat, ready to devour one another, than to their having no idea of any thing beyond themselves and their immediate sphere of action . . . Having no circulating libraries to exhaust their love of the marvelous, they amuse themselves with fancying the disasters and disgraces of their particular acquaintance . . . The common people in civilized countries are a kind of domesticated savages . . . They are taken out of a state of nature, without being put in possession of the refinements of art . . . If the inhabitants of the mountainous districts described by Mr Wordsworth, are less gross and sensual than others, they are more selfish. Their egotism becomes more concentrated, as they are more insulated, and their purposes more inveterate, as they have less competition to struggle with. The weight of matter which surrounds them, crushes the finer sympathies. Their minds become hard and cold, like the rocks which they cultivate. The immensity of their mountains makes the human form appear little and insignificant . . . Nor do they regard one another more than flies on a wall. Their physiognomy expresses the materialism of their character, which has only one principle – rigid self-will. They move on with their eyes and foreheads fixed, looking neither to the right nor to the left, with a heavy slouch in their gait, and seeming as if nothing would divert them from

their path. We do not admire this plodding pertinacity, always directed to the main chance. ('The Same Subject Continued ['Observations on Mr Wordsworth's Poem, "The Excursion"']', *SWWH*, 2:123–5)[23]

This description is arresting for a number of reasons. The most obvious is its marginalising and fatalistic rhetoric. If social reformers like Hannah More and Anna Barbauld can be accused of encouraging the poor to accept their station and wait for redemption in Heaven, Hazlitt takes it for granted that the rustic poor are doomed to be miserable in their lot whether they accept their lot or not. He leaves little consideration for their redemption on earth or in the afterlife. Here, 'self-denial' is dissociated from virtue and cast solely as self-neglect or slovenliness. The passage is also strangely un-Romantic. A 'love of the marvelous' nurtured in the private imagination is second to one satisfied by books in circulating libraries. The state of nature is a barbaric condition if the 'refinements of art' are absent. Competition is said to alleviate egotism rather than promote it. Mountains do not awe the rustic (who is insensible of the sublime) but diminish his or her respect for the 'human form'. A physiognomic reading of the rural character leads to 'one principle – rigid self-will'. Even the faces and gaits of country-dwellers are subject to a uniform sluggishness. Clearly 'Hazlitt has no time for the pastoral ideal'.[24] Essays like this one, written for the *Examiner* and collected in *The Round Table*, were 'abused by reviewers for their vulgarity' and 'rancorous politics'.[25]

Generalising – leaving out details about actual rural inhabitants – seems to have allowed Hazlitt more room for scorn and intolerance. And yet one scholar claims that Hazlitt is 'convinc[ed] of the harm arising from the contemporary emphasis upon generality'.[26] How can this be? How can the same author who excoriates '[a]ll country people' realise the harm in generalisation? Perhaps Hazlitt is of two minds. He writes elsewhere that the familiar essayist should avoid 'sounding generalities' ('On Familiar Style', *SWWH*, 6:220). The periodical essayist should avoid 'sweeping clauses of proscription and anathema' in favour of 'nice distinctions and liberal constructions'; and should 'not try to prove all black or all white', but 'la[y] on the intermediate colours, (and most of them not unpleasing ones)' ('On the Periodical Essayists', *CWH*, 6:91–2). Hazlitt condemns 'vague conclusions' and 'hate[s] people who have no notion of any thing but generalities'

('On Reason and Imagination', *SWWH*, 8:40). But what is his description of country people if not 'sweeping ... anathema'? What is possibly 'nice' or 'liberal' about it? I suggest that any hatred Hazlitt has for generalities applies more to his understanding of character as it exists in art, than character as it exists in life. He prefers a painted portrait, for instance, that welcomes the particularities of time and place in lieu of one that suppresses incident and detail for the sake of general harmony or conformity to a type – the aesthetic advocated by Joshua Reynolds.[27] No abstract principle, that is, should neutralise the particularising elements of a work of art. Peculiarities of form and circumstance are welcome – as long as they remain organic to the basic idea of the piece. But in several essays on human types, Hazlitt loses this sense of balance. Particulars of form and circumstance become lost in a more dogmatic enforcement of the general. His typological essays seem to abuse what John Savarese has called Hazlitt's 'mindreading', or his 'ability to attribute mental states like beliefs or desire to people' through the 'projective imagination'.[28] Savarese studies the *Essay on the Principles of Human Action* to suggest that Hazlitt promotes 'mindreading' because it is the key to benevolence and sympathy. In the case of the rustic character sketch, however, Hazlitt exploits imaginative mindreading at the cost not only of benevolence and sympathy, but of all 'nice distinctions and liberal constructions'.

Hazlitt's inflammatory typological rhetoric did not go unnoticed by contemporaries. A reviewer of *Political Essays, with Sketches of Public Characters* (1819) in the *Quarterly Review* complains that Hazlitt is prone to sweeping generalisations when he is not slandering public figures. The reviewer cites several passages from the *Political Essays* to support his case: '"To be a true Jacobin man must be a good hater"', '"A Tory is not a man, but a beast"', '"A Whig is . . . a coward to both sides of the question"' and so on. What astonishes this contributor is that among Hazlitt's 'effusions' on 'abstract character[s]' he can make the 'veracious assertion' that '"*We do not wish to say any thing illiberal of any profession or set of men in the abstract*"'.[29] While it may seem like politics as usual that someone writing for the *Quarterly Review* should target Hazlitt (whom he or she casts as a 'forlorn drudge of the Examiner'), what the author observes of *Political Essays* could well be applied to many of Hazlitt's essays in other collections.[30] Hazlitt warns readers against the dangers of 'sweeping clauses' as often as he relies on them in his own polemics.

I noted above that his theory of abstraction helps Hazlitt naturalise a typological view of personal character. His understanding of what he calls 'coalescence' works to the same end. In his essay 'Paragraphs on Prejudice', Hazlitt writes that our 'habitual impressions, from being made up of a few particulars always repeated, grow together into a kind of concrete substance, which will not bear taking to pieces, and where the smallest deviation destroys the whole feeling'. A 'grossness' of ideas forms in the mind. These 'ideas by habit and the dearth of general information coalesce together into one indissoluble form', so that 'insignificant' details become 'inseparably bound up with the main principles as the most important, and to give up any part [is] to give up the whole'.[31] Hence one Christian sect will wage war against another Christian sect over trifling differences of opinion, although both are in full agreement concerning the fundamental articles of faith. The details have acquired as much importance as the 'main principles'. All details are 'bound up' together in a single mass. Hazlitt makes the case that coalescence is largely responsible for personal prejudices.

Whatever merit coalescence has as an explanation of how prejudices form in the mind, it certainly sheds light on Hazlitt's penchant for the Theophrastan 'character'. If one grants coalescence, then all the trivial behavioural details one applies to a certain 'type' are in some sense excusable. They can be viewed as indissolubly attached to one's conception or 'whole feeling' of that type. To extract one or more petty details from the 'main principles' of a human type would be counterintuitive, even unnatural. What becomes important – and what I discuss below in the next section – is that Hazlitt occasionally undermines his own cavalier application of abstraction and coalescence. In certain cases he acknowledges the limits of typologies and congenital biases. As John Whale has rightly observed, Hazlitt had his 'doubts as to whether all instances provide [a] clear-cut substitution of individual for general'.[32]

Interrogating Ethology

In essays like 'On Personal Character' and 'On the Knowledge of Character', Hazlitt maintains an essentialist of view of human character as the source and primary determinant of individual thought and behaviour. Circumstance and education can do little to alter the nature and extent of its influence (though education can present rational alternatives to unhealthy or unsocial behaviour). In his *Essay on the Principles of Human Action*, Hazlitt argues that all habits are unreflectively assumed: that the 'original disposition' of a given mind (which is 'fixed and invariable') determines how and to what extent that mind avoids or acquires its habits.[33] But was Hazlitt always comfortable with such biological determinism in light of his passion for human freedom? I suggest that he had reservations on the subject; that he occasionally viewed his own theory of character as the lesser of two evils. Character was a matter of *internal* necessity; the greater evil was a necessity that was *external*.

Fredrick Burwick has compared Hazlitt to Friedrich Schelling in terms of their responses 'to the ideological shifts manifested in the French revolution and the Napoleonic Empire'. According to Burwick, both authors tried to rescue human freedom from 'the mechanistic implications of associationist doctrine' and the Helvetian dictum that '[a]ll behaviour ... is motivated by self-interest'. Schelling, for his part, believed in personal freedom but not without 'the counter-force of necessity'. He saw the two not as diametrically opposed but working symbiotically:

> If the individual ... acts in accord with inner nature, or following that part of external necessity which is subsumed in the Identity of self and nature, the act is free so long as it arises from the laws of one's own being, and is not determined by any other factor. In the concept of inner necessity Schelling claims that the opposition of freedom and necessity is resolved. Inner necessity is independent of the causally determined scheme operating outside the self.[34]

However comforting this resolution of individual freedom and external necessity may seem, inner necessity is still a kind of necessity. The unalterable 'laws of one's own being' still legislate private thought and action inexorably. Recall that, for Hazlitt, a drunk is always drunk. His predisposition ('inner necessity') to alcohol abuse remains in all its strength no matter how much or for how long he alters his drinking habits (as with Thomas Hardy's 'Man of Character', Michael Henchard, whose alcoholism persists like a sword of Damocles through twenty years of sobriety). Like Hazlitt,

Schelling also considers the possibility of moral reformation in his *Philosophical Investigations into the Essence of Human Freedom* (1809). According to Schelling, 'Man, even if born in time, is indeed created into the beginning of the creation'. As 'a man acts here so has he acted from eternity . . . His action does not *become*, just as he himself does not *become* as a moral being, but rather it is eternal by nature'. So a person cannot *become* a 'moral being' but he either is one or is not one eternally. Schelling then asks whether this view prevents a person from 'turning . . . from evil toward good, and vice versa' in this life. He answers in the negative: a good person who has acted badly may indeed reform his behaviour; and even if his behavioural 'transformation' 'has not [yet] taken place', 'the good principle' in him, 'that inner voice of his own better nature', is never 'completely extinguished'. It is there for eternity. The man himself must choose whether he will allow or not allow that 'good . . . spirit in him' to act. This 'allowing-to-act-within-himself' constitutes human freedom.[35]

In other words, a person may either will or not will the eternal spirit of good or evil within him or her to act. This ability to decide and direct the eternal spirit inside oneself makes one free. But the fact remains that he or she who allows a spirit to act is not that spirit. He or she has control over the reins but not over the strength and speed of the horse. And then there is the astonishing fact – which seems to undercut the entire concept of human freedom as Schelling views it – that whether and to what extent a person is likely to reform himself or herself in this life *are determined in advance*. If

> human or divine assistance – (man always requires some assistance) – may destine an individual to convert to the good, then, [the fact] that he grants the good spirit this influence and does not positively shut himself off from it, lies likewise already in the initial action [of creation] whereby he is this individual and no other.

In other words, the extent to which I am likely to allow human or divine assistance to help me reform has been predetermined in the initial act of my creation in eternity. It is I who allow or do not allow that assistance, but not I, strictly speaking, who acts: 'given how man is in fact created, it is not he himself but rather the good or evil spirit in him that acts'.[36] Insofar as I operate within the laws of my self

I am free from external necessity, but at the same time I am powerless to act outside these laws by which I am constituted as I and no other.

This concept of internal necessity – I may act freely provided I act within the laws of my own being – is similar to what Hazlitt calls the congenital bias of character. Both concepts suggest a dynamic process of growth and development set in motion within strict metaphysical or quasi-metaphysical boundaries. Hazlitt writes:

> I shall not undertake to decide exactly how far the original character may be modified by the general progress of society, or by particular circumstances happening to the individual; but I think the alteration (be it what it may) is more apparent than real, more in conduct than in feeling.

The ordinary circumstances of life probably affect our predetermined abilities and desires as little as they do our physical appearance: '[w]e do not change our features with our situations; neither do we change the capacities or inclinations which lurk beneath them' ('On Personal Character', *SWWH*, 8:220, 216). Here we can see the influence of the article in Rees's *Cyclopædia* on 'Life'. Why, for Hazlitt, are we unable to change our 'capacities or inclinations'? Because they are under the strict control of certain psychological arch-faculties: 'essential faculties, such as will, imagination, &c', 'original independent principles, necessarily interwoven with the nature of man as an active and intelligent being'. These essential faculties are what 'give effect and direction to our physical sensibility', in which 'capacities or inclinations' are rooted ('Mind and Motive', *CWH*, 20:44). How do the essential faculties operate? For the phrenologist, all mental faculties (whether 'essential' or not) function autonomously – each within its own brain organ. But recall that Hazlitt refuses to localise mental faculties. For Hazlitt, faculties operate not independently but under the control of a unified mind with an autocratic power: 'some single, superintending faculty or conscious power' that controls all other mental powers ('On Dr Spurzheim's Theory', *SWWH*, 8:128). In a word, the mind is a hierarchy. A supreme active power rules over all essential faculties (arguably compromising their status as 'independent principles'). The 'essential faculties' rule over physical sensibility (capacities and inclinations). In sum: superintending faculty; essential faculties (will and imagination); some, presumably, nonessential faculties; and capacities and inclinations – in that order.

This hierarchy becomes a bit less steady when Hazlitt introduces the idea of *fascination*. As Hazlitt describes it:

> The attention which the mind gives to its ideas is not always owing to the gratification derived from them, but to the strength and truth of the impressions themselves, i.e. to their involuntary power over the mind. This observation will account for a very general principle in the mind, which cannot, we conceive, be satisfactorily explained in any other way, we mean the *power of fascination*. ('Mind and Motive', CWH, 20:45)

The brain receives sense impressions from its environment and these impressions become ideas in the mind. Occasionally, the 'strength and truth' of certain 'impressions' can have an 'involuntary power over the mind' and its faculties. What I find interesting is that with the notion of fascination Hazlitt problematises his own hierarchical psychology. He said earlier that faculties like imagination and will regulate our 'physical sensibility' – give it 'effect and direction'. Here he claims that sense impressions (even displeasing ones) can sometimes 'fascinate' our minds despite the efforts of will and imagination. The 'essential faculties' that are supposed to regulate 'physical sensibility' automatically can be rendered temporarily powerless by the 'strength and truth' of fascinating impressions.

Hazlitt's faculty psychology raises important questions. Where does the 'bias' of character fit into it? Does that bias determine the strength, depth or breadth of the 'superintending' power that rules all other faculties (or vice versa)? Does the fact that neither will nor imagination can operate outside this superintendence somehow compromise the 'original[ity]' or 'independen[ce]' of either one? Is consciousness the same thing as the all-ruling 'conscious power' in the mind? I would say that the specific answers to these questions are ultimately less important than what the questions imply – that the mind seems to operate at a distance from some preferable immediacy of experience, or pure agency; that, in spite of (or because of) his repeated insistence on the all-powerful governance of character, Hazlitt opens up his rigid ecology to debate and doubt.

I have argued that Hazlitt's essays as a whole define the limits and authority of character but not without reservations. In no text does Hazlitt seem to divorce himself from his professed ethology more energetically than in the sensational *Liber Amoris* (1823). As Hazlitt himself claimed toward the end of *Liber Amoris*, 'a more complete experiment on character was never made' (*Liber Amoris*, *SWWH*, 7:71). In this autobiographical tour de force, Hazlitt produces the longest, most impressionistic and most imaginative 'portrait' (or 'portrait-character') of his career – that of Sarah Walker. It is unlike anything he had ever written or would write. In composing it Hazlitt suspends both his belief in character as a calculable object of experience that determines individual thought and action for life, and his belief in character as an intuitable, superintending principle inherent in a work of art that unifies all aesthetic details. In *Liber Amoris*, he treats character as a mode of becoming rather than a state of being. In the midst of this freedom there emerges an ideal of character as protean, undetectable, unbounded by strict chains of internal or external necessity, even in a sense nonexistent in persons and in art. I have said that Hazlitt is far more willing to make bald generalisations about human types than he is about aesthetic representations. Walker is unique in that she seems to have neither a personal nor a textual-aesthetic character. She falls under no human 'type' because she is as much the creation of a Pygmalion artist as she is human. Yet as an idealised creation, she so abounds in ever-shifting particulars that no aesthetic principle – aesthetic character – can possibly unify these particulars (as Hazlitt claims happens in the painting of Cromwell). David Bromwich summarises the story of Sarah Walker succinctly:

> For most of two years, in his early forties . . . [Hazlitt] had become infatuated with the serving girl who brought him his tea in a lodging house, and who startled him one day by sitting in his lap. This was Sarah Walker, nineteen years old and a flirt . . . [F]or her sake he made a wreck of his life. With friends and acquaintances, almost indifferently, he carried on a desperate correspondence about his pursuit of her . . . he tried every possible means to resolve Sarah's character into that of angel or demon, going so far as to test her faithfulness by laying a trap in the shape of a hired seducer; but when, after humiliating delays and contrivances, he procured a divorce from his wife and proposed marriage to Sarah, he was flatly rejected. Of all this we have an almost daily record, in the diaries of Hazlitt and of his wife, in his correspondence, and in his verbatim transcriptions of meetings with Sarah, which with the correspondence and some brief stretches of narrative he published in 1823, as soon as he was certain of his loss, under the title *Liber Amoris; Or, the New Pygmalion*.[37]

Two years before the publication of *Liber Amoris*, Hazlitt alludes to Walker in his essay 'On the Knowledge of Character' (1821):

> The greatest hypocrite I ever knew was a little, demure, pretty, modest-looking girl, with eyes timidly cast upon the ground, and an air soft as enchantment; the only circumstance that could lead to a suspicion of her true character was a cold, sullen, watery, glazed look about the eyes. ('On the Knowledge of Character', *SWWH*, 6:273)

Everything about the young Walker is perfectly enchanting – everything but her eyes. They alone reveal the dark secret of her 'true character'. Here Hazlitt as confident (or self-defensive) essayist implies that Walker habitually concealed her real (that is, evil) character long enough for him to became one of its 'fascinated' victims. But in *Liber Amoris*, Hazlitt's Pygmalion persona 'H' happily creates all her shades of character – evil and good and everything in between – and shows his hand in the process. If 'S' is an angel or a devil, it is because 'H' self-consciously makes her so. This much is obvious. But it becomes particularly important when one considers what 'Hazlitt' has spent a career saying about the truth and knowability of character.

Dart has observed that, as both a 'domestic angel and a "common trader"', Walker 'cut an ambiguous figure in the household . . . in terms of . . . character'.[38] Ultimately, this 'ambiguity' frees Hazlitt from his ethological foundationalism. 'H' exclaims: 'I will make a Goddess of her, and build a temple to her in my heart, and worship her on indestructible altars, and raise statues to her: and my homage shall be unblemished as her unrivalled symmetry of form; and when that fails, the memory of it shall survive' (*Liber Amoris*, *SWWH*, 7:43). How should we interpret this statement – as empty sentiment or as real but misguided affection? Some of his sympathetic contemporaries erred on the side of the latter. The painter Benjamin Robert Haydon thought Hazlitt was 'really downright in love with an ideal perfection, which has no existence but in his own head!'[39] Mary Shelley observed that

> when I saw him I could not be angry – I never was so shocked in my life, [for he was] gau[nt] and thin, his hair scattered, his cheek bones projecting – but for his voice & smile I sh[oul]d not have known him – his smile

brought tears into my eyes, it was like a sun-beam illuminating the most melancholy of ruins – lightning that assured you in a dark night of the identity of a friend's ruined & deserted abode.[40]

Hazlitt is literally devastated by the affair, but he possesses nonetheless the Byronic glamour of a once-glorious human being reduced to ruin. Shelley casts him as a Manfred figure, a 'noble wreck', sunlight amid the ruins of a dead but once glorious civilization. In constructing his idealised beloved, 'H' has allowed himself to be counter-constructed as the ideal lover. He notes that the 'S' that he himself fashions can, in turn, 'mould [him] as [she] like[s]', and that

> *I* was transformed too, no longer human (any more than she, to whom I had knit myself) my feelings were marble; my blood was of molten lead; my thoughts on fire. I was taken out of myself, wrapt into another sphere, far from the light of day, of hope, of love. I had no natural affection left. (*Liber Amoris*, SWWH, 7:64)

Thus his Pygmalionism has set in motion a counter-Pygmalionism: the artist has become art.

The instability of 'marble' as a signifier becomes increasingly important as 'H' begins to feel disillusioned in the relationship. In the last-quoted passage, 'H' refers to his private 'feelings' as 'marble'. Does he mean hard or soft? numb or elastic? Intuitively the stronger sense is numb: after all, he has 'no natural affection left'. But at the same time his blood is 'of molten lead' and his thoughts are 'on fire'. On another occasion he describes the sky as marble: '[t]he sky is marble to my thoughts; nature is dead around me'. Is the sky metaphorically dead to him, unsympathetically marble to his pain, or does he see marble in the sky because he projects Walker's marble form everywhere he looks? Sometimes the word suggests graceful beauty, as when 'H' tells 'S' that her form 'resemble[s] some graceful marble statue, in the moon's pale ray!' Other times it can imply emotional frigidity, like when 'H' asks his friend Peter George Patmore to 'call . . . and see whether or no she is quite marble – whether I may go back again at my return, and whether she will see me and talk to me sometimes as an old friend'. Basically he asks Patmore to find out whether Walker will receive him or be marble-cold to his advances.

But the word as used in the letter to Patmore involves important conflicting connotations. Marble-as-coldness here cannot be strictly separated from marble-as-grace, marble-as-plasticity, marble-as-lifelessness. It becomes difficult to tell what exactly 'H' asks his friend to determine about Walker. The meaning of the word is particularly indeterminate when 'H' tells Patmore that he has 'had her face constantly before [him], looking so like some faultless marble statue, as cold, as fixed and graceful as ever statue did' (*Liber Amoris*, *SWWH*, 7:35, 11, 32, 48). Which bears more meaning in this instance – 'cold' and 'fixed', or 'faultless' and 'graceful'? Lahey argues that, since Hazlitt was writing to Patmore on this subject shortly after completing his essay 'On the Elgin Marbles', what he had admired about the Elgin Marbles is precisely what he was admiring about Walker: her transcendent grace – not, on the other hand, her 'humanity turned to stone', 'dead and . . . inert'.[41] But it seems to me that both senses (among others) are equally legitimate here and in any of Hazlitt's uses of the word throughout *Liber Amoris*.

Hence the word 'marble' can signify vitality, beauty, gracefulness, coldness or deadness in human form or temperament, or all of these at once and more. It also reminds us that we are reading a self-consciously Pygmalion text. The writer-artist persona 'H' has fallen in love with a young female, 'S', whose 'character' he fashions and refashions as if from a block of Parian marble. In one sense *Liber Amoris* portrays character as a malleable construct that can be chiselled and shaped in the creative imagination. In another it hints that character is marble-hard, congenitally fixed, 'true to itself' in spite of crafty efforts to conceal it. All of this suggests that for Hazlitt, anticipating Nietzsche and Postman, mental/verbal abstraction is inherently prone to deception or myopia. In *Liber Amoris*, words like 'marble' and 'character' are not valid markers of things in the world, but metaphorical place-holders falsely thought to 'contain' a set of unequal qualities, to 'contain' an infinitely divisible set of events.

In most of his essays, it is true, Hazlitt insists that character does exist as a kind of *qualitas occulta* that can be read physiognomically in faces (contra Nietzsche) and perceived in works of art (poems, paintings, sculptures). Yet he also admits that '[w]e believe things not more because they are true or probable, than because we desire, or . . . because we dread them' ('Belief, Whether Voluntary', *CWH*, 20:367). It seems to follow that when Hazlitt portrays character as an absolute and unchanging substance, it may be because that view happens to suit his inclinations or fears at a given moment (most moments). This same flexibility applies, as *Liber Amoris* testifies, when the word 'character' – for instance, the character of a 'marble' female who is both person and art-object and neither – operates playfully as a signifier with an infinitely deferred signified. At first, 'H' finds himself in a position to want to believe that Walker is an angel, and so he makes her an angel.[42] But when he is ultimately disillusioned and wants to believe that Walker has all along been a whore/devil, he makes her a whore/devil. So how real and automatic, for Hazlitt, are abstracting, coalescing, typologising? For the author 'Hazlitt' they are natural, necessary and involuntary mental processes. But 'H' seems to think and feel beyond the pale of strict mental processes and 'biases' of character – as if all ethological observations, terms and conclusions postulated by 'Hazlitt' are the discursive products of 'Hazlitt', not universal truths with which all discourses must come to terms.

Notes

1. Locke, *Some Thoughts concerning Education*, p. 41.
2. Rousseau, *Émile*, p. 227.
3. Eliot, *Middlemarch*, p. 454.
4. See Knight, 'Hazlitt's Use of the Character Tradition'; Haefner, '"The Soul Speaking in the Face"'; and Mulvihill, 'Character and Culture'. Haefner claims that 'character is a keystone of [Hazlitt's] aesthetics because it is the means by which artist, writer, and audience are bound together' ('"The Soul Speaking in the Face"', p. 661). Manning seconds this point (*Poetics of Character*, p. 124).
5. See Feuer, 'John Stuart Mill as a Sociologist', p. 94; and Carlisle, *John Stuart Mill and the Writing of Character*, p. 170.
6. Hazlitt, 'On Personal Character', in Duncan Wu (ed.), *The Plain Speaker*, vol. 8 of *The Selected Writings of William Hazlitt*, p. 215. *The Selected Writings of William Hazlitt* will hereafter be abbreviated as *SWWH*. Individual essays within this multivolume collection will be cited parenthetically within the main body of the text by volume and

page number(s). Knight suggests that Hazlitt's doctrine of character can be considered 'a kind of organic determinism' ('Hazlitt's Use of the Character Tradition', p. 47).

7. Hazlitt, 'Originality', in P. P. Howe (ed.), *Miscellaneous Writings*, vol. 20 of *The Complete Works of William Hazlitt*, p. 299. *The Complete Works of William Hazlitt* will hereafter be abbreviated as *CWH*. Individual essays within this multivolume collection will be cited parenthetically within the main body of the text by volume and page number(s).

8. A few critics underestimate the extent to which Hazlitt stresses the congenital and ineffaceable influence of character. Mulvihill claims that for Hazlitt 'character is not *a priori*; it is more than the sum of its parts, but it does not precede them' ('Character and Culture', p. 294). Alan Richardson likewise observes that a '"biological view"' of character – according to which 'the child's character is "genetically determined at conception"' – 'rarely appears in literary or other texts of the [Romantic] period' (*Literature, Education and Romanticism*, p. 10). Yet Hazlitt repeatedly – though not without important qualifications discussed in the second half of this chapter – describes character as an irreducible *a priori* core grounded in the body and barely (if at all) alterable by circumstances or education.

9. Coleridge, *General Introduction; Or, Preliminary Treatise on Method*, p. 6.

10. Dart, *Metropolitan Art and Literature*, p. 81.

11. Rorty, 'A Literary Postscript', p. 318.

12. Mee, '"Reciprocal Expressions of Kindness"', pp. 113, 110.

13. Spurzheim, *The Physiognomical System of Drs. Gall and Spurzheim*, pp. 557–8.

14. David Bromwich, on the contrary, claims that in his descriptions on character Hazlitt 'tell[s] us what he saw, with the extravagance of belief and not of system' (*Hazlitt: The Mind of a Critic*, p. 79).

15. Hazlitt, 'On Prejudice', p. 93.

16. Knight, 'Hazlitt's Use of the Character Tradition', p. 48.

17. Hazlitt's explanation of abstraction remarkably anticipates the study of abstraction by Polish-American philosopher and scientist Alfred Korzybski. In his *Science and Sanity: An Introduction to Non-Aristotelian Systems and General Semantics* (1933), Korzybski argues that language is a means of abstraction at several removes from the levels of reality that it would neatly and conveniently symbolise. As Neil Postman summarises:

[w]e abstract at the neurological level, at the physiological level, at the perceptual level, at the verbal level; all of our systems of interaction

with the world are engaged in selecting data from the world, organizing data, generalizing data. An abstraction, to put it simply, is a kind of summary of what the world is like, a generalization about its structure. (*The End of Education*, p. 180)

18. Nietzsche, 'On Truth and Lies', pp. 83–4.
19. See Knight, 'Hazlitt's Use of the Character Tradition'; Stapleton, *The Elected Circle*, pp. 104–5; Kinnaird, *Hazlitt: Critic of Power*, p. 274; and Story, 'Emblems of Identity', pp. 81–90.
20. Knight, 'Hazlitt's Use of the Character Tradition' p. 7.
21. Story, 'Emblems of Identity', p. 84.
22. Boyce observes that

    [t]o speak of a portrait-character may seem a solecism. In theory, the [Theophrastan] Character exists in order to typify a group; the [biographical] portrait, to separate a man from the group. But human experience is relative, and the essence of some men is perfect conformity to others. Nature created many duplicates, and a portrait of one may be a Character of all. Hence a portrait-character is possible. (*The Polemic Character, 1640–1661*, p. 46)

23. Duncan Wu speculates that this diatribe was 'coloured by [Hazlitt's] unfortunate experiences in the Lakes in 1803' (*SWWH*, 2:361, n. 6).
24. Dart, *Metropolitan Art and Literature*, p. 80.
25. Cronin, *Paper Pellets*, p. 90.
26. Park, *Hazlitt and the Spirit of the Age*, p. 2.
27. See Haefner, '"The Soul Speaking in the Face"', pp. 660–1.
28. Savarese, 'Reading One's Own Mind', pp. 438, 443.
29. Anon., 'Art. VIII. – *Political Essays*', pp. 358, 360–1.
30. Ibid., p. 359.
31. Hazlitt, 'On Prejudice', pp. 85–6.
32. Whale, *Imagination under Pressure*, p. 134.
33. Hazlitt, *An Essay on the Principles of Human Action*, p. 48.
34. Burwick, 'Schelling and Hazlitt', pp. 150, 137–8, 148–9.
35. Schelling, *Philosophical Investigations*, pp. 51–4.
36. Ibid., p. 54.
37. Bromwich, *Hazlitt: The Mind of a Critic*, p. 12.
38. Dart, *Metropolitan Art and Literature*, pp. 98, 85.
39. Benjamin Robert Haydon to Mary Mitford, 8 September 1822, qtd in P. P. Howe, *The Life of William Hazlitt*, p. 349.
40. Mary Shelley to Marianne Hunt, 10 October 1824, qtd in Duncan Wu, *William Hazlitt: The First Modern Man*, p. 355.

41. Lahey, Appendix A.1, pp. 264, 263.
42. Cronin argues that 'all readers' of *Liber Amoris* observe that Walker oscillates between 'virgin' and 'whore' so that the distinction between the two becomes 'unstable' (*Paper Pellets*, pp. 63, 72). Dart similarly claims that Hazlitt 'couldn't be satisfied until he had revealed her in one guise or another' (*Metropolitan Art and Literature*, p. 89).

Chapter 5

'The Loved Abortion of a Thing Designed': Hartley Coleridge and the Drive for Dissolution

> The feel of not to feel it,
> When there is none to heal it
> Nor numbed sense to steel it,
> Was never said in rhyme.
> John Keats, 'In drear nighted December' (1829)[1]

> To live in death and be the same
> Without this life, or home, or name,
> At once to be, & not to be,
> That was, and is not – yet to see
> Things pass like shadows – and the sky
>   Above, below, around us lie
> John Clare, 'An Invite to Eternity' (comp. by 1847)[2]

In a letter to the Reverend John Dawes, S. T. Coleridge writes about his son, (David) Hartley Coleridge, that

> the absence of a Self . . . the want or torpor of Will . . . is the mortal sickness of Hartley's being, and has been for good & for evil, his character – his moral Idiocy – from earliest Childhood. . . . . He has neither the resentment, the ambition, nor the Self-love of a man – and for this very reason he is all too often as selfish as a Beast – and as unwitting of his own selfishness. With this is connected his want of a salient point, a self-acting principle of Volition.[3]

This is an amazing, and a little heartbreaking, appraisal of a son by his father. Coleridge denies his son any claims to a 'moral' character. Hartley's 'mortal sickness' is that he has little or no 'Will', no 'self-acting principle of Volition'.⁴ Not unlike the characterless characters of Walter Scott, Hartley is thought most often to bend to the sway of his passions, to the expectations of others, to external circumstances. Even since 'earliest Childhood' his 'character' has been defined by its 'moral Idiocy'. Up to this point it seems that Coleridge is only talking about Hartley's 'character' in a moral sense. But one could also draw from this letter that – as far as his father is concerned – Hartley has no character in the constitutive sense of the word either. He has, in fact, no actual 'Self' to which character traits can be ascribed. At the same time, however, Hartley is called 'selfish' – but only in the way that a 'Beast' is selfish. He is a creature, that is, run primarily by the dictates of instinct, passions and environment and has no moral agency.

How are we supposed to interpret this paternal 'portrait'? One could say that Hartley has become precisely what Coleridge and Wordsworth intended he should become: a living Æolian harp, the 'human embodiment' and 'chosen child' of Nature – only his wise passivity before the genial winds of Nature has dwindled into something unexpectedly prosaic: 'torpor of Will' and 'moral Idiocy'.⁵ A few critics I discuss in this chapter take pains to argue that Hartley eventually overcame the 'character' chosen for him in advance by the older Lake poets. For our purposes, however, whether Hartley successfully 'transcended' the character created for him by Wordsworth and Coleridge (a feat that Robert Owen claimed was impossible) is less important than that his poetry portrays the very concept of character as a kind of inherited entrapment, a powerful if 'fictitious entity'. His poems imagine what it would be like for one to be characterless, and it is from this creative effort to elude signification, appreciation, appraisal, that his poetry gets its power. Hartley dramatises the being without a will, a moral centre, a constitutive set of traits, not as a 'mortal sickness' but a desideratum, a prospect of freedom. He does this not so much – as some critics argue – by dissolving his ego into the pantheistic oneness that pervades all things (that would amount to his being a version of Wordsworth), but by fantasising a-spiritually about his own annihilation, his own return to self-less, characterless matter that retains a spark of consciousness just so as not to be an absolute thing. His poetry gestures toward the possibility (or the desire, or both) that character is as much an empty signifier, a conceptual snare, as it is a fact justifiable empirically and/or rationally. I have explored how writers like Lamb and Hazlitt oscillate between granting 'character' as a firm principle grounded in bodies, and suggesting character's referent-less existence in language. Hartley is less interested than Lamb and Hazlitt in working out the concept of character per se, and more interested in trying to escape the implications of that concept. Many of his poems are attempts to isolate the idea of consciousness not only from its psychosomatic situation – from a state of being that enables it, conditions it – but also from its attachment to something damningly predictable, legible, knowable.

I

The past twenty years have witnessed something of a mini-Renaissance in the critical study of Hartley Coleridge, poet, essayist, teacher and firstborn son of S. T. Coleridge whose work has been sorely neglected by scholars until relatively recently. Two major recovery projects were published respectively in 2008 and 2012.[6] Both take it for granted that Hartley has been unfairly marginalised and that his literary productions merit reexamination in their own right, irrespective of who his father was. Lisa Gee published a new selection of his poetry, together with a revitalising introduction, in 2000.[7] A year later, Judith Plotz included an extensive chapter on Hartley in her book on Romanticism and childhood, which brought to light an archival trove of unpublished essays, poems, marginalia, annotations, notebook entries and letters collected at the University of Texas at Austin.[8] Four significant articles on Hartley appeared between 2006 and 2010, the most recent of which surveys the reception of his poetry from 1833 to the present.[9] It is clear, therefore, that at least a few scholars have taken a serious interest in Hartley as a writer in the twenty-first century, finding ways to minimise the giant shadow of his father that has eclipsed his work and shaped its reception since first it appeared in print in 1833.

Although Hartley has traditionally been read as a good but unfortunate poet and a faithful Christian, his work has become open to radically new interpretations. Healey has summed up over a century and a half of Hartley reviews/criticism, paving the way for new scholarly discussions of his life and works. Her main points are as follows: Hartley can be associated with what Anne Mellor has called feminine Romanticism; he was held as a poet of 'immense stature' in his day; his critical reputation has subsequently dwindled, mainly due to the memoir his brother Derwent published in 1851, which 'infantilis[ed]' Hartley as Coleridge and Wordsworth had done earlier (not to mention the fact that Tennyson eclipsed Hartley in the 1830s); that a strictly 'text-based strand of criticism' stands to reveal that Hartley was actually a highly competent and original artist struggling to free himself from his public identity as a weak, amateurish writer who might have been; and that – relevant to the present chapter – Hartley 'manag[ed] to pre-empt the best part of later Victorian verse, and more modern schools of poetry'.[10]

I agree with Healey's and Keanie's major revisionist claim: that critics need to pay closer attention to the words Hartley actually wrote (via a 'text-based strand of criticism'). His family life is obviously important, but not the only or necessarily the best avenue to understanding his poems. One need not hold any more, for instance, that the philosophical preoccupations of Coleridge and Wordsworth (which Derwent reinforced in his memoir) basically wrote Hartley into existence, kept him an overgrown child throughout his adult life and prevented him from thinking or creating anything original. He is not, that is, simply a failed Romantic child who became a poetaster but never a man.[11] Keanie and Healey insist, on the contrary, that Hartley breaks from the character prepared for him in advance by the Lakists and succeeds as an artist on his own terms.[12]

I do find it problematic, however, that both critics consider Hartley to be a pantheistic poet, more alive even than the early Wordsworth to the 'something far more deeply interfused' behind the phenomenal world.[13] Keanie writes that Hartley was especially sensitive to 'the infrastructure of links interanimating the visible and invisible, a panoramic *feeling* of the whole, the one, the indivisible aliveness of Everything'.[14] Healey claims that Hartley could intuit this 'infrastructure' without the aid of philosophical reflection or the egotistical sublime that Wordsworth needed. The unity of all things just came to him, effortlessly, almost thoughtlessly. Although these readings do justice to Hartley as a thinker in his own right, they are still visibly indebted to the ideology of natural supernaturalism. What is needed – and what I offer here – is a new critical/philosophical vocabulary for treating Hartley's approach.

Healey reads the pantheistic trends in Hartley's poems as part of a larger discourse: what she calls his innate sense of 'relational selfhood' or 'self-in-relation'. Her main point is that Hartley is 'driven by relationship and community, the antithesis of the critical stereotype of Hartley as a self-absorbed, childlike figure'. Since he viewed personal identity as 'externally grounded and affected', his poems 'reinven[t] ... the sublime' as a finding of the self in its dynamic relationship with others. The Hartleyan sublime is thus less about the ego that responds to nature only to transcend it, and more about a divine intuition of the self in other persons, in nature, in the universe: 'a recognition of, and participation in, a larger "wholeness"'. His sense of interconnectedness with all living and nonliving things 'brings him into being', convinces him that he is part of 'a more permanent and meaningful universal entity'. All of this, Healey concludes, relates to his 'continuing theory of pantheism', a theory that Wordsworth before him 'struggle[d] to sustain'.[15]

I would add that Hartley struggled to sustain it too. One of the foremost aims of this chapter is to examine the nonspiritual, even the deistic or atheistic undertones in some of the poetry that Hartley wrote. One can easily read several of his pantheistic and orthodox Christian poems as strained, as centres that do not always hold. When Healey says that Hartley 'accepts', even more than his father, 'the apparent ego-diffusion, even annihilation, which a relational selfhood engenders', she invites discussion of another, what we might call a darker, drive in the poems.[16] For Healey, the idea of self-in-relation actually 'brings [Hartley] into being'. But I prefer to emphasise the aesthetic experiments in which he tries to write himself – to write whatever 'character' he imagines or doubts he has inherited – *out of* being. Much of his verse reads as 'dark' Lucretian/Swinburnian/Freudian fantasies about the 'pleasurable' dissolution of character into inorganic matter after death: what it would 'feel like' to exist as a material thing, to be paradoxically conscious of unconsciousness, to experience what Keats famously called the 'feel of not to feel it'. The Christian/neo-Platonic/pantheistic poems that struggle against materialist or atheistic discourses only reinforce their dangerous appeal. I will argue that it is no coincidence that Hartley obsesses over infancy, imagines what it would feel like to be deaf or blind, identifies himself with natural phenomena (both organic and inorganic), seems strangely uncomforted by his religious convictions and fantasises about death. He has *literalised* the nature tropes that Wordsworth and his father imposed on him as a child – whether the one called him a dew-drop or the other a wandering breeze. His poems occasionally de-mystify these tropes, dilute their pantheistic content, as part of an effort to escape through the imagination into a 'pleasurably' insensate, amoral, structureless, characterless state.

Lucretius, Swinburne and Freud each offer differing but equally useful models for understanding Hartley's preoccupation with dissolution. For Lucretius, the soul is mortal matter. It dies when it separates from the body, and both soul and body are reduced to atoms in a godless world. Hartley wrote two poems that say something directly about Lucretian materialism – challenge it – but many others that engage Lucretius's poem imaginatively and indulgently. Much of Hartley's verse nominally embraces Christian doctrine, but there are also several poems that take it to task and suggest that his relationship with Anglicanism is strained; the speakers in these poems seem more seduced by the quiet calm of a Lucretian world where 'dead men rise up never'.[17]

Hartley shares with Lucretius, Swinburne and Freud an interest in understanding our simultaneous attachments to life and to death, and in reconciling these attachments to one another. As James Porter has argued, Lucretius accepts but is critical of our involuntary attachment to reproduction and biological existence. We cling to life not because it is worth living, but because we are instinctively and non-emotionally bound to organic existence. And woven into the very fabric of organic existence is an incomprehensible drive against it. In this light, Porter compares Lucretius to Freud, whom he calls 'a latter-day Lucretian in more than a few respects'.[18] Both writers view an immanent urge toward death as 'a permanent element in the logic of life' (Lucretius observes that the embodied spirit, '[i]f shaken loose by something' during life, 'often seems to want to go/ And to be freed from the body altogether', referring to the fact that we become unconscious when struck by a severe blow).[19] Swinburne is important in this context because his poems capitalise on the paradox that we are simultaneously bound to life and death, blurring the boundaries between existence and nonexistence. As an atheist poet, Swinburne repeatedly celebrates the peaceful dissolution of organic into inorganic matter (almost always the sea) at death – and yet keeps the human person 'alive' after death, in and through the matter into which its body has been assimilated. My point is that we can read the regressive and self-effacing tendencies in Hartley's poems as evidence against the univocality of his spiritual convictions. His 'death drive' appears inextricably tied to his drive to life, in this world and the next; both seem to operate in the service of a conservative principle, an *'urge inherent in organic life to restore to an earlier state of things* which the living entity has been obliged to abandon under the pressure of external disturbing forces'.[20]

A caveat: my aim is not to legitimate or justify the existence of the death drive as Freud described it in *Beyond the Pleasure Principle* and *Civilization and Its Discontents*. I am certainly not trying to read Hartley psychoanalytically with outdated psychoanalysis. My argument is rather that some ideas advanced in the writings of Lucretius, Swinburne and Freud can serve as a new grammar with which to understand Hartley's poems, and their interest in characterlessness, more comprehensively. I don't want to deny his conscious devotion to the immortality of the soul, but to emphasise the tendencies in his poems that complicate that devotion, and in some ways even enrich it. If the soul is anything like the character – a constitutive, readable, partly determining principle – then it is simply *not* something that Hartley is enthusiastic about retaining for all eternity.

II

Derwent seems to have given the following poem by Hartley its title: 'Lines Written by H. C. in the Fly-Leaf of a Copy of Lucretius Presented by Him to Mr. Wordsworth':

> In the far north, for many a month unseen,
>   The blessed sun scarce lifts his worshipp'd head;
> No hardy herb records where he hath been;
> But pale cold snows, with dim abortive sheen,
>   Show like the winding-sheet of Nature dead.
>
> Yet ofttimes there the boreal morning gleams,
>   Flickering and rustling through the long, long night;
> So hid from truth, and its all-cheering beams,
> The mind, benighted, dawns with gorgeous dreams,
>   Cold, restless, false, unprofitably bright.

> If such delusion held thy earthly thought,
>   Lucretius, still thou wast a lofty mind;
> For, spurning all that hopes and fears had taught,
> Thy venturous reason, hopeless, fearless, sought
>   In its own pride its proper bliss to find.
>
> Oh! was it fear of what might be in realms
>   Of blank privation made thee seek the peace
> That the dead faith affords? – fear that dishelms
> The vessel of the soul, and quite o'erwhelms
>   The spiritual life, that rather would surcease,
>
> Or be an atom, motion, air, or flame,
>   Whose essence perishes by change of form,
> Than wander through the abyss without an aim,
> Duty, or joy – to feel itself the same,
>   Though naked, bodiless, weak, amid the storm?[21]

On a basic level, the poem praises the genius of Lucretius but questions his Epicureanism. Brilliant yet benighted (that is, pre-Christian) minds like his are subject to 'gorgeous dreams', satisfying to 'venturous reason' but not to common emotional experience (what 'hopes and fears had taught'). Epicurean philosophy is really no more than a dream, a pretty show, as 'unprofitably bright' as the Aurora Borealis when it showers the Arctic north in mock-sunlight. The last two stanzas ask (and simultaneously suggest) what could possibly have motivated Lucretius to champion such a 'dead faith'. Maybe he was afraid that his posthumous soul, its 'essence' still intact, would drift meaninglessly through a cold and impersonal universe, stripped of its protective armour and 'o'erwhelm[ed]' in the chaos. In such a place of 'blank privation', it would be better to be 'an atom, motion, air, or flame' than some kind of undead spiritual 'essence'. A spiritual essence, 'naked, bodiless, weak', can still feel pain. Mere matter cannot. The prima facie position of these lines is that fear of what happens in the afterlife is no good reason to maintain the illusion of its nonexistence.

But at the same time the poem seems somewhat unsure of itself. It calls Epicureanism the product of a 'delusion[al]' mind 'hid from truth', but Lucretius still has the Romantic appeal of Satan on the lake of fire: the great philosophical rebel who invites our admiration as much as our pity. The language ennobles him in a way that suggests more than just a Christian nod to a pagan genius. His mind was 'lofty', 'restless' and 'venturous', and the epic poem burst on it gloriously like the dawn. The lines, moreover, are somewhat ambivalent about what motivated Lucretius to write *The Nature of Things*. The speaker imagines that because he 'fear[ed]' the trials his disembodied spirit would endure in an abysmal universe, he denied the immortality of the soul. Whatever belief he had in immortal existence must have been weaker than his fear of the unknown. But the third stanza undermines the claim that fear motivated his atheism. There the speaker says that it was only in 'spurning all that . . . fears had taught', in being 'fearless', that Lucretius could possibly have composed so iconoclastic, so cheerless a poem. The discrepancy is important because it supports the idea that Hartley was more tentative, more open-ended in his spiritualty than he lets on. Lucretius is initially said to be motivated by a fearless quest for his 'own proper bliss', and then by a personal dread of the afterlife. The first incentive valorises him; the second diminishes him. In the end we know where Hartley, as a Christian, ideally *wants* to or *should* stand with respect to Epicurean philosophy, but there is some doubt as to whether his poem helps him get there.

Nowhere in *The Nature of Things*, of course, does Lucretius express anxiety over the possibility that a disembodied soul will remain trapped 'alive' in a postmortem chaos. He says the exact opposite: that these kinds of fears belong only to the superstitious. He presumes that most his audience will have read and believed what Ennius erroneously said of Hell: that 'there we neither in the flesh nor in the spirit dwell/ But, rather, something wraithlike of us lingers, wan and weird' (*NT*, Book I, 6). Part of the pleasure of the Epicurean is that he can let go of such irrational fears. It's quite possible that the anxiety Hartley ascribes to Lucretius comes from within: that Hartley displaces his own doubts or fears about the Christian afterlife onto a pagan materialist philosopher whom he admires but feels obliged to reject.[22] Whatever sense Hartley and others had of his own inalienable 'character' hardly served him in life, if the consistent pattern of self-deprecation in his poems is any evidence. Why should he want to retain anything like it after death? For Hartley there seems to be something pacifying in the thought of ethological annihilation. The anxieties that come with moral agency, legibility, constitutive properties, 'inner necessity', all come to an absolute end, a sleep, like 'Nature dead' beneath funeral shroud of 'pale cold snows'.[23] I am not trying to reverse the basic thrust of the poem: clearly it wants to challenge Lucretius on a fundamental level. But its theistic challenge is hardly more compelling than the atheistic ideology it questions. Lucretianism holds its own in a poem that tries to deny it.

Images of life, love and reproduction in Hartley's poems are usually finely blended with the language of sterility and death. A Prodigal Son figure in Sonnet 'X' leaves his home rich in '[y]outh, love and mirth', but once in the world he finds 'each seeming joy a mere abortion', and compares 'every smile' he sees to a 'barren womb' ('X', *PHC*, 1:14). Sonnet 'X' is basically a sentimental poem about the fleeting passage of youth and happiness, but this language seems disproportionately strong. If the word 'abortion' is used to describe a 'seeming joy', its meaning (one imagines) is probably mostly figurative: abortion as the '[f]ailure or abandonment' of a joy that might have been.[24] But the 'barren womb' mentioned a few lines later in the sonnet lends an eerily literal sense to the word 'abortion' that precedes it. The smiles the Prodigal sees in foreign lands are so many barren wombs, things made for carrying life but showing no signs of it. Joyful expressions appear not just fake or transient but aborted, expelled or removed from the barren wombs of smiling faces.

Other poems feature the same striking conflation of life and death. One speaker says that the birthday of a wayward child often represents a 'cenotaph of hope' to its frustrated parent ('The Birth-Day: To James Brancker, Esq.', *PHC*, 1:138). Another laments a posthumous infant who lost his father 'ere/ [its] little breath/ Was drawn from atmosphere of death' ('To a Posthumous Infant', *PHC*, 1:143). The phrase 'atmosphere of death' most immediately refers to the death of the father that precedes the birth of his posthumous child. But 'atmosphere of death' also suggests in this context – rather eerily – the state of existence in utero of the unborn child. The rhyming of 'breath' and 'death', too, invokes more than the apparent circumstances: a father dead before his child is born. It mingles breathing and dying, depolarises them, renders death 'a permanent element in the logic of life'. A similar rhyme occurs in 'The Sabbath-Day's Child', whose speaker refers to a sleeping infant girl as the 'image of a happy death'. Her quiescent state is so 'absolute', so 'pure', that she seems altogether beyond organic existence: beyond the 'vital *breath*' that 'by the act of being *perisheth*' ('The Sabbath-Day's Child', *PHC*, 1:100, my italics). Still another poem about stillborn twins describes the womb that held them as a 'brief imprisonment' and a 'fertile tomb' ('Twins', *PHC*, 2:121). In the light of these poems, the 'atmosphere of death' described in 'To a Posthumous Infant' more readily suggests an atmosphere *from* which the infant emerges (womb/tomb), as well as an atmosphere *into* which it emerges (death of the father).

In one of his most powerful, self-castigating sonnets, Hartley describes a seed blown about by the wind but never sown, '[w]afted along for ever, ever, ever' without finding 'soil or water' (alluding to his own unproductive life). The wind that carries the seed along makes a sound like 'the last note of a trembling lute,/ The loved abortion of a thing design'd' (Sonnet 'LIV', *PHC*, 2:56). Here, the falling sound of a lute is being compared to the exquisite ending ('loved abortion') of 'a thing design'd' – presumably the lute-song designed to come to an end. This is another case in which Hartley exploits the figurative senses of the word 'abortion' in an immediate context, and then lets its literalness bleed into the poem as a whole. The lute-song is the thing aborted: in the sense of finished too soon, terminated. But we also recall that, all the while, the wind is blowing a seed along, a seed destined never to germinate. So not just the song, but the seed too, becomes associated with 'a thing design'd' that ends up aborted. The idea of a loved abortion is at first contained in a metaphoric vehicle describing only a song, until that vehicle comes to extend itself beyond its immediate figuration. The seed, Hartley himself, human life, human character, is implicitly figured as a 'loved abortion of a thing design'd'. Love, generation, Eros, is fixed to its own undoing, its own dissolution. A seedling denied its growth and development (aborted) is entangled in the natural force of union and reproduction (love).

These and similar poems amount to more than just Hartley feeling sorry for his wasted or 'aborted' life. They allow for if not suggest the possibility that organic development serves the broader aim of organic dissolution and regression. Plotz observes that Hartley 'depicts adulthood as a state of steady decline best conveyed through metaphors of impoverishment, death, and even abortion'.[25] I would say that not only adulthood but Eros, generation, life itself is depicted in these terms. According to Freud, 'all the organic instincts . . . tend towards the restoration of an earlier state of things'. The instinctual forces that seem to be driving our growth and change are actually helping us regress. We *would* stay exactly as we are (our repetition compulsions are evidence of this) were it not for the 'disturbing and diverting influences' of the external world. Over time these influences have, as it were, coerced the organism into biological development. They have forced certain 'modification[s]' on it that only complicate or reroute its fundamental regressive impulses. Freud elaborates:

> The hypothesis of self-preservative instincts, such as we attribute to all living beings, stands in marked opposition to the idea that instinctual life as a whole serves to bring about death. Seen in this light, the theoretical importance of the instincts of self-preservation, of self-assertion and of mastery greatly diminishes. They are component instincts whose function it is to assure that the organism shall follow its own path to death, and to ward off any possible ways of returning to inorganic existence other than those which are immanent in the organism itself. We have no longer to reckon with the organism's puzzling determination . . . to maintain its own existence in the face of every obstacle. What we are left with is the fact that the organism wishes to die only in its own fashion.[26]

So the organism has always been hardwired to return to an inorganic state, a primitive state that antedates (that is, lies 'beyond') the pleasure principle: '*inanimate things existed before living ones*'. Growth and development (the growth of a body, and what Eliot calls the growth of a 'living and changing' character) have become more or less diverting obstacles on the path toward dissolution. In this light Hartley can be read as more than just a self-pitying Christian whose poems repeatedly lament his own failures. His verse moves beyond the personal and beyond despair, sometimes treating inorganic existence as the destination toward which even Christian souls may feel themselves driven in spite of hope and spiritual training. The poems wrestle with the possibility that 'everything living dies for *internal* reasons – becomes inorganic once again', that '*the aim of all life is death*'.[27]

Many of the poems Hartley wrote can adequately be described as backward-looking or regressive. Some of his favourite subjects are children, prenatal existence and the collapse of the living being back into the inorganic world.[28] As for children, he composed

> dozens of poems to newborn babies, to two-, three-, or four-year-olds on their birthdays, to his many godchildren, as well as meditations on the mystery of birth and elegiac songs and sonnets about his own infant self and childhood reading.[29]

Hartman acknowledges Hartley as 'the laureate of children', and Plotz makes the massive claim that his poems 'represent the most unqualified and extravagant vision of the beatitude of childhood to be found in all Romantic literature'.[30] Most critics agree that Hartley wrote so much about children because saw them as especially holy and intuitive, as creatures of 'stability and permanence in a changing world', even to the extent that he 'identifie[d] religious salvation with man's re-attainment of the infant state'.[31] Keanie observes that the 'child's intuition' Hartley maintained as an adult helped him discern the 'complex and subtle totalities' behind the phenomenal world. According to Healey, '[t]he purity of childhood and the child's unself-consciousness is clearly emblematic to Hartley of pure being and his ideal state of a regenerative "one life" that integrates humanity'.[32] In other words, the child simply, purely *is* in a way that becomes impossible for adults. This 'pure being' is an emblem of that undifferentiated life-force that connects all living and nonliving things.

But is Hartley really fascinated with children exclusively as emblems of Christian blessedness or the 'one life'? No doubt many orthodox themes underlie his paeans to childhood innocence: the 'Suffer little children to come unto me' mentality is definitely present. But these poems can just as easily be seen as part of a regressive drive. Hartley may imply a desire to return to an infant state, but not necessarily or exclusively because infancy encapsulates religious purity or the 'regenerative "one life" that integrates humanity'. His retrogressive imagination travels beyond the womb and beyond even organic life. Porter's account of Lucretius is immensely suggestive for a reading of Hartley: 'something like a subjective desire or willingness to die, the soul's unequivocal wanting to be released from the body it also clings to, as if the fragility of life at the organic level (the tendency to dispersion) were a sign of a drive to return to the inanimate condition of the world itself'.[33]

In certain poems, Hartley mixes Lucretian language about the dissolution of constitutive/moral character with the language of Christian hope in the afterlife; desires for regression and dispersion with desires for transcendence. The following lines are a paradigmatic example:

> man,
> By sinning, made out of himself a self
> Alien from God, that must be self-destroy'd
> Ere man can know what freedom is, or feel
> His spirit enfranchised, – general as the light
> Diffused through ether in its purity,
> And by the various sympathies of earth,
> Blent and dissected into various hues
> That all are light
>
> ('Why Is There War on Earth? Written on a Calm and Beautiful Day in May, 1848', *PHC*, 2:152)

The first five lines lightly poeticise the Christian paradox that he who humbles himself will be exalted. The lines that follow suggest, in part, the dispersion of the material soul at death. The word 'general' (and the simile that follows) refers to 'spirit'. By 'general' Hartley probably means 'affecting all, or nearly all, the parts of a specified whole', as light does when it seems to permeate the air.[34] He imagines that the freed soul, like light, is '[b]lent and dissected into various hues' by 'the various sympathies of earth'. His simile here is unclear, but the general drift of it seems more Lucretian than Christian. First, only something made of matter can properly be said to be 'dissected'. For Lucretius the material spirit permeates the body, so that when the body is split deeply enough the spirit is likewise split and the person dies. And what you can 'sever/ Obviously relinquishes all claims to last forever' (*NT*, Book III, p. 91). A human spirit, moreover, that has certain 'sympathies' with the earth may suggest more than Wordsworthian pantheism. Perhaps what the two have in common is that both are made of the same stuff – atoms and void. The spirit dies but its atoms are some of the deathless building blocks of the universe.

So according to this poem sin alienates us from God by individuating us, and we have to destroy this sinful self and be born again: but not into a resurrected human self so much as a self-and-non-self, a self lost – dead but somehow conscious – in a merger with the natural world. Hartley also mentions in this poem the 'old Epicurean fantasy/ Of waving atoms hook'd into a world' ('Why Is There War on Earth?', *PHC*, 2:151–2), alluding to the Lucretian notion that atoms are the 'seeds of things that make the sum,/ The basic elements the universe is fashioned from' (*NT*, Book I, p. 17). That he calls this idea a 'fantasy' is no strong evidence against his sustained investment in it. The evidence rather suggests that Hartley doth protest too much.

A merger with the natural world in a part-Christian (dualism), part-Lucretian (monism) sense is a standard trope in the poems. Consider the following sonnet subtitled 'Prayer':

> There is an awful quiet in the air,
> And the sad earth, with moist imploring eye,
> Looks wide and wakeful at the pondering sky,
> Like Patience slow subsiding to Despair.
> But see, the blue smoke as a voiceless prayer,
> Sole witness of a secret sacrifice,
> Unfolds its tardy wreaths, and multiplies
> Its soft chameleon breathings in the rare
> Capacious ether, – so it fades away,
> And nought is seen beneath the pendent blue,
> The undistinguishable waste of day.
> So have I dream'd! – oh, may the dream be true! –
> That praying souls are purged from mortal hue,
> And grow as pure as He to whom they pray.
>
> (Sonnet 'LIII. Prayer', *PHC*, 2:55)

No one would deny the presence of religious devotion in this sonnet. The speaker says that he has often dreamt of losing his body in and through the act of prayer: maybe 'praying souls are purged from mortal hue,/ And grow as pure as He to whom they pray'. But these are just the last two lines; the rest of the poem is written in a very different register. The whole sonnet, in fact, is more or less a single metaphor, the first eleven lines forming a complex vehicle and the last three lines establishing the tenor. The tenor, however, seems inadequate to the vehicle: the imagery in the first eleven lines has a searching, wilful and expansive quality to it that the conclusion somehow fails to translate into Christian sentiment.

In the first quatrain, the earth is identified with a weeping mourner whose patience has been tried. Then a 'blue smoke' rises from the ground, suggesting a kind of incense or burnt offering, a 'secret sacrifice' to the heavens above (it is unclear whether the 'sad earth' itself is responsible for the sacrifice or some other agent). But the skies appear unresponsive ('pondering'), perhaps because the offering has come too late, its wreaths 'tardy'. In any case, the blue smoke '[u]nfolds' itself and 'multiples/ Its soft chameleon breathings in the rare/ Capacious ether', until finally it 'fades away,/ And nought is seen beneath the pendent blue,/ The undistinguishable waste of day'. What are these lines trying to image? The smoke is blue and the upper air ('ether') is blue, which explains the fact that the 'breathings' of the former are 'chameleonic'. The tendrils multiply themselves, disperse themselves, become smaller and smaller until they fade away entirely in air. And what is left beneath the 'pendent blue'? Only 'nought', which I read in apposition to the 'undistinguishable waste of day'.

There is something undeniably Lucretian about these lines: not, of course, that the smoke manoeuvres as a 'voiceless prayer' sent up to God, but that it dissolves in air and leaves behind 'nought', the 'waste of day'. Rising blue smoke has blent indissolubly with blue ether. How fitting is all this initial imagery to the sentiment in the closing lines? Is the blue smoke meant to correspond to the praying human spirit? Is the '[c]apacious ether' meant to correspond to the God into whose essence that spirit becomes assimilated through prayer? Is the 'waste of day' meant to correspond to the 'mortal hue' the spirit sheds? The poem reads as a strange mix of panentheism and Lucretianism. The speaker prays to a God (a 'He') that seems both to interpenetrate the universe and to be greater than and independent of it. But the relationship between supplicant and deity is cast in the language of inorganic matter. God is ether, the praying spirit is smoke and the body is the 'waste of day'.[35] The first eleven lines strongly suggest a return to an inorganic state, a dispersion of material self in material air, while the tenor ropes the preceding images into a fantasy about becoming one with a panentheistic God through prayer. The point is that poems like this one are less clear, less neatly orthodox than others. They have a Lucretian, a probing materialist edge to them.

Another poem with similar themes describes a still spring day, so quiet that 'the sweet Nun, diffused in voiceless prayer', can '[f]eel her own soul through all the brooding air' ('V. May, 1840', *PHC*, 2:65). The person of the nun is extended, dispersed, when and as she prays silently, and can somehow feel her disembodied soul through the air that interpenetrates it. This could just be a flight of the Christian imagination: anyone who prays earnestly enough may feel (or want to feel) taken, as it were, by God into the 'brooding air' and blent there with him, in an ecstasy like that of the two lovers on the '[p]regnant banke' whose souls drift aloft and make 'a new concoction' in air.[36]

But even if the scene amounts to Christian wish fulfilment, it is interesting that the nun is said to be 'diffused', albeit in such a way that she can still 'feel her own soul'. Lucretius observes that mind and spirit (along with the body) decay with age. At death the spirit, made of ultra-fine particles, leaves the body and is 'scattered on the high winds like a puff of smoke' (*NT*, Book III, p. 85) – not unlike the praying spirit above imaged as blue smoke. After its separation from the body, the spirit cannot sense or feel anything: it has no existence outside the flesh. Lucretius is firm on this point: 'There's no possibility/ That spirits by themselves can feel; indeed, they cannot *be*' (*NT*, Book III, p. 90; italics in original). The nun is described as an essence diffused in air yet still able to feel her own soul. Thus the lines join dispersion and retention, regression and transcendence, material and immaterial. None of this means that Hartley is trying to make room in his verse for a nascent materialism, but the poems do suggest his emotional investment in at least the possibility of death after death, of death as dispersion or sleep.[37] The idea lingers in the shadows behind his more pronounced hope in the Christian resurrection. Resurrection may imply being burdened with one's recognisable, readable character for all eternity, a common fear according to Lucretius: 'each man is running from himself, yet still/ Because he clings to that same self, although against his will,/ And clearly can't escape from it, he loathes it'. Why not accept eternal death with pleasure? 'What is it there that looks so fearsome?' Lucretius asks: 'What's so tragic? Isn't it more peaceful than any sleep?' (*NT*, Book III, pp. 104, 101).

Hartley often associates sleep with deathlike tranquillity and occasionally with blessedness. One speaker cherishes the 'golden time' of youthful love because it seems 'bare of incident as dreamless sleep' ('Leonard and Susan', *PHC*, 1:71). A fallen woman in another poem longs for the time when she 'sleeps in silent death' ('The Forsaken to the Faithless', *PHC*, 1:146). This is not to say that Hartley ever abandons his hope in Heaven: it persists, only sometimes as a semi-consoling afterthought. In one sonnet the speaker calls death '[d]ecomposition – dust, or dreamless sleep', even though a few lines later he hopes that he can 'reach the blessed sky' and reunite with his long-dead parents (Sonnet 'XII', *PHC*, 2:14). On another occasion Hartley records his ambivalent impressions on visiting the coffin of the Reverend Owen Lloyd in the Lake District: Lloyd, his speaker says,

> rests in peace; in Langdale's peaceful vale
> He sleeps secure beneath the grassy sod;
> Ah, no! he doth not – he hath heard 'All hail
> 'Thou faithful servant', from the throne of God!
> ('A Schoolfellow's Tribute to the Memory of the
> Rev. Owen Lloyd', *PHC*, 2:189)

In this instance, the orthodox Hartley gets the last word but, as is often the case, in a context that gently rubs against the grain of orthodox sentiment.

When Hartley writes in a neoclassical vein, his imagination seems richer, less inhibited, more lucid. The description of the scene in 'Prometheus. A Fragment' mentions a chorus of sylphs (air spirits) who travel to a 'desolate spot, supposed to lie beyond the limits of the habitable earth', where they discover Prometheus chained to a rock ('Prometheus. A Fragment', *PHC*, 2:285). One sylph describes the flight to this lone spot as a 'sleep of endless blessedness', and the spot itself – '[a]t the last confines of the fair creation' – as a place where '[t]he thick, dark air,/ Still pressing earthward, closes o'er our heads/ With dull and leaden sound, like sleepy waters'. This is essentially a Swinburnian description of death. The sylph and her crew have just flown through an aerial 'sleep of endless blessedness' only to end up in another soporific place, at the ends of the earth, where the skies enclose them as if in an airy grave. The 'habitable earth' just ends at this point, with the loose threads of creation unwoven before an infinite blank, '[w]here tired Nature left her work half done' ('Prometheus: A Fragment', *PHC*, 2:290). Nature herself is tired, sleepy, spent, like her elements ('sleepy waters'). There is an eerie implication in these lines that the journey toward death resembles a return to the beginning of things (which is also the end of things): to a place where the world has yet to form or will never form, where the elements – earthward air that asphyxiates like water – enshroud souls in the sleep of death.

Hartley is imagining what it would feel like not to feel it; to transition from an organic substance with a legible 'character' to an inorganic substance without one. He may have been inspired by the Keats poem we now know as 'In drear nighted December', which he probably read when it was first published as 'Stanzas' in *The Literary Gazette* in 1829. His own poems, in fact, were being advertised regularly in *The Literary Gazette* around the same time.[38] There is also the fact that he admired and identified with Keats as an author who craved literary immortality but felt he could never achieve it. Of course, if he had, in fact, read Keats's poem as it was originally published, he would not have encountered the line 'The feel of not to feel it', but its 'corrupted' alternative, 'To know the change and feel it'.[39] This seems inconsequential, however, since the implications of the original line are still present in the rest of the poem, which would have appealed to Hartley for basically the same reasons.

Hartley wrote a tribute poem to Keats: 'I Have Written My Name on Water. The Proposed Inscription on the Tomb of John Keats':

> And if thou hast, where could'st thou write it better
> Than on the feeder of all lives that live?
> The tide, the stream, will bear away the letter,
> And all that formal is and fugitive:
> Still shall thy Genius be a vital power,
> Feeding the root of many a beauteous flower.
>
> (PHC, 2:168)

The basic point of the lines is more or less clear: the speaker suggests that Keats will receive some kind of immortality in spite of his own self-doubt. *How* the poem makes this suggestion is what I find compelling. On one level the poem agrees that Keats is right to be diffident: the 'tide' or 'stream' of Time will, in fact, 'bear away' his name and 'all' else that is 'formal'[40] and 'fugitive': mind, body, character – everything constitutive of or contiguous to the subject 'John Keats'. These things may be carried off, lost, forgotten; but the 'Genius' of the poet will remain as a 'vital power,/ Feeding the root of many a beauteous flower'. So 'John Keats' will indeed die, but his poetic authority and influence, compared here to water as the source of life, will live on in the writings ('beauteous flower[s]') of numerous other like-minded, sensitive poets. His 'Genius' will become part of the cycle of life. The subject is sacrificed to exalt his nourishing, vivifying influence.

The tribute to Keats implies that a gain compensates for a loss. What happens long after Keats's death justifies his dissolution. But this subsequent state of affairs is framed not in spiritual but in material terms, and with – I would argue – Lucretian undertones. According to Lucretius, the constitutive character or '[e]ssence' of any person, like all combinations of atoms and void that interlock to form a single, recognisable individual, is mortal, but the atomic building blocks of that essence are deathless. Atoms 'survive infinite time to make things new' and 're-power/ The world' (*NT*, Book III, p. 80; Book I, p. 19) – not unlike water, which Hartley calls 'the feeder of all lives that live'. In other words, the atoms that make up a living person remain long after that person has ceased to be, creating new life for all time. The poem offers a similar consolation: just as water continually gives life to new flowers, so some elemental or impersonal part of Keats (his 'Genius') endures after the man himself is dead and gone, giving life to new poets. Thus both this poem and *The Nature of Things* overcome the fear of death in terms of nonspiritual processes, and without recourse to the traditional notion of Christian afterlife that Hartley champions so often in his poetry.

I have proposed a critical alternative to the claim that Hartley tends always to spiritualise or mystify the material world. Keanie claims that Hartley found 'nothing inherently safe or solid about the sensible world', which he thought 'cohere[d] not by physical but by mental agency'.[41] What did this alleged pantheism do for Hartley? According to Healey it allayed his fears of a 'sensory and emotional numbness that signals disconnection from the rest of human life, and thus, more disturbingly, from the "one life" itself'.[42] I have tried to acknowledge the many poems that decentre the 'one life' from organic existence and imply at least some comfort in solidity, materiality, the absence of deathless mystical and personal agencies. I have also marked poetic language that suggests a regressive or conservative drive, a primal urge toward a state of senselessness, characterlessness. One poem, in bold reversal of Donne's famous meditation, calls a deaf and dumb girl

> a loose island on the wide expanse,
> Unconscious floating on the fickle sea,
> Herself her all, she lives in privacy.

In a basic sense the girl (tenor) is compared to an island (vehicle) to indicate her isolation from others, her solitariness. But the island image also brings insensate matter to mind. Consider the word 'unconscious'. Grammatically it can modify both 'she' and 'island', which makes sense insofar as both entities are to some extent unconscious: the girl of sound waves, and the island of everything. The speaker also mentions that the girl-as-unconscious-island 'looks so calm and good' in her state ('To a Deaf and Dumb Little Girl', *PHC*, 2:119). Hartley seems attracted here to the lessening of sensory stimulation, to privation, to the advance of unconsciousness. Plotz claims that the poem views 'privation' as 'presence not absence'.[43] But perhaps the lines value privation simply as privation, precisely because it *is* an absence. On some level Hartley is reluctantly pacified by the very possibilities he fears to embrace: eternity without a character; life whose aim is death; organic development indistinguishable from organic dissolution; and the return to a primitive and insensate state beyond pleasures and pains, where Christian stoicism is no longer required as an engine against the wayward mind and body, and where every 'thing designed' becomes a 'loved abortion'.

Notes

1. Keats, 'In drear nighted December', in *John Keats: Complete Poems*, p. 163, lines 21–4.
2. Clare, 'An Invite to Eternity', in *The Later Poems of John Clare, 1837–1864*, p. 349, lines 18–24.
3. Qtd in Taylor, '"A Father's Tale"', p. 49.
4. For the sake of clarity, I will refer to Samuel Taylor Coleridge in this chapter as 'Coleridge', and Hartley Coleridge as 'Hartley'.
5. Plotz, 'The *Annus Mirabilis*', p. 184; and Plotz, *Romanticism and the Vocation of Childhood*, p. 216.

6. See Keanie, *Hartley Coleridge*; and Nicola Healey, *Dorothy Wordsworth and Hartley Coleridge*.
7. See Gee, *Bricks without Mortar*.
8. See Plotz, *Romanticism and the Vocation of Childhood*, chapter 5, 'The Case of Hartley Coleridge: The Designated Genius'.
9. See Keanie, 'Hartley Coleridge: Son of the Mariner'; Healey, '"A living spectre of my Father dead"'; Keanie, 'Hartley Coleridge and His Art of Dovetailing Miscellaneous Particulars'; and Healey, 'The Reception of Hartley Coleridge's Poetry'.
10. Healey, 'The Reception of Hartley Coleridge's Poetry', pp. 25–6, 39. As to his anticipating later Victorian verse, this chapter compares Hartley (his orthodoxly pious poems aside) to A. C. Swinburne as a poet who makes repeated, obscure and sometimes pained efforts to reconcile the drives to life and death. Plotz mentions Swinburne twice in connection with Hartley to suggest the respect both poets share for the preciousness of childhood (*Romanticism and the Vocation of Childhood*, pp. 20, 206).
11. Plotz reminds us that Coleridge expected his son to be both one with the natural world and to transcend it, a 'human embodiment of and mediator of nature' ('The *Annus Mirabilis*', p. 184). Elsewhere she elaborates: '[a]lmost from his birth, poems by Coleridge and Wordsworth marked Hartley as a chosen child both of Nature (in the spirit of the philosopher for whom he was named) and of the self-reflective philosophic mind' (*Romanticism and the Vocation of Childhood*, p. 216). As the argument goes – one that Healey and Keanie take pains to discredit – the Lake poets effectively prevented Hartley from establishing his own character as either a person or an artist. He could never live up to their twofold ideal and he never substituted another in its place. While his father became 'the productive and grand sage of Highgate', he himself ended up 'wander[ing] in exile, drunk and disheveled through the mountains around Grasmere, a pitiful miniature, echoing his father's phrases' (Taylor, '"A Father's Tale"', p. 47).
12. The force of this claim becomes evident as we understand the critical commonplaces it challenged. Earl Leslie Griggs asserts that Hartley never 'reach[ed] the real literary position for which his high intellectual gifts fitted him' ('Hartley Coleridge on His Father', p. 1246). Herbert Hartman calls him, 'both as poet and man of letters, a signal failure' who 'scarcely fulfilled the promise of his birthright' (*Hartley Coleridge: Poet's Son and Poet*, p. vii). Lucy Newlyn does acknowledge the 'pathos ... in [Hartley's] acceptance of a symbolic role' set by his father, but also the fact that he 'never gr[ew] beyond it' ('The Little Actor and His Mock Apparel', p. 38). Plotz's assessment of Hartley is arguably

the most severe, referring to him as 'a successful child who became an abject adult failure, a shambling, drunken, superannuated boy' ('The *Annus Mirabilis*', p. 181).
13. Wordsworth, 'Lines Written a Few Miles from Tintern Abbey', in *Lyrical Ballads and Other Poems*, p. 92, line 97.
14. Keanie, *Hartley Coleridge*, p. 115.
15. Healey, *Dorothy Wordsworth and Hartley Coleridge*, pp. 3–4, 64, 16, 22, 43.
16. Ibid., p. 22.
17. Swinburne, 'The Garden of Proserpine', in *Algernon Charles Swinburne: Major Poems and Selected Prose*, p. 132, line 86. Twentieth-century critics have taken Hartley's Christian stoicism as an unyielding force in his poetry. Mary Joseph Pomeroy mentions his 'reverence for ... Almighty God' in spite of all odds (*The Poetry of Hartley Coleridge*, p. 39). Griggs admits that Hartley might have been seduced by his sense of his own 'weakness' and his 'self-condemnation', without his 'humble devotion' and 'belief in Christian redemption' (*Hartley Coleridge*, pp. 181–2). For James Reeves, Hartley is nothing short of a 'convinced Christian' ('Hartley Coleridge', p. 141).
18. Porter, 'Love of Life: Lucretius to Freud', p. 116.
19. Porter, 'Love of Life: Lucretius to Freud', p. 136; and Lucretius, *The Nature of Things*, Book III, p. 89. *The Nature of Things* will hereafter be cited as *NT*. Passages from the poem will be cited parenthetically within the main body of the text by book and page number.
20. Freud, *Beyond the Pleasure Principle*, p. 43.
21. 'Lines Written by H. C. in the Fly-Leaf of a Copy of Lucretius Presented by Him to Mr. Wordsworth', in *Poems by Hartley Coleridge*, 2:154–5. *Poems by Hartley Coleridge* (1851) will hereafter be abbreviated as *PHC*. Individual poems within this two-volume work will be cited parenthetically within the main body of the text by volume and page number(s). The first volume of *PHC* contains Derwent's *Memoir*, followed by a reprint of Hartley's 1833 *Poems*; the second volume features previously unpublished verse by Hartley selected by Derwent.
22. Reeves claims that Hartley's poems suggest 'a too easy belief in the consolation of Heaven', and that his religion was 'only a part of his personality, and ... should only be seen in terms of the rest' ('Hartley Coleridge', p. 143). The 'rest' of his personality – or, for our purposes, his personality as manifested in the collective substance of his not-quite-Christian-sounding poems – suggests that he was something less than a convinced theist. The speaker of the sonnet 'Fear' claims that fear can serve both good or evil ends: it can 'fight for either God or Devil'. Apparently this speaker has indulged the wrong, devilish kind of fear,

and uses the poem to confess his sins. In the spirit of Christian humility, he identifies his own person as the very embodiment of Fear (whom he apostrophises): 'As goblin, ghost, or fiend I ne'er have known thee/ But as myself, my sinful self, I own thee' ('Fear', *PHC*, 2:54). In another poem, Sonnet 'XI', the speaker claims that it would be 'too terrible' for a person to acknowledge that he has 'no precedent, no chart, or plan', and to 'think himself an embryo incomplete,/ Or else a remnant of a world effete,/ Some by-blow of the universal Pan,/ Great nature's waif, that must by law escheat/ To the liege-lord Corruption' ('XI', *PHC*, 2:13). By saying how terrible it would be to acknowledge these things, of course, the speaker is already acknowledging them. The word *waif* is used here in several senses: as '[s]omething borne or driven by the wind' ('waif, n.³'. *OED Online*. Oxford University Press, December 2014, <http://www.oed.com> (last accessed 22 December 2014)); as a 'piece of property which is found ownerless and which, if unclaimed within a fixed period after due notice given, falls to the lord of the manor' ('waif, n.¹ and adj.'. Def. A1a. *OED Online*. Oxford University Press, December 2014, <http://www.oed.com> (last accessed 22 December 2014)); and as a 'person who is without home or friends' ('waif, n.¹ and adj.'. Def. A2b. *OED Online*. Oxford University Press, December 2014, <http://www.oed.com> (last accessed 22 December 2014)). The 'liege-lord Corruption' refers to the lord on whose estate the speaker-as-waif has been arbitrarily left or discarded, and to whom the speaker (as a piece of unclaimed property) is to be reverted by escheat. Perhaps Hartley is thinking like Letitia Landon, who, according to Adriana Craciun, 'reveal[s] inherent corruption and decay at the heart of all origins, even female ones', and so 'undermines the essentializing distinction between patriarchal surface (culture) and prediscursive female depth (nature)' (*Fatal Women of Romanticism*, p. 198). For Landon, Craciun argues, female poets are not blessed with a well of a heart overflowing with pure emotion. The corruption at the root of their feelings bleeds into their verse. And for all his orthodoxy Hartley is never too far from this line of thinking. He feminises his speaker as the insignificant byproduct of an 'effete' pantheist world, whose only law is to become the property of an indifferent 'liege-lord'. And under the grim rule of that lord the speaker will only be effaced, dissolved.

23. Cf. Swinburne's 'Hymn to Proserpine (After the Proclamation in Rome of the Christian Faith)': 'there is no God found stronger than death; and death is a sleep' (*Algernon Charles Swinburne: Major Poems and Selected Prose*, p. 104, line 110).

24. 'abortion, n.'. Def. 1b. *OED Online*. Oxford University Press, December 2014, <http://www.oed.com> (last accessed 22 December 2014).

25. Plotz, 'Childhood Lost, Childhood Regained', p. 139.
26. Freud, *Beyond the Pleasure Principle*, pp. 45–7.
27. Ibid., p. 46. Italics in original.
28. His feelings about the possibility of prenatal existence were ambiguous at best. See, for instance, 'Fragment' (*PHC*, 1:106–7), Sonnet 'XIX' (*PHC*, 2:21) and 'To an Infant' (*PHC*, 2:117).
29. Plotz, 'Childhood Lost', p. 138.
30. Hartman, *Hartley Coleridge*, p. 101; and Plotz, *Romanticism and the Vocation of Childhood*, p. 206.
31. Plotz, *Romanticism and the Vocation of Childhood*, pp. 210–11.
32. Keanie, *Hartley Coleridge*, p. 114; and Healey, *Dorothy Wordsworth and Hartley Coleridge*, pp. 55–6.
33. Porter, 'Love of Life', p. 124.
34. 'general, adj. and n.'. Def. AI1. *OED Online*. Oxford University Press, December 2014, <http://www.oed.com> (last accessed 22 December 2014).
35. According to Lucretius, the human person can be explained in terms of mind, spirit and soul. The 'mind [*animus* or intelligence] and spirit [*anima* or vital principle] are bound up with one another,/ And . . . together they combine to form a single nature [the soul]'. The mind is located 'in the mid-region of the chest' and is connected to the spirit, which extends throughout the body. Both mind and spirit are material entities made up of particles (*NT*, Book III, p. 76).
36. Donne, 'The Extasie', p. 130, lines 2, 27.
37. Willard Spiegelman notes that Wordsworth, with whom Hartley is often compared, 'discovers his perfect serenity in the eternity of death'. His 'golden moments, the hoped-for relief from emotional and physical upheaval, the bliss of solitude and the peace that passeth understanding, derive as much from Wordsworth's Epicurean as from his Stoic leanings' ('Some Lucretian Elements in Wordsworth', p. 32). The influence of Lucretius on Wordsworth has been well documented: see Kelley, 'Wordsworth and Lucretius' *De Rerum Natura*'; Jacobson, 'Lucretian Encomia in Wordsworth's *Prelude*'; and Dix, 'Wordsworth and Lucretius'.
38. Hartley published pieces in the up-and-coming literary annual, *The Winter's Wreath*, for 1829 and 1830. *The Literary Gazette* featured advertisements for both of these volumes a month in advance and mentioned Hartley as a contributor (612 [11 October 1828] and 664 [10 October 1829]). On another occasion, the *Literary Gazette* announced and reviewed the literary contents of *The Gem* for 1829, passing over poems by Walter Scott and Charles Lamb but transcribing a 'song' by Hartley 'so pretty that we quote it in preference to the higher names before' (Anon., '*The Gem, A Literary Annual*', p. 661).

39. The line 'To know the change and feel it' was apparently written by an unknown author who felt dissatisfied with the original, and it was this revised line that made its way into the early print publications. See Jones, 'Keats and "The Feel of Not to Feel It"', pp. 185–6.
40. The word 'formal' is tricky in this context. It can refer to 'the form or constitutive essence of a thing' ('formal, adj. and n.'. Def. A1a. *OED Online*. Oxford University Press, December 2014, <http://www.oed.com> (last accessed 22 December 2014)); or, quite the opposite, the 'form, arrangement' or 'external qualities' of a thing ('formal, adj. and n.'. Def. A1c. *OED Online*. Oxford University Press, December 2014, <http://www.oed.com> (last accessed 22 December 2014)). If Hartley uses the word in the first sense, the poem seems more Lucretian than Christian: the very 'constitutive essence' of Keats is permanently annihilated at death.
41. Keanie, 'Hartley Coleridge: Son of the Mariner', p. 57.
42. Healey, *Dorothy Wordsworth and Hartley Coleridge*, p. 52.
43. Plotz, *Romanticism and the Vocation of Childhood*, p. 208.

Chapter 6

'A Series of Small Inconstancies': Letitia Landon and the Politics of Consistency

> Constancy is made up of a series of small inconstancies, which never come to any thing; and the heart takes credit for its loyalty, because in the long-run it ends where it began.[1]
> Letitia Landon, *Romance and Reality* (1831)

I

In James Gillray's 1791 print, 'A Uniform Whig' (see Fig. 6.1), Edmund Burke appears as an emblem of Inconsistency. His right arm rests on a pedestal featuring a bust of George III (who looks rather arrogantly at Burke); his right hand holds his recently published *Reflections on the Revolution in France* (1790); the pockets on the right side of his body – which is covered in a gold-laced coat – are overflowing with coins (perhaps a government pension from George III). The left half of his body, on the other hand, is decrepit; its empty pockets hang inside out; his left hand holds the staff and red cap of Liberty. In the background is a windmill perched on what is probably Mount Parnassus, on one sail of which a personified Fame stands delicately balanced. On the bottom of the print is a slightly misquoted passage from the end of the *Reflections*: 'I preserve consistency, by varying my means to secure the unity of my end'. The actual passage from *Reflections* reads: '[M]y opinions ... come ... from one who wishes to preserve consistency; but who would preserve consistency by varying his means to secure the unity of his end'.[2] The print calls attention to the fact that the same man who had endorsed a series of revolutions in America, Ireland, Corsica and Poland now suddenly condemns the revolution in France, defending the French clergy and their rights to

Figure 6.1 James Gillray, 'A Uniform Whig' (1791). © Trustees of the British Museum.

Church property. Whether or not Burke actually maintained an essential consistency throughout his political life is less important for our purposes than consistency itself as a prevailing contemporary topic. The political 'apostasies' of Wordsworth and Southey are too well known to require comment. The fact is that numerous cases of ideological inconsistency among prominent public figures – arising mainly from the hopes raised and dashed throughout the Revolution, Coalition Wars and Napoleonic Wars – were known and deplored in the early nineteenth century. Among those who eventually made '*voluntary, sincere changes of mind and political opinion*', Kenneth Johnston includes Wordsworth, Coleridge, Archibald Hamilton Rowan and James Mackintosh. Amelia Alderson Opie (along with Wordsworth and Coleridge) similarly underwent a '*significant revision or outright erasure of "juvenile errors"*' during this time. Charles Lloyd, Charlotte Dacre and Humphry Davy also underwent a '*dramatic, calculating adoption of contrary conservative and/or outright pro-government positions*'.[3] Johnston emphasises that, as the reform movement of the 1790s was effectively crushed by the reactionary backlash, a host of changes of mind, revisions, erasures and backslidings were necessary casualties.

Not that inconsistency itself was uniformly suspect among first-generation Romantics. Its moral quality depended on the intellectual attitude of the individual. Godwin (like Emerson after him) made a virtue of inconsistency. After his relationship with Mary Wollstonecraft, he 'abandoned his belief in impartiality' – instantiated in the 'famous fire cause' outlined in Book II of *Political Justice* – realising that his 'long loveless childhood ... had blinded him to the role of the emotions in human psychology'.[4] As far as Godwin was concerned, his change of heart was 'not only an illustration of the necessitarian influence of early environment on opinion and behaviour, but a triumphant vindication of the eventual power of truth'.[5] According to Julie Carlson, Godwin 'made "the alleged demerit of inconsistency" the measure of honest enquiry, the sign that the writer is motivated by truth, not self-concern'. The '"active and independent mind" will "inevitably pass through certain revolutions of opinion"' in the course of its perfectibility.[6] What this implies is that there is nothing inherently wrong with inconsistency – provided that one is intelligently inconsistent or inconsistent in the right direction. To proceed back and forth between an old opinion and its opposite is a sign of intellectual ignorance or the force of prejudice. The eponymous hero of Godwin's second novel, *St. Leon* (1799), count, patriot and knight of France, fights for the honour and glory of king and country at the siege of Pavia, but witnesses such bloody scenes of human destruction in Italy that he almost 'abjure[s] the trade of violence for ever'. Almost, but not quite: his pacifism is only 'temporary' (as are many of his self-professed mental 'revolutions' throughout the novel). The 'military passion return[s] upon [him] in its original ardour' so soon after it departed that he seems to have become, in his own words, 'a monument of . . . inconstancy'. But his is an inconstancy in a cyclical or progressive-regressive sense. He never synthesises old and new perspectives towards some dialectical progress, but takes one step forward and another step back. The problem in St Leon's case is that '[t]he force of [his chivalric] education, and the first bent of [his] mind, were too strong' for him not – ultimately – to crave military honours.[7]

All of this raises an important question: 'Why are representations of inconsistency in character so disconcerting?' For Manning, the answer is that 'consistency across time' 'confers confidence in character'. 'Expectation raised by custom is our only guide in deciding the truth': '[w]hat kind of confidence can be placed in a character not sustained either by the progressive flow of narrative, or . . . a fixed position in a social network?'[8] This is where the work of Letitia Landon becomes important. Her texts flout the unimportance of constancy as a holder of ethological value in print and in life. They question the power or even the need of 'character' to make individual ideas and behaviours cohere over time. Cronin has observed that, 'by 1823, consistency of character no longer served to confer authenticity so much as to reveal the presence of an accomplished author'.[9] What he means is that fictional characters calculated to appear 'consistent' in texts no longer seemed quite 'real', or 'authentic', to seasoned reading audiences in 1823. By that time the reading public had changed. Predictability, conservation, continuity of character all seemed stale and unreal (even if they were the sign of an 'accomplished author'). Readers became

> so practiced, so familiar with all those techniques that novelists, poets, and essayists have used to body forth the reality of their inward lives upon the page that only the most patently inauthentic cadences retain the power to produce the shock of the real.[10]

Cronin goes on to say that *Liber Amoris* is one work that did meet the needs of veteran readers who expected more out of 'real' characters than consistency. Hazlitt's autobiographical text produced 'the shock of the real' precisely because its characters were so disjointed: 'H' and 'S' 'remain discontinuous, jumping erratically between quite different verbal registers'.[11] Landon bursts into fame right around the publication of *Liber Amoris*, and her work likewise undermines the value of consistency – only its 'shock of the real' is somewhat different from the one that Cronin describes. Inconsistency for Landon is more than an ultra-realistic attribute found in disjointed fictional characters: it is also a value-neutral fact of life. Conflicting attitudes and behaviours in texts and in the real world are not necessarily products of an unprincipled character so much as surface phenomena problematically traced to an inner real as the source of moral value. The work of Landon as a whole bears out the fact that constancy itself (in relationships or in anything) is an idea that has only as much moral worth as one is willing to grant it. Inconsistency is neither virtuous because it is ultimately truth-seeking (Godwin) nor vicious because it is unprincipled. It is open to valuation but inherently valueless.

II

The epigraph to this chapter appears in Landon's first 'silver fork' novel, *Romance and Reality* (1831). The passage seems to refer primarily to romantic relationships (one 'heart takes credit for its loyalty' to another heart), and to suggest that no lover is ever quite faithful to his or her partner in a strict and absolute sense. As a comment on love, the statement flies in the face of conventional notions of female constancy (compare Anne Elliot's speech at the end of Austen's final novel, *Persuasion*). Consider what the author of 'The Female Character' says about female affection in *The Mirror* (1823): '[c]onstancy . . . is . . . that in which . . . the nobleness of the female heart [is] chiefly remarkable'. The author means constancy in love. Love, to the female character, is

> second nature, the business of her life, the motive of her actions, the theme of her waking thoughts . . . the innate principle of her constitution, it is born with her, it grows with her heart-strings . . . Constancy is then, in her, almost an unavoidable virtue, for her happiness consists in loving and being loved, which latter constancy best ensures.[12]

It is clear that the epigraph is a pessimistic challenge to conventional beliefs like this one about female love and loyalty. But Landon's immense literary output goes much further than this. It tends to blast all essentialising categories out of existence. Her literary corpus suggests that not just constancy in love, but constancy itself is theoretically and practically impossible. To be 'constant' to anything – a lover, an opinion, a character, an ideal object – is simply to be abortively *in*constant to it, to be perennial unfaithful in small ways that never get noticed or never amount to anything.

This view of constancy turns the much-lauded firmness or 'decision' of character on its head. Perhaps a lifetime of what looks like constancy is not what it appears to be. Perhaps a given set of ideas and behaviours can never be reliably traced to and reconciled within an ethological source. Landon is one of many reform-era artists whose extended critique of character has yet to be understood. Her interest in constancy and the 'properties of . . . interiority' makes sense when we consider that she rose to fame in a world of stifling fashionable exteriors – shortly after the ascension of George IV to the British throne (1820). The Regency was still fresh in her mind (she was nine in 1811 and eighteen in 1820), a time when the corpulent Prince Regent drained the treasury to expand and refurbish his impossibly decadent Brighton Pavilion, and Beau Brummell became a national hero owing to the genius of his toilette. The 1820s also witnessed the rise and immense popularity of the literary annual, to which Landon was one of the most prolific contributors of her day. Her usual task was to write companion poems for the plates featured in a given annual. Many of these plates were engraved portraits of aristocrats or famous figures, so that Landon was used to seeing face after face aestheticised in the midst of miscellaneous art and advertisements.

Most students of Romanticism have at least heard of Landon by now. A few of her poems appear in Romantic-era anthologies published within the last twenty years, thanks to the surge of critical interest in Romantic women writers in the 1990s. One of her essays may occasionally show up in a companion to nineteenth-century literature and culture. But I would hesitate to call her canonised – at least in the same way that other female authors like Mary Robinson and Felicia Hemans are canonised. I would also argue that her work is now marginally anthologised but often misunderstood. A tiny fraction of her corpus serves to encapsulate her role as an artist wherever she appears in edited collections. Most of her prose stays out of the classroom, and her sentimental love-poetry alone tends to get read.

This chapter makes three claims about Landon. The first is that it is unusually difficult to make critical statements about her private opinions or allegiances based on evidence from her literary output or correspondence. Her poems, prefaces, novels, essays, footnotes and even private letters yield no reliable self-portrait.[13] The second claim is that if we want to make any sense of her work, we have to examine not this or that poem, nor this or that large group of similarly themed poems, nor even just poems. We have to consider all the genres in her oeuvre and account for what deep-seated assumptions seem to generate a lifelong host of logical contradictions. The student of Landon is best served who reads her poetry against the background of her prose (especially her novels), and vice versa: the novels, virtually unread, tend to debunk the ideologies advanced in her poems, and the poems tend to do the same to the novels. The third claim is that there *is* one reliable and consistent fact evident throughout her giant corpus – its shameless inconsistency of persuasion. One of her speakers promotes the Wordsworthian sense of an occult relationship between the human and vegetable worlds and another thinks the idea absurd; one touts Protestant theology and another sounds pagan; one is a neo-Platonist (à la Percy Shelley) and another a firm materialist; one lists the obvious advantages of British imperial expansion and another launches heartfelt attacks on it. Consider the following remarkable dichotomies we can trace throughout her work:

Hardship Inspires Good Art	Hardship Inhibits Good Art
Neo-Platonism	Materialism
Man/Nature Metaphysically Related	Man/Nature Analogously Related
Pro-Industrialism	Anti-Industrialism
Pro-Imperialism	Anti-Imperialism
Nationalistic	Unpatriotic
Pro-Picturesque	Anti-Picturesque
Christian	Pagan
Memory as Salvific	Memory as Destructive
Love's Mutability Celebrated	Love's Mutability Censured
Sympathy/Benevolence	Scepticism/Selfishness
Good Poetry is Imaginative	Good Poetry is Realistic
Poetry Remedies Selfishness	Poetry Promotes Selfishness

This is a striking 'series of inconstancies'. I ascribe them not to a confused mind or to an artistic sell-out (a common and – in my view – all-too-easy critical conclusion about Landon) but to a mindset emancipated from reform-era notions about the value of a 'good' (legible/principled/consistent) character. Her 'inconstancies' question the moral worth of the 'decided' character and the nature and usefulness of character as a concept. The entire career of Landon can be seen as a playful engagement with the Owenite claim – with which she can never be said quite to agree or disagree – that 'insanity is inconsistency'.

III

Landon holds an exceptional place in the British Romantic canon since critics disagree completely on basic points about her aesthetic and cultural allegiances. Anne Mellor argues that Landon is 'entirely complicit in her culture's construction of female beauty, rewriting her own life and subjectivity to conform to preexisting categories. Sorrow, Beauty, Love, Death – these are the subjects of Landon's poetry'.[14] Cronin leaves out sorrow, beauty and death, claiming that Landon 'writes almost exclusively of love', 'self-consciously transform[ing] herself into a cultural icon of womanhood'.[15] Glennis Stephenson agrees that Landon writes a lot about 'love, erotic passion, feelings' – but stresses that her love-centredness is an act merely to secure 'popularity with the public'. Behind the scenes, Stephenson goes on, Landon is an 'astute businesswoman with a pressing need to make a living' and a 'keen sense of the literary market'. I think that Stephenson is right here – but her seminal book on Landon (*Letitia Landon: The Woman Behind L. E. L.* [1995]) studies only Landon's poetry (leaving her novels completely out), so that it comes as no surprise when Stephenson claims that, instead of 'distinguishing the various figures' in her texts, Landon 'tends to draw them closer and closer together until they all appear as subtexts of one highly personalised, feminised primary text – a primary text that is, basically ... L. E. L. speaking the heart'.[16] Tricia Lootens has been one of the first critics to challenge this homogenisation of Landonian voices. According to Lootens, Landon 'did more than write or enact poetic femininity' in her verse: she was also a satirist, a moralist and an artist who 'indulg[ed] in cosmic weariness and epigrammatic, often bleak humor'.[17] I take this claim for granted and suggest that it has critical implications yet to be addressed. It is a fact that Landon seems to wear many 'masks' and to write in many modes. It is also a fact that her poems reproduce a variety of popular sentiment. But we need not conclude from these facts that her career is primarily an affair of opportunism and personal regret.[18] There is instead a liberal (Hazlitt might call it a 'French') mobility in her writing – in its casual disregard for the value or even the possibility of 'decisive' characters in print/life.

The eponymous protagonist of *Rameau's Nephew* by Denis Diderot – who, we recall, undermined Kant's distinction between 'natural' and 'moral' characters – embraces and anticipates this particular mobility. Diderot wrote *Rameau's Nephew*, a philosophical dialogue, in the 1760s and 1770s. Goethe translated it into German in 1805 and an authentic French version of it appeared in 1823. Landon published her famous *The Improvisatrice* in the following year (1824). Whether she read *Rameau's Nephew* must be a matter of speculation (although she knew French), but she did rise to fame during what Virgil Nemoianu calls the Age of Biedermeier (1815–48), an epoch partly characterised by its 'return to eighteenth-century attitudes'.[19] Her novel *Romance and Reality* is more or less one long conversation of sparkling wit and badinage – a recreation of Enlightenment salon culture. Her mature novel *Ethel Churchill* (1837), set in the early eighteenth century, features social landscapes modelled after the paintings of Antoine Watteau, aristocratic duels, and a cast of characters including Lavinia Fenton, Sir Robert Walpole and Alexander Pope.

Diderot models the main character of his dialogue, *Lui*, after Jean-François Rameau, nephew to the great composer Jean-Philippe Rameau. *Lui* is a bizarre and unpredictable performer-extemporiser of culture, ethics, life. He recognises that 'every man takes one or another "position" as the choreography of society directs', and '[w]ith the mimetic skill which is the essence of his being, [he] demonstrates how he performs the dance upon which his survival depends'. Importantly, it is precisely because he is mimetic that *Lui* possesses that 'liberty . . . we wish to believe is inherent in the human spirit . . .

in its consciousness of itself and its limitless contradictions'. As an improvising artist, *Lui* 'invokes . . . moral categories at the same time that he negates them'.[20]

I would describe the Landonian 'I' in similar terms. It evokes aesthetic/political/moral categories and negates them – though not as immediately and overtly as *Lui* seems to do. Its negation of these categories lies in its many casual, tongue-in-cheek contradictions of its own professed doctrines. Landon's 'I' uses a rhetorical posture of sincerity to advocate for the position x in, say, a novel. Within that very novel it may use the same rhetorical posture of sincerity to argue for a position opposite to x. Or it may be that two first-person poetic speakers advance opposite ideologies in two different poems within a single collection, in whose preface Landon identifies herself as author and 'I'. I don't mean to imply that Landon was devilishly conscious of each instance of ideological contradiction and the trick it may play on her readers. My point is rather that her countless clashing 'I's compromise the value of constancy and suggest a certain arbitrariness at the root of all private conviction, all personal advocacy.

Rameau's Nephew consists of the nephew *Lui* and the narrator *Moi* having a long and funny philosophical conversation in a fashionable Parisian café. Rameau enters the scene having just lost his position as a sort of clown-servant in the house of the wealthy state treasurer, Bertin, for insulting his mistress (the actress Mademoiselle Hus) in a moment of weakness and exasperation. The narrator, more or less an upright, respectable and practical bourgeois, urges Rameau to return to the house of Bertin, apologise for his offence and perhaps get his job back before he is replaced:

> All the same, I should go along with that ravaged face, those wild eyes, shirt torn open, tousled hair, in fact in the really tragic state you are in at the moment. I should throw myself at the goddess's feet, glue my face to the ground, and without raising myself address her in a low, sobbing voice: 'Forgive me, Madame, forgive me, I am an unspeakable wretch. It was just an unfortunate moment' . . . (The funny thing was that while I was holding forth to him in this way he was doing the actions. He flung himself down with his face pressed to the ground, he seemed to be holding the point of a slipper between his hands, and he wept and sobbed, saying: 'Yes, my little queen, yes, I promise, never in my life, in my life'. Then suddenly rising to his feet he went on in a serious and thoughtful tone.)[21]

Exactly as *Moi* advises him, *Lui* is busy melodramatically performing the actions (his behaviour recalls that of Hazlitt's naturally 'characterless' mademoiselle). Throughout the dialogue, in fact, he is nearly all show: when it is his turn to speak he enacts his own words, occasionally beating his forehead with his fist, or cracking his joints, or performing a sonata with an invisible violin and sweating heavily – '[o]ne passion after another flitt[ing] across his face . . . tenderness, anger, pleasure, grief'.[22]

Rameau's Nephew invites readers to ask important ontological questions. It is unclear just who or what Rameau is or means to be. He seems to be only what he performs, but at the close of the conversation he exhibits a plausible affection for his young son. In the end, the dialogue makes no dogmatic assertions about human life or 'character' – although it *suggests* that most physical or verbal expressions may be postured or spontaneous. Diderot imagines a world where all behaviour is random but never absolutely discounts the possibility of sincerity, of true-to-self-ness. The narrator (who in one sense stands for the reader) cannot decide if he should criticise or pity the spectacle Rameau makes of himself. And yet perhaps the nephew is not meant to be pitied. Perhaps he is not the sad fatalist he appears to be, 'aping' what his patrons expect and despising himself for it. He is just as likely a happy hedonist who embraces whatever sense of 'character' his expressions happen to convey. At one point he admits that his character is an undecidable mystery – '"Devil take me if I really know what I am"' – and there is existential courage in this admission.[23] It prevents him from being like the narrator: fixed, inflexible, patterned after a single persona and set of habits that make him both stable and stagnant.

The Diderot model sketched here may serve as a hermeneutic supplement to Angela Esterhammer's claims about the role of spontaneity and improvisation in Landon's work. Esterhammer has associated Landon with the improvisational tradition in eighteenth-century Italy.[24] In a somewhat recent essay, she writes that 'the figure of the improviser allows [Landon and her British contemporaries] to reflect on their own relation to an audience, the often vulnerable status of poets and poetry, and the problematics of celebrity'.[25] While I agree with this statement, I would add that Landon may have had a deeper, more lived relationship with improvisation than Esterhammer implies. First, as an essayist, novelist and dramatist she is more than a poet writing about what it means to be a poet. Second, her texts seem to not only to appropriate an improvisational tradition for rhetorical purposes, but to resemble improvisations that 'enact cultural identities' as a matter of course.[26]

IV

Landon's best-known statement on the role of the poet is a short article, 'On the Ancient and Modern Influence of Poetry', published anonymously in *The New Monthly Magazine* in 1832. In this article she claims that throughout history poetry has had two main functions: in the ancient world it civilised savages, and in the modern world it prevents civilisation from 'growing too cold and too selfish'. Poetry elevates our human nature: it nurtures our rational, ethical and beautiful qualities, and suppresses whatever in us is crude or degenerate. The 'best and most popular ... poetry makes its appeal to the higher and better feelings of our nature'. It is made up of 'spiritual awakenings, and deep and tender thoughts' that the poet can enlist in a war against materialism, utilitarianism, selfishness, the 'hurry and the highways of life'. In a word, poetry brings spiritual heat back to a population of cold Utilitarians; and although it should be both beautiful and original, beautiful poetry alone is better than none at all.[27]

In her preface to *The Venetian Bracelet, The Lost Pleiad, The History of the Lyre, and Other Poems* (1829), written a few years earlier than the essay, Landon anticipates 'On the Ancient and Modern Influence of Poetry':

> A highly cultivated state of society must ever have for concomitant evils, that selfishness, the result of indolent indulgence; and that heartlessness attendant on refinement, which too often hardens while it polishes. Aware that to elevate I must first soften, and that if I wished to purify I must first touch, I have ever endeavoured to bring forward grief, disappointment, the fallen leaf, the faded flower, the broken heart, and the early grave. Surely we must be[come] less worldly, less interested, from this sympathy with sorrow in which our unselfish feelings alone can take part.[28]

In this preface Landon casts herself as a poet whose mission is to extend human sympathies. What is interesting is that she justifies her use of clichés ('the fallen leaf, the faded flower, the broken heart, and the early grave') on the grounds that they are ethically motivated. She lists a few of the macabre images and plots recycled in her poems as if half-admitting how formulaic and lifeless they become with overuse. But she also implies that they are necessary as medicine to the sick or punishment to the recalcitrant. Her poems are supposed to work by the steady and gradual administration of the same effect, again and again, exposing the self-absorbed reader to one opportunity for imaginative sympathy after another, until he or she is healed by small doses of textual tenderness. One of the poems in the *Venetian Bracelet* volume, 'A Summer Evening's Tale', aestheticises the premises advanced in the preface:

> . . . the smooth surface of society
> Is polish'd by deceit, and the warm heart
> With all its kind affections' early flow,
> Flung back upon itself, forgets to beat,
> At least for others: – 'tis the poet's gift
> To melt these frozen waters into tears,
> By sympathy with sorrows not our own
> . . . .
> Young poet, if thy dreams have not such hope
> To purify, refine, exalt, subdue,
> To touch the selfish, and to shame the vain
> Out of themselves . . .
> . . . .
> If thou hast not some power that may direct
> The mind from the mean round of daily life,
> Waking affections that might else have slept,
> Or high resolves, th[at] petrified before,
> Or rousing in that mind a finer sense
> Of inward and external loveliness,
> Making imagination serve as guide
> To all of heaven that yet remains on earth, –
> Thine is a useless lute: break it, and die.[29]

According to these lines, the poet is the moral and aesthetic saviour of a cold and calculating civilisation. In moral terms the poet is sent to heal the small-minded, the covetous, the selfish and the unambitious. In aesthetic terms the role of the poet is to 'rous[e] in th[e] mind a finer sense/ Of inward and external loveliness'.

In all three locations, article, preface and poem, an 'I' argues that poetry should generate human sympathies and promote high-cultural ideals.[30] A humanist aesthetic is preached. But how do we reconcile this voice with other voices that seem set on contradicting it – in texts that provide no good reason for us to suppose that the voices do not belong to Landon? The narrator of *Romance and Reality*, a pessimistic, Rochefoucauldian 'I', writes that 'the poet feeds the fever in his veins – works himself up to the belief of imaginary sorrows, till they are even as his own'.[31] This statement seems to challenge the sympathetic programme advanced in 'A Summer Evening's Tale'. The poet who, in the words of that poem, encourages our 'sympathy with sorrows not our own', is here more delusional than didactic: he writes to 'fee[d] the fever in his veins'. The same narrator says elsewhere that 'Fear and sorrow are the sources of sympathy; the misfortunes of others come home to those who are anticipating their own'.[32] These are powerful words, which ascribe commiseration to selfish fears and seem to be part of a distinctly *anti*-sympathetic ethos.

The imagination is another ambivalently described concept in the Landon canon: alternately divine and Satanic. In 'A Summer Evening's Tale', we recall that the imagination is 'a guide/ To all of heaven that yet remains on earth'. The narrator of the novel *Francesca Carrara* (1834) seems to agree, referring to it as 'man's noblest and most spiritual faculty', one that 'ever dwells on the to-come'. And yet that same narrator writes that '[n]othing ... frames such false estimates as the imaginative temperament. It finds the power of creation so easy, the path it fashions so actual ... and the fancied world appears the true copy of the real'.[33] The implication here (à la Samuel Johnson) is that the imagination is verisimilar to a fault. The eponymous heroine of *Francesca Carrara* speaks of the wiles of the imagination,

> 'which, like a spring confined to one spot, collects its pure waters, and is at once a beauty and a blessing; but which, allowed to spread abroad in every direction, oozes through the marshy earth, becomes stagnant, and is habited by the loathsome reptile'

until what 'would have been a green haunt, with its fair fountain, is a dreary and useless quagmire'.[34] The point of Francesca's simile seems to be that the imagination is harmless, even beautiful when under control, but toxic when overindulged. And worse, it is very hard for a person *not* to overindulge it. By nature it is a serpentine and elusive power. When active it does whatever it can to resist the control of the mind that operates it: '[t]he imagination shuns to reveal its workings, unless it can clothe them in some lovely and palpable shape'.[35] One and the same novel conceives of the imagination as a guide to both heaven and hell.

Through her poetic speakers and narrators, Landon encourages readers to imagine that she is a firm materialist. One of her speakers laments

> . . . the so false exterior of the world!
> Outside, all looks so fresh and beautiful;
> But mildew, rot, and worm, work on beneath,
> Until the heart is utterly decay'd.
>
> ('Roland's Tower', *PWL*, p. 276)

Some critics read passages like this and agree that the persona of the melancholy, lovesick poetess is a sham, only to assume that the next step is to lend most or all credence to its opposite – the disillusioned artist who is all polish, wit and coldness. Riess claims that Landon treats 'the Romantic vision of a poetry which transcends commercial exploitation [as] an illusion'; McGann and Riess, that her 'self-consciously quotational writing works to demystify the ancient authority of poetry'; Mellor, that she '[i]mplicitly embrace[s] David Hume's sceptical argument that the mind can only know the empirical sensations transmitted through the body'; and Craciun, that she exposes the 'material properties of imagination, corporeal properties that Wordsworth tried to put to sleep'.[36] I would say that such pronouncements as these can only be made by presuming that one set of like-minded speakers represents the 'Landonian ethos'. But these criticisms contain just partial truth. We cannot use Landon's language in a few passages as evidence of her materialism any more than we can use some of her other, more vaporous and metaphysical language as evidence of her neo-Platonism.

Speaking of neo-Platonism, Landon just as often writes of delicate and *im*material realities, as if roused by the same speculative passions as Percy Shelley,[37] whose influence in the following excerpts is clear:

> Beauty is the shadow flung from heaven on earth – it is the type of a lovelier and more spiritual existence, and the broken and transitory lights that it flings on this our sad and heavy pilgrimage, do but indicate another and a better sphere, where the beautiful also will be the everlasting.[38]

> I am often tempted to liken our mental world to a shadow flung on water from some other world – broken, wavering, and of uncertain brightness.[39]

> love, which, though tried, thwarted, and turned aside from its perfectness in the wayfaring below, is still the animating spirit of the universe.[40]

These passages view earthly life as the shadow of a heavenly or quasi-Platonic reality. In the sublunary world, one can feel only intimations of a wonderful existence beyond comprehension. Mortal pleasures and beautiful objects are evanescent tastes or fractions of Eternity. The language here has Christian affiliations, but it is obscure enough to suggest the pleasure Landon feels in dwelling in the uncertainty or liminality of faintly resonant imagery. It is not the crisp and clear-cut Christianity touted by her poetic speakers in *Fisher's Drawing Room Scrap-Book*, who condemn eastern idolatry in the name of Church and King. There, 'Christ' and 'God' are named; here, the closest we come to Christian doctrine is the mention of human life as a pilgrimage, of heaven and eternity. The first and second passages may have been inspired by Shelley's 'Hymn to Intellectual Beauty', which Landon could have read in the *Examiner* in 1817 as an impressionable girl of fifteen. The third excerpt, holding that 'love' is the 'animating spirit of the universe', may similarly have been inspired by Percy Shelley's reworking of *Queen Mab*, *The Daemon of the World* (1816), in which the daemon or intermediary spirit, Love, comes to the sleeping Ianthe in a chariot and grants her temporary access to the Platonic flame behind the veil of life and the senses. Keeping this third excerpt in mind, I think it is fascinating how Landon dramatically qualifies the idea that love is the 'animating spirit of the universe', spoken by the narrator of *Francesca Carrara*, in her poem 'The Lost Pleiad'. In that poem the speaker observes that 'Love is of heavenly birth,/ But turns to death on touching earth' (*PWL*, p. 198). Surely the spirit that animates the universe cannot itself be dead! Is Landon changing her mind all the time, changes evident in each of her textual voices? Are her narrators and speakers – involved in some kind of ongoing ideological war – meant to have nothing to do with her own views? Both claims may have some truth. But I think it is more accurate to say that Landon associates conviction, advocacy, constancy, decidedness – the metaphorical 'position' where one presumes one stands, and from which one imagines one decides, opines, declaims – with spur-of-the-moment expressions unattached to an inner source, expressions generated all but exclusively from social or discursive context.

Landon imitates not only the neo-Platonism of Shelley but also his style, as described by William Keach. She uses imagery to express the operations of the human mind, making sensory images the tenors of metaphors or similes and mental activities the vehicles (as in a cloud that moves as swift as thought); or she describes images and objects in a way that makes them seem to evanesce or dissolve in our imagination; or she writes reflexively, analysing an 'object or action' by comparing it, 'implicitly or explicitly, to an aspect of itself'.[41] A good example of reflexive writing occurs in her song-poem 'The Dream', spontaneously recited by a Scottish minstrel in the long poem *The Golden Violet*, in which the 'lowering sky' 'gather[s] darkly', '[a]s if fearing its own obscurity' (*PWL*, p. 130).

V

Most of the poems I cite in the rest of this chapter were originally published in the fashionable literary annual *Fisher's Drawing Room Scrap-Book* between 1832 and 1838. Landon excels at writing for an annual (a mélange of genres and modes) because she is a master of ideological variety. She can express in short lyric poems whatever popular idea or belief a given engraving suggests to her, or whatever idea/belief she imagines it would suggest to someone else. Often her poems read as ideological advertisements: straightforward, catchy, digestible. Considered in the collective, they suggest an author who half-expects the reading public to extract ideologies from them and fetishise these ideologies along with the knick-knacks and second-hand art advertised in the same volumes. In my view – though it may seem paradoxical to say it and though it is certainly fair to argue the reverse – this is what gives Landon her power. Her speakers are made of earnestness and conviction, and she allows if not encourages readers to interpret their sentiments as her own – which they customarily did.[42] But her various literary modes and all the incompatible ideas she appears to endorse indicate that her view of art has little or nothing to do with the character of the artist (contra Hazlitt). Instead, she comes across as a faceless shuffler of 'principled' statements. On one level Landon gives readers the clichéd poems they expect in the shortest and simplest way possible. On another she mocks them from an epistemological high ground – 'mocks' in its dual sense of 'imitates' and 'ridicules' (as the sculptor of Ramses II in Percy Shelley's 'Ozymandias' mocks his tyrant's features in the stone) – playing the *Lui* to her readers' *Moi*. I would argue that both levels are continuously operative in the *Fisher's* poems and fundamentally inseparable.

Landon's 'poetic illustrations' – short lyric poems meant to describe or somehow complement the engravings in the *Fisher's* volumes – reveal a lot about the artistic relationship she had with William Wordsworth. Landon was often assigned to write companion poems for engravings depicting natural scenery, and she made use of Wordsworthian ideas and language to drive her points home. But in the end, her texts do not add up to some stable trajectory of thought and taste. One of her speakers (she almost always uses the 'I') is all but a disciple of Wordsworth and another seems long ago to have dismissed his philosophy as naïve and inadequate. Each poetic 'disposition' has the feel of something extemporised and – for all we can tell – inspired and validated by the author. Or at least Landon permits these speakers to speak without subjecting them to a sustained critique in the way that Tennyson or Browning might have done. Ultimately, her views on Wordsworth are ambivalent and indeterminable. Perhaps a love of nature really does emerge from a lived relationship with rocks, stones and trees: from powerful associations built on associations through a long series of early impressions. Or perhaps love of nature is always too postured a sentiment to deserve lasting credit. There is simply no way to tell. Both the 'I' that seems to profess a heartfelt love of nature and the 'I' that seems merely caught up in the tide of fashion can be carefully imitated or spontaneously produced or some mixture of both.

Consider the poem 'Linmouth' (1833), a companion piece to an engraving of a small rural valley in north Devon. The poem is an encomium on London life mixed with some light derision of rural sensibilities. One short credo in it stands out:

> There's more for thought in one brief hour
> In yonder busy street,
> Than all that ever leaf or flower
> Taught in their green retreat.[43]

These lines speak directly to a moral sentiment in 'The Tables Turned', a short poem by Wordsworth from the *Lyrical Ballads* (1798):

> One impulse from a vernal wood
> May teach you more of man;
> Of moral evil and of good,
> Than all the sages can.[44]

It is clear that 'Linmouth' is something of a response to 'The Tables Turned', which stands as a sort of predecessor-poem. Each text uses the meter of the ballad stanza and its less common rhyme scheme (*abab* instead of *abcb*). The syntactic structures of the two stanzas are similar. Both poems make affirmations about environments that initiate deep thought. The speaker of 'The Tables Turned' is clearly a more solitary figure, a lover of nature who 'watches and receives' the wisdom inherent in her 'beauteous forms'.[45] He is a bit unclear as to how a 'vernal wood' can transmit didactic impulses to a person, but insists nonetheless that an individual can learn more from nature than from books (written by 'sages').

'Linmouth' troubles the argument advanced in 'The Tables Turned' when it suggests that an urban scene is full of more useful mental stimulants nowhere to be found in the country. In strict form it is a dramatic monologue: an 'I' tells readers that London, not a lone spot in southwest England, is where she prefers to learn about human 'sorrow, suffering, and thrall', where she can hear and feel the 'hearse [that] passes with its dead' and the 'homeless beggar's prayer'. For this speaker, the city is an exciting melting pot of human faces:

A busier scene for me!

I love to see the human face
Reflect the human mind,
To watch in every crowded place
Their opposites combined.
     ('Linmouth', F33, p. 40)

Landon attaches a (Hazlittian) footnote to the poem that echoes its speaker:

[T]hat melodramatic morality which talks of rural felicity, and unsophisticated pleasures . . . Your philosophers inculcate it, your poets rave about it . . . I do own I have a most affectionate attachment for London – the deep voice of her multitudes 'haunts me like a passion' . . . The country is no more left as it was originally created, than Belgrave Square remains its pristine swamp. The forest has been felled, the marsh drained, the enclosures planted, and the field ploughed. All these . . . are the work of man's hands; and so is the town – the one is not more artificial than the other. ('Linmouth', F33, p. 40)

Here the idea of the country is divested of its romantic grandeur. It is no more natural or pristine or marked by the hand of God (as Burnet – whom Wordsworth admired – argued in his *Sacred Theory of the Earth*) than its counterpart the city. Landon even borrows a few lines from 'Tintern Abbey' to make her point: in that poem 'the sounding cataract/ Haunted [the speaker] like a passion', but here the rushing sound of human crowds is said to have the same effect.[46]

This counter-Wordsworthianism seems strange alongside two companion pieces also published in *Fisher's Drawing Room Scrap-Book*: 'Glengariffe' – a poem that appears in the same 1833 volume as 'Linmouth' – and 'Rydal Water and Grasmere Lake, the Residence of Wordsworth' (1838), both of which feature first-person speakers who more or less profess an allegiance to Wordsworthian philosophy. And yet again Landon makes no real effort to distance herself from her speakers. She does not ironise either one or emphasise their status as dramatic characters, as organic minds that utter only what seems necessary or natural to them. She chooses to use the 'I' but not so as to signal an entity clearly apart from the author.

'Glengariffe' is a lyrical reflection on the picturesque beauties of Glengarriff Bay in Co. Cork, Ireland, written as a companion piece to an engraving after the British artist William Henry Bartlett. The poem bears similarities to ones by Keats and Wordsworth, a tribute to the healing properties of natural beauty. It reproduces some of the familiar language and imagery of Keats's 'Ode to a Nightingale', if not the exact sense of that poem. Its speaker tells us that a mind beset by 'feverish moods of discontent' and a 'sense of personal nothingness' can find solace in the image of Glengariff Bay. The mental vision of its beauty 'haunt[s]' her imagination so pleasurably that she can picture herself nestled comfortably in the 'summer solitude' of its 'small wood', a safe, darkened place blanketed with grass and flowers and charmed with the 'music' of raindrops heard but not felt ('Glengariffe', *F33*, p. 33). The wood is depicted as a natural shelter that almost entirely conceals an interior space from the elements, except where traces of sunlight filter through the apertures of trees stripped of their leaves by time and lightning. All of this approximates the poetic situation in 'Ode to a Nightingale'. In that poem, the poet-speaker finds himself in a state of 'drowsy numbness' owing to the rich, almost unbearable happiness he feels when he hears the nightingale sing, and he would perpetuate this calming numbness (acquired through poetry) as long as possible in order to escape the 'weariness, the fever, and the fret' of life. He follows the song of the nightingale to a forest glade very similar to the one described in 'Glengariffe' – a 'forest dim' in midsummer, where

>   there is no light,
> Save what from heaven is with the breezes blown
> Through verdurous glooms and winding mossy ways.[47]

Keats's ode ends on an ironic note, when the speaker reveals his suspicions that fancy may be no more than an illusory escape from the inescapable real world. He is not sure what to believe. Some of this uncertainty or negative capability is operative in 'Glengariffe' as well, whose speaker poeticises the pockets of sunlight stealing into the bower (by means of its dead border trees) as 'death/ . . . let[ting] in light and life'. The absolute security of the haven now feels somewhat compromised. But on the whole, the poem ends on a note of Wordsworthian confidence in the animating powers of nature. Nature – itemised in 'Glengariffe' as 'flowers; green grass, and aged tress' – no longer inspires mixed thoughts of life, repose and death, but 'fills the mind/ With natural love, and sweet and gentle thoughts', the sort that 'soothe, and calm, and purify,/ E'n 'mid a busy wilderness of streets' ('Glengariffe', *F33*, p. 33). These impressions may suggest the central argument of Wordsworth's unfinished *Recluse* – that love of Nature leads to love of mankind – but more likely recall the notion in 'Tintern Abbey' that envisioning the 'forms of [natural] beauty' can redeem individuals cramped in 'lonely rooms, and mid the din/ Of towns and cities'.[48]

The speaker of one of Landon's final poems, written in the year of her death, 'Rydal Water and Grasmere Lake, the Residence of Wordsworth', positions herself as a sort of prodigal-daughter poet lying prostrate before an old master – the now sixty-eight-year-old Wordsworth – to do worship and receive guidance:

Great poet, if I dare to throw
My homage at thy feet
. . .
As wayfarers have incense thrown
Upon some mighty altar-stone,
Unworthy, and yet meet,
The human spirit longs to prove
The truth of its uplooking love.
('Rydal Water and Grasmere Lake, the Residence of Wordsworth', *F38*, p. 30)

Landon's speakers' vacillating judgements so far on the subject of Wordsworthian poetry and poetics should lead us to expect that this speaker attitudinises as carelessly as the rest. I read the poem, in fact, as an enactment of unworthiness, a postured or spontaneous apostrophe to the ageing sage of Rydal Mount. One contemporary critic, however, had the opposite impression, claiming that the poem 'draw[s] forth a burst of homage, which we can easily believe Miss Landon cordially cherishes towards Wordsworth'.[49] The mistake in this case is that the reviewer confuses act with actuality, language with a source in thought; but it is an excusable error. Most readers will 'easily believe' that the author of 'Rydal Water and Grasmere Lake' *is* behind the words, maybe because by this stage in her career (she died in 1838) Landon has perfected the art of *Lui*. Frederic Rowton, in his anthology *The Female Poets of Great Britain* (1853), cannot seem to get past the idea that Landon's verses can be anything but sincere: 'We cannot believe her sadness to have been put on like a player's garb: to have been an affectation, and unreality: it is too earnest for that. We must suppose that she *felt* what she wrote: and if so, her written sadness was real sadness'.[50] But perhaps Landon's sadness is neither 'real' nor unreal, principled nor unprincipled, since all such descriptors measure her success as a poet in terms of how she reproduces the contents of personal or dramatic 'characters' – concepts she has destabilised before the act of composition.

Landon discusses Wordsworth directly and at length in her novel *Romance and Reality*. The characters in that novel appreciate him as a moral poet whose business is to extend human sympathies by means of the doctrine that love of nature leads to love of man. Montague Delawarr, a somewhat self-centred opportunist, admires the poetry of Wordsworth for its 'mountain range of distant hill and troubled sky – or the lonely spot of inland shade, linked with human thought and human interest'. Lady Mandeville notes that Wordsworth 'wanders through the fields, and calls from their daily affections and sympathies foundations whereon to erect a scheme of the widest benevolence'. The narrator herself even makes casual observations worthy of a Lakist poet: 'it is from the wood and the field, the hill and the valley, that poetry takes that imagery which so imperceptibly mingles with all our excited moods'.[51] The affinities in this last statement seem pretty clear. The narrator claims that some of the best poetic imagery is drawn from natural forms and the elevated moods in which those forms are first perceived and then recollected. It seems reasonable to infer that Landon is speaking through the narrator in this sentence – or, more accurately, that she encourages readers to think she is. Otherwise, this silver fork narrator has little reason to interrupt the story and tell us about poetic imagery.

The truth is that the narrator of *Romance and Reality* is as sufficient a stand-in for Landon herself as she is for any other one of Landon's speakers. No one voice or discourse in the Landon corpus has hegemonic authority over the rest. The voice of 'Rydal Water and Grasmere Lake' describes Wordsworth's poetry as 'music' that can '[call] that loveliness to life,/ With which the inward world is rife', 'Music that can be hush'd no more', a 'gushing melody forever', 'music [that] do[th] impart/ . . . freshness to the world-worn heart', 'song' that 'Forth flows . . . as waters flow' ('Rydal Water and Grasmere Lake, the Residence of Wordsworth', *F38*, pp. 30–1). Yet Lady Mandeville calls Wordsworth 'deficient in . . . passion' and a poet who 'never fills the atmosphere around with music'.[52] In her personal and private letters, Landon echoes Lady Mandeville: she refers to Wordsworth as 'rugged and mountainous', as 'a poet that even Plato might have admitted into his republic . . . the most passionless of writers'.[53] In the end, the only way to reconcile all these conflicting voices is to admit that Landon has no interest in reconciling them: to admit that, as far as Landon is concerned, it makes no sense 'to speak of a self that precedes its expression', but only of 'selves [that] come into being through cultural forms, such as poems' – or, in Landon's case, every conceivable genre of text.[54]

It may be that critics have neglected Landon's work (especially her novels) because she has refused to give critics what they want – a clear sense of authorial voice, or 'character': a voice whose authority makes it easy for readers to understand when the author is speaking sincerely, when the author is speaking ironically, when the author approves of a dramatic speaker's sentiments or when the author ironises a dramatic speaker's sentiments. We can view Landon's 'characterlessness' as an unfortunate sort of self-effacement, or selling out, or we can see it as the revelation of something important and far ahead of her time: the idea that character is a vexed concept whose signifieds and referents are glaringly problematic. Ralph Waldo Emerson writes that 'Character is centrality, the impossibility of being displaced or overset'.[55] Landon's novels, essays, poems, letters and footnotes amount to one long, perhaps long overdue, unravelling of this Romantic dream – not an absolute denial of it, but a slow chipping away at its foundations. Emerson calls character 'a Familiar or Genius, by whose impulses the man is guided but whose counsels he cannot impart'.[56] Landon flaunts her refusal to go along with this position. She inherits the British – particularly the Wordsworthian – version of this 'Genius' and consistently compromises it without killing it, dampens it without extinguishing its flame. Her work repeatedly suggests the possibility that what is known about character comes predominantly (if not entirely) from what has been written about it. Character and its associated concepts, for Landon, are more or less what Bentham calls 'fictitious entit[ies]', which culture loves to reify time and again in various ways and for various political, literary and ideological ends.

Notes

1. Landon, *Romance and Reality*, vol. 3, p. 111.
2. Burke, *Reflections on the Revolution in France*, pp. 249–50.
3. Johnston, *Unusual Suspects*, pp. 13–14. Italics in original.
4. St Clair, *The Godwins and the Shelleys*, p. 175.
5. Ibid., p. 176.
6. Carlson, *England's First Family of Writers*, p. 62.
7. Godwin, *St. Leon*, p. 73.
8. Manning, *Poetics of Character*, p. 146.
9. Cronin, *Paper Pellets*, p. 75.
10. Ibid., pp. 74–5.
11. Ibid., p. 75.
12. Anon., 'The Female Character', p. 314.
13. Serena Baiesi, on the other hand, argues that Landon 'assert[ed] her own ideas, aesthetics, and personality through her poetry', that she 'express[ed] her own subjectivity as a woman who actively took part in the literary, social, and also political community of her century' (*Letitia Elizabeth Landon and Metrical Romance*, p. 40). One part this statement is more or less factual: that Landon 'actively took part in the literary, social, and political community of her century'. But I disagree with what Baiesi extrapolates from this observation – that Landon uses literary texts to assert her 'personality'. Claims about her political allegiances – Watt calls her a 'staunch Tory' – are also highly problematic (Watt, 'We Did Not Think That He Could Die', p. 129).
14. Mellor, *Romanticism and Gender*, p. 113.
15. Cronin, *Romantic Victorians*, pp. 84, 94.
16. Stephenson, *Letitia Landon: The Woman behind L. E. L.*, pp. 2, 14, 4, 72–3.
17. Lootens, 'Receiving the Legend', pp. 243, 254–5.

18. Angela Leighton considers Landon a poet who *knows* that she has 'wasted her gifts instead of nurturing them' (*Victorian Women Poets*, p. 66). McGann and Riess observe that her 'rehears[al] [of] established forms and ideas' is part of 'a poetical discourse of personal disillusionment' (introduction to *Letitia Elizabeth Landon: Selected Writings*, p. 23). Riess supposes that Landon is '[d]isgusted by the degradation of poetry by the annuals, yet dependent upon them for her continued existence', so that '[t]he result is a poetry of self-destruction' ('Laetitia Landon and the Dawn of English Post-Romanticism', p. 823). For Cronin, Landon is haunted by a 'sense that she has not fulfilled her talent' (*Romantic Victorians*, p. 89).
19. Nemoianu, *The Taming of Romanticism*, p. 6.
20. Trilling, *Sincerity and Authenticity*, pp. 31–3.
21. Diderot, 'Rameau's Nephew', p. 48.
22. Ibid., p. 54.
23. Ibid., p. 79.
24. In 1824 Landon published one of her most popular works, *The Improvisatrice*, a long poem about a female Florentine poet who extemporises verse for her audiences. *The Improvisatrice* was largely influenced by Madame de Staël's novel *Corinne; or Italy* (1807). In turn, de Staël based her fictional heroine Corinne on the real Italian improvisatrice Corilla Olympica (1728–1800), who was crowned at the Capitol in Rome in 1776. De Staël wrote her novel in French, including the spontaneous verses performed by Corinne before audiences (readers were invited to imagine that the French prose was an inferior version of the unknown Italian poems Corinne 'actually' sang). Landon converted the French prose songs from *Corinne; or Italy* into iambic pentameter verse in English for an 1833 translation of de Staël's novel.
25. Esterhammer, 'Spontaneity, Immediacy, and Improvisation', p. 334.
26. Burroughs, *Closet Stages*, p. 19.
27. Landon, 'On the Ancient and Modern Influence of Poetry', in *Critical Writings*, p. 62.
28. Landon, preface to *The Venetian Bracelet, The Lost Pleiad, The History of the Lyre, and Other Poems*, p. 102.
29. Landon, 'A Summer Evening's Tale', in *Poetical Works of Letitia Elizabeth Landon, 'L.E.L.'*, pp. 330–1. This edition of Landon's poems is hereafter abbreviated as *PWL* and cited in the text by title and/or page number.
30. Judith Pascoe observes that Landon is 'more interested in theatrical effect than hortative value' (*Romantic Theatricality*, p. 235). Pascoe's

comment seems inapplicable here. The essay, preface and poem all stress the 'hortative value' that poetry has or at least should have.
31. Landon, *Romance and Reality*, vol. 2, p. 44.
32. Ibid., vol. 2, p. 13.
33. Landon, *Francesca Carrara*, vol. 2, p. 265; vol. 1, p. 113.
34. Ibid., vol. 1, pp. 168–9.
35. Ibid., vol. 1, p. 227.
36. Riess, 'Laetitia Landon and the Dawn of English Post-Romanticism', p. 824; McGann and Riess, introduction to *Letitia Elizabeth Landon: Selected Writings*, p. 23; Mellor, *Romanticism and Gender*, p. 120; and Craciun, *Fatal Women of Romanticism*, p. 242.
37. Michael O'Neill has been the first critic to write at length about the intertextual relationship between Landon and Percy Shelley. His claim is that Landon both 'sympathizes' with and 'qualifies' Shelley's poetry. See his '"Beautiful but Ideal"', p. 211.
38. Landon, 'No. 8. – Isabel Vere', pp. 114–15.
39. Ibid., *Romance and Reality*, vol. 2, p. 242.
40. Ibid., *Francesca Carrara*, vol. 2, p. 265.
41. Keach, *Shelley's Style*, p. 79.
42. Stephenson notes that nineteenth-century readers were quick to identify the 'poet with the poem', especially when the poet was female (*Letitia Landon: The Woman behind L. E. L.*, p. 6).
43. Landon, 'Linmouth', in *Fisher's Drawing Room Scrap-Book, 1833*, pp. 39–40. All subsequent references to particular volumes of *Fisher's Drawing Room Scrap-Book* will be hereafter cited in the text with an 'F', the last two digits of the year of publication and page number(s).
44. Wordsworth, 'The Tables Turned', in *Lyrical Ballads and Other Poems*, p. 83, lines 21–4.
45. Ibid., p. 83, lines 32, 27.
46. Wordsworth, 'Lines Written a Few Miles above Tintern Abbey', in *Lyrical Ballads and Other Poems*, p. 92, lines 77–8.
47. Keats, 'Ode to a Nightingale', in *John Keats: Complete Poems*, pp. 279–80, lines 1, 23, 20, 38–40.
48. Wordsworth, 'Lines Written a Few Miles above Tintern Abbey', in *Lyrical Ballads and Other Poems*, p. 90, lines 24, 26–7.
49. Anon., 'Art. XXIII. – *Fisher's Drawing-Room Scrap-Book*', p. 452.
50. Rowton, *The Female Poets of Great Britain: Chronologically Arranged with Copious Selections and Critical Remarks*, 1853, qtd in Stephen Behrendt, 'Mary Shelley, *Frankenstein*, and the Woman Writer's Fate', p. 77.

51. Landon, *Romance and Reality*, vol. 1, p. 314; vol. 2, p. 119; vol. 3, p. 299.
52. Ibid., vol. 2, p. 118.
53. Landon, *Letters: by Letitia Elizabeth Landon*, pp. 46, 145.
54. Forbes, *Sincerity's Shadow*, p. 47.
55. Emerson, 'Character', p. 98.
56. Ibid., p. 90.

Chapter 7

Character and Paranoia in Beddoes' *Death's Jest-Book* and Peacock's *Crotchet Castle*

In 1829 Thomas Carlyle voiced his concern that the French physiologist Pierre Jean George Cabanis dared to 'la[y] open our moral structure with ... dissecting-knives and real metal probes'.[1] In the same year, Thomas Lovell Beddoes completed his macabre drama *Death's Jest-Book*. Cronin has observed that a young Beddoes went to Germany to conduct 'medical researches ... [in] an unavailing attempt to find physical evidence for the immortality of the soul'.[2] His drama reflects that research. The body in *Death's Jest-Book* is portrayed as 'a machine that even the ghost has deserted'.[3] At one point in the play, the spies of the autocrat Isbrand 'enter human skulls like insects intruding into an abandoned, empty house'. One of the subordinate conclusions that Cronin draws is that the play 'explores ... the idea of masculinity, and finds that it is vacuous, empty of meaning'.[4] I would also say that the idea of character is subject to a similar sense of vacuity in this play. *Death's Jest-Book* suggests that if 'character' refers exclusively to a result of organised matter (immanentism), it is an insufficient medium, or grounding principle, of experience; and that if, moreover, it refers to a vital force superadded to the body (transcendentalism or vitalism), it is likewise insufficient or constrictive. The play, in fact, may be read as one long, desperate scratching against the walls imposed by all such 'human' concepts.

There has been a recent resurgence of interest in the 'self-styled anatomist poet' and dramatist Thomas Lovell Beddoes, nephew to the Irish novelist Maria Edgeworth, devotee of Percy Shelley and author of the play *Death's Jest-Book,* completed in 1829 but not published until 1850. Several studies on Beddoes have appeared in the past twenty years, including a substantial collection of his poems edited by Susan Wolfson and Peter Manning (2003); a modern reprint of the 1829 *Death's Jest Book* edited by Michael Bradshaw (2003); the world premier of the play scripted by Jerome McGann and directed by Frederick Burwick at UCLA, Grasmere and New York with a full orchestra (2003); the *Ashgate Research Companion to Thomas Lovell Beddoes* (2007); *Science, Politics and Friendship in the Works of Thomas Lovell Beddoes* (2012), a book-length examination of his entire corpus by Ute Berns; and several article-length studies.

Many Beddoes scholars examine his plays in light of his radical politics or his study of human anatomy and life sciences in Germany in the 1820s and 1830s. I am interested in the ways that his major work, *Death's Jest-Book*, interrogates the concept and implications of 'character', whether it is considered primarily as a physiological or as a metaphysical structure. Burwick has noted that, as a trained anatomist, Beddoes 'believed man was fully determined by physical nature and his own physical being'.[5] Such beliefs, however, are not always comfortably maintained in creative texts. The play seems both to acknowledge character as the product of material organisation and to dramatise its dissolution as such. Its dramatis personae seek freedom from determination – from both material and immaterial centredness. They imagine or claim to experience instances of being invisible, characterless, unmade, reborn or recreated perpetually as new species. Neither human body nor human soul is a medium of experience amenable to the demands of the imagination. In one instance in the play, the tyrant Isbrand finds his human will too limiting and claims to have invented another, superior will to control his original one. He and others in the drama rebel against humanness, containment, structurality, a moral universe run by laws, imagining instead a Dionysian state of being without any clear sense of a 'self' or its – to use Hegel's terms – personal and executive aspects of character.

Beddoes was the second child of the physician and author Dr Thomas Beddoes, who was supposed to have 'educated his children in comparative anatomy with displays and dissections of human and animal bodies'.[6] He took his degree at Oxford and achieved recognition for his Jacobean drama *The Brides' Tragedy* (1822), but soon sank into literary obscurity. He emigrated from England in 1825 to study physiology, surgery and chemistry at Göttingen University in Germany. In 1829 he completed his five-act play *Death's Jest-Book, or, The Fool's Tragedy*, and probably would have published it then had not his friends Bryan Waller Procter, Thomas Forbes Kelsall and J. G. H. Bourne strongly objected to its indecency. Depressed and expelled from Göttingen for several bouts of intemperance, Beddoes went on to earn his doctor of medicine degree at Würzburg in 1831. Around this time he became involved in the Burschenschaft movement for a united Germany. He visited England briefly in 1846–7 and returned afterwards to Frankfurt. In 1848 he tried to commit suicide by opening an artery in his leg in the Cigogne Hotel in Basel, developed gangrene and had his leg amputated. His second suicide attempt (probably by curare) in 1849 was successful.

The characters in *Death's Jest-Book* maintain a peculiar habit of trying to un-write or un-constitute themselves as characters. To some extent critics have acknowledged this feature of the play.[7] O'Neill argues that the *dramatis personae* 'long to lose their egos in the larger world of death'.[8] Burwick claims that the 'boundaries between life and death are repeatedly challenged in the play, particularly when the knight Sir Wolfram suggests that 'an organism is maintained by a constant process of cellular replacement, as cells die and new cells are generated'.[9] Nat Leach comes closest to our own point of view when he argues that the 'depthless characters' in *Death's Jest Book* 'play out a series of roles unrelated to any essential identity as Beddoes parodies the kind of attempt to reduce character to a knowable essence typified by [Joanna] Baillie's "Introductory Discourse"'. According to Leach, Beddoes parodies the tyrant Isbrand when Isbrand attempts to 'reduce the encounter with the Other to the status of knowledge'.[10] Such an attempt seems foolish to the duke Melveric, for instance, for whom one can 'never hope to learn the alphabet,/ In which the hieroglyphic human soul/ More changeably is painted than the rainbow' (*DJB*, III, ii, 93–5). Melveric 'insists on the alterity of character ... not [as] a transcendent essence but an unreadable materiality resistant to the anatomizing gaze'.[11] I fully agree with Leach that Beddoes parodies the reduction of character to some kind of knowable 'essence'. But I also think that the play is up to something even more radical than denying character's knowability (though it does this). *Death's Jest-Book* loosens the conceptual ligatures that 'character' and all such customary 'human-nature' words establish over time. Perhaps human character refers strictly to a 'materiality' – something inscribed on the body though unreadable – or perhaps it does not. Maybe it is simply striking that a word with so much cultural capital has so dramatically unreliable a referent. The play expresses these doubts. It also addresses the problem that to accept some version of the concept of character is to accept whatever ideological baggage happens to come along with that version.

The play's opening lines introduce the idea of metamorphosis: 'Am I a man of gingerbread that you should mould me to your liking?' (*DJB*, I, i, 1–2.) The speaker is Homunculus Mandrake, a jester who is interested in alchemy and works for quack-doctor. Mandrake is on the verge of leaving both his profession and his native Italian town of Ancona, and setting out for Egypt with Sir Wolfram to rescue the duke Melveric, who has been captured by pagans during a trip to Jerusalem. Egypt, for Mandrake, has intellectual advantages: 'There . . . in that Sphynx land', he claims, 'they made the roads with the philosopher's stone. There be wise crocodiles whose daughters are more cunning than the witches of Lapland'. The soon-to-be dictator Isbrand (disguised at the onset of the play as another court fool) enters the scene and, overhearing Mandrake, indulges Mandrake's new resolve ironically: 'how art thou transmuted!', Isbrand tells him; 'thou commencest philosopher' (*DJB*, I, i, 23–6; I, i, 35, 52).

When Mandrake asks his friend Kate whether people really think of him as a 'man of gingerbread', he implies that no other person or persons can rightfully 'mould' *him* into a 'zany' against his will (*DJB*, I, i, 7). He feels he can become a master of alchemy in Egypt if he so chooses. It is telling that the phrase 'man of gingerbread' can mean an 'unsubstantial' person: in a literal sense, this is just what Mandrake becomes in the second act.[12] During his sea-voyage back from Egypt, a pot containing the 'oil of invisibility' (which Mandrake himself concocted there) falls on his body, 'bath[ing] him from head to foot'. His servant-boy, having arrived in Italy ahead of his master, tells Mandrake's friends of the incident in advance. They decide to mock Mandrake when he arrives by pretending not to see him. Feigning to hear his voice but not to see his body, they soon convince the jester-turned-alchemist that he has, indeed, become invisible: 'I am no Mandrake', he cries, 'I am nothing'. For the rest of the play he continues to process his 'new state' with limited success:

> Well, what is, is, and what is not, is not; and I am not what I was – for I am what I was not; I am no more, for I am no more: I am no matter . . . and nobody at all, but poor Mandrake's pure essence.

It is unclear what Mandrake means by 'pure essence'. Does he imagine that he is a ghost (there are more than one in this play), or possibly what Sir Wolfram refers to as a 'hieroglyphic human soul' disembodied? Mandrake is unsure. Later he calls himself an 'amateur goblin' and a 'young angel, as yet unfledged' (*DJB*, II, i, 81–2, 149; II, ii, 53–7, 91, 96–7). What is important is that his language has a probing, punning, postmodern edge to it that undermines the metaphysics of presence in spite of the phrase 'pure essence', which becomes drained of its conventional meaning by the equivocal language that precedes and follows it. 'I cannot possibly be what I was', Mandrake reasons, 'since I am something altogether different now. And yet I am (quantitatively) no more than what I was, because I am (exist) no more. I am no matter (I have no body and I have no significance)'. The pure essence into which he has supposedly transformed becomes a laboured construct unravelled in the process of its formulation. Christopher Moylan observes that Mandrake is a practically inconceivable being, describing him in Lacanian terms as 'visible-invisible, alive-dead, piebald and hermaphroditic . . . a monstrous and uncategorizable otherness, an appearance from something beyond the symbolic order'.[13]

That Mandrake becomes 'invisible' to others makes sense in the context of the play and particularly with respect to his name. When, in Egypt, his servant asks him whether he will apply the invisibility balsam on himself, he responds: 'Who would ever lose sight of himself? 'Tis scarce possible nowadays' (*DJB*, I, iv, 27–8). He seems to mean that no one would ever choose to be invisible, but only because there is no reliable way to attempt it. If there were, one could certainly be persuaded to free himself from the 'sight of himself' – 'scarce possible' but, on some level, desirable. His Christian name 'Homunculus' can mean 'a diminutive man'.[14] The surname 'Mandrake' can refer to the Mediterranean plant credited with medicinal properties, used as an aid in conception and supposed to have a human-shaped root that shrieks when uprooted. It can also refer to 'the root of white bryony, *Bryonia dioica*, as formerly cut into the shape of a mandrake root and so called in order to deceive people into buying it for medicinal purposes'.[15] The second definition is in keeping with Mandrake's work in the nostrum business (what he refers to as 'retail conjuring'); he might have actually marketed white bryony root as mandrake root at some point (*DJB*, I, iv, 6). Hence his name suggests diminution, insubstantiality and deceit. Even before he is rendered 'invisible' to his friends he is already cast as a sort of inessential being, or present absence. The opening lines of *Death's Jest-Book* are also redolent of the reform-era March of Mind (discussed in more detail below), to the extent that Mandrake is the rough equivalent of a working-class individual who aspires to transcend class and 'character' through the acquisition of increasingly available scientific knowledge.

Several characters in the play experience or claim to experience the sensation of being dissolved, unmade, remade; of moving beyond bodily or metaphysical structures (ego, soul, character, essence, presence, absence). In most cases the sensation is pleasurable and has quasi-religious undertones. The beautiful Sibylla, beloved of both Wolfram and Melveric, identifies her sleep and awakening on the African coast as a sort of death and rebirth: '[a]s one who doth go down unto the springs/ Of his existence and there bathed, I come/ Regenerate up into the world again' (*DJB*, I, ii, 65–7). When Wolfram arrives in Egypt to rescue the captive duke Melveric, the latter is so thrilled that he feels as if he is experiencing powerful emotions for the first time. He calls 'Joy' and 'Gratitude'

> silly hypocrites:
> They understand me not; and my soul, dazzled,
> Stares on the unknown feelings that now crowd it,
> Knows none of them, remembers none, counts none,
> More than a newborn child in its first hour.
>
> (*DJB*, I, ii, 162–3, 164–8)

The night before he plans to overthrow the dukedom of Ancona, Isbrand considers himself on the verge of a new state of existence: 'Tomorrow, with what pity and contempt,/ Shall I look back new-born upon myself!' (*DJB*, IV, iv, 23–4). On the following day he appears to have transformed himself from a mere 'm[a]n of muscle' into a Nietzschean overman:

> I found that first
> I was but half created; that a power
> Was wanting in my soul to be its soul,
> And this was mine to make. Therefore I fashioned
> A will above my will, that plays upon it,
> As the first soul doth use in men and cattle.
>
> (*DJB*, V, i, 47, 49–54)

All three examples of rebirth use similar language – regenerate, new-born – though in very different contexts. Sibylla associates virtual rebirth with profound rest and refreshment; Melveric with experiencing emotions as if for the first time; Isbrand with newfound political and psychological power. For Isbrand, ordinary men and animals are controlled ('play[ed] upon') by their souls, in what he considers a 'half created' state of existence. His own soul was no different than theirs before his political empowerment. But as a dictator he has forged a 'will above [his] will' and a second, more powerful soul, a soul-within-a-soul that could reign over the first and place him on a superior ontological stratum. All three accounts of rebirth suggest a desire to overreach, to escape confinement in the actual, to out-nature nature.

Perhaps the most dramatic 'transformation' occurs after a remorseful Athulf (son of the usurped duke Melveric) kills his brother Adalmar over a woman in the penultimate act. In his grief, Athulf experiences an astonishing metamorphosis:

> What's going on in my heart and in my brain,
> My bones, my life, all over me, all through me?
> It cannot last. No longer shall I be
> What I am now. Oh! I am changing, changing,
> Dreadfully changing! Even here and now
> A transformation will o'ertake and seize me.
> It is God's sentence whispered over me.
> I am unsouled, dishumanized, uncreated;
> My passions swell and grow like human beasts conceived;
> My feet are fixing roots, and every limb

> Is billowy and gigantic, till I seem
> A wild old wicked mountain in the sea
> ...
> I break, and magnify, and lose my form.
>
> (*DJB* IV, iii, 356–67, 376)

Unlike the previous examples of rebirth, in which a character becomes newly human or newly more-than-human, this transformation suggests an endlessly deferred ontological state – a state of endless becoming, reinforced by the confusion of grammatical tenses. There is the repetition of the present progressive tense ('I am changing, changing,/ Dreadfully changing!'); the future tense qualified by adverbs denoting present space and time (a 'transformation will o'ertake' him 'here and now'); the simple present ('My passions swell and grow'); and so on. The imagery is chaotic and inconclusive. If Melveric felt that he was experiencing human feelings as an infant does – feelings unsatisfactorily captured by the 'hypocritical' signifiers 'joy' and 'gratitude' – Athulf feels as if passions are conceiving themselves and growing inside him like 'human beasts'. In vivid, Ovidian imagery, his feet are identified with roots, his limbs with giant waves and his state of being with a 'wicked mountain in the sea'. This is a strange image. What is a wicked mountain? How strongly should we read in this passage an allusion to the mountain that Christ claimed could be cast into the sea through the power of faith? In these lines, Athulf is not the pious caster but the thing cast; not the faithful agent but the mute inglorious object. Athulf construes his transformation as a divine punishment for fratricide: he calls himself 'damned before [his] time' (*DJB*, IV, iii, 379). Read in the immediate context of the murder, the transformation can be understood in this way. But read in the context of the entire play, the passage implies that Athulf on some level desired or was internally driven to his 'punishment', his dissolution. He murders his brother Adalmar immediately after Adalmar saves his life; and, standing over the corpse, feels that his existence has come to a sort of tranquil climax:

> I know not whether I have slept,
> Or wandered through a dreary cavernous forest,
> Struggling with monsters. 'Tis a quiet place,
> And one inviting strangely to deep rest.
> I have forgotten something; my whole life
> Seems to have vanished from me to this hour.
>
> (*DJB*, IV, iii, 335–40)

With fraternal blood still on his blade, Athulf finds himself in a 'quiet' and 'inviting' place of post-homicidal repose. The 'something' he has forgotten seems to be life itself, eclipsed at once by a single action. In an instant, life has become an insignificant prelude to the peace of quiet confusion and impending dissolution.

Most critics who discuss *Death's Jest-Book* draw special attention to a 45-line song sung by Isbrand in the third act, named after its first line: 'Squats on a toad-stool under a tree', or just 'Squats on a toad-stool'. This is the song that drew particular hostility from the friends (Procter, Kelsall and Bourne) to whom Beddoes sent his play. The poem is sung by something like an unborn foetus – a 'bodiless childfull of life in the gloom' – who is trying to decide as a member of what species he would like to enter existence. He tells us that his 'mother killed [him]/ Scarcely alive in her wicked womb' and asks, 'What shall I be?' He imagines entering the world as a crocodile, a hog, a serpent, a nightingale, a camel and a duck until finally he settles on the unimaginable:

> 'I'll be a new bird with the head of an ass,
>   Two pigs' feet, two men's feet, and two of a hen;
> Devil-winged; dragon-bellied; grave-jawed, because grass
>   Is a beard that's soon shaved, and grows seldom again
>   Before it is summer; so cow all the rest;
>   The new Dodo is finished. O! come to my nest'.
>   (*DJB*, III, iii, 323, 325–7, 362–7)

According to Burwick, the poem suggests that 'no harmonious order of man and universe is taken for granted'.[16] O'Neill claims that the song 'celebrates, with a grim desperate wit, the inescapability of the entrapment within the physical'.[17] Berns argues that the speaker 'insists on self-creation in an emphatic if not triumphant sense that celebrates the grotesque as defiance'.[18] According to Moylan, the voice of the poem

> decides . . . to escape from the symbolic order into a place where something can be created from nothing, and nothing created from something. That is, the choice is not to chose, not to settle for an illusory form of closure . . . Identity establishes itself not through affirmation, but through erasure and effacement.[19]

I disagree with O'Neill that the poem '*celebrates* . . . the inescapability of entrapment within the physical' (emphasis added). The poem seems to 'celebrate' nothing. Anyone who is created (whether by himself, a supernatural being or a natural process) is subject to the limitations of creatureliness: finitude, linear development, embodiment, organisation. Isbrand would avoid not only physical but metaphysical containment: avoid recognising himself, that is, as what Derrida calls a centred structure – a metaphysical structure with a 'center' that 'orient[s]' and 'organize[s]' it. That centre – which, in the case of 'Squats on a toad-stool', may be called consciousness, character, essence and so on, 'limit[s]' the '*play*' of the 'elements' within the structure even as it 'permit[s]' that play.[20] Isbrand would have the impossible: he would be a structure both with and without a centre, an infinitely deferred being that somehow possesses or has access to a single consciousness.

This is what he *would* be; but what is he actually? Berns calls him a 'fundamental, protean and indestructible' life-force 'whose range includes the movement out of dead and into new living bodies'.[21] But if he is such a 'life-force' he still has a consciousness (a pure force cannot sing a song). And if he has a consciousness he must at least resemble a structure that is centred in some principle. However we define and delimit the state of existence that Isbrand imagines in this song, he seems to privilege that elusive state over one that is comparatively determinable or finite. He is not upset because he is less than substantial (a 'childfull of life') or even because he was murdered: he cries out because he must continue in a cycle of physical and metaphysical (re)incarnation. His temporary disembodiment has encouraged him to desire an existence beyond not only bodiliness but structurality itself. The song suggests that the more closely one can identify – however elusively – with a state of pure freeplay or potentiality, the freer he or she is from the shackles of structurality. Notice that the speaker does not call the mother 'wicked', but her 'womb'. This is more than a transferred epithet. The womb in this song suggests determination, delimitation, the formation of a discrete and organised being whose physicality brings with it immutable laws and limitations. It forces upon the speaker an origin, a derivation.

The singer refers to himself as a '[p]oor unborn ghost'. The *OED* gives the word 'unborn' three basic meanings: 1) 'still to be born'; 2) 'deprived of birth' and 3) 'existing without having been born'.[22] All three meanings are relevant here in fascinating ways. The second meaning is most clearly present: the speaker is un-born or has been 'deprived of birth' because his 'mother killed [him]/ Scarcely alive in her wicked womb'. But the other two meanings are subtlety interwoven with this one. That the speaker must, and is soon to be, born again (meaning number one) causes him anxiety and frustration. So does the fact that he might – in an ideal world – have 'exist[ed] without having been born' (meaning number three), a definition the OED draws exclusively from Percy Shelley's verse drama *Hellas* (1822), which Beddoes – verse dramatist, admirer of Shelley and guarantor for the publication of Shelley's *Posthumous Poems* in 1824 – most likely read. In *Hellas*, the wandering Jew Ahasuerus advises the Turkish sultan Mahmud, who laments his doomed Ottoman Empire, to 'look on that which cannot change – the One,/ The unborn and the undying'. By these phrases Ahasuerus means 'thought'. Thought alone, he claims, is the 'cradle and . . . grave' of all things; thought is 'the stuff whence mutability can weave/ All that it hath dominion o'er, worlds, worms,/ Empires, and superstitions – what has thought/ To do with time or place or circumstance?'[23] In these lines, thought is like the Power behind Shelley's Mont Blanc: pure contingency or causality. Isbrand's speaker identifies with the 'unborn' stuff of the material Universe: he would exist beyond time, place and circumstance, only he would prefer (because he knows nothing different) to maintain his consciousness in the process. To pass from consciousness without a strong physical or metaphysical centre, to an embodied being tied to language and linear development, is a grave descent.

The main question becomes: is there any good reason why this speaker refuses the bodies of whole creatures and elects instead to become a sort of grotesque hybrid with the name of an extinct species – the Dodo? He admits, after all, that it would be 'pleasant to need no shirt, breeches or shoe' like the snake, that a camel has a 'beautiful back' and that the natural cry of the duck is 'music' (*DJB*, III, iii, 350, 359–60). So his aversion to these creatures seems *less about the disadvantages peculiar to a given species* and more about *the unfreedom inherent in organisation itself*. He ultimately selects (or at least fancies) a creature whose existence and anatomical structure are barely imaginable. In creating the form of this 'new Dodo', he is not so much romanticising the hybrid for the hybrid's sake, as using it to mock the fact that existence is conceivable only in and through structures – linguistic, anatomic, metaphysical. Bodiliness, as well as the 'character' or 'temperament' or 'organising principle' that seems to result from the balance of biological elements, may be facts of life to Beddoes the anatomist, but to this speaker they are 'facts' that invite imaginative reconstruction and revaluation. Furthermore, a metaphysical existence is not the opposite of a physical one insofar as it achieves purity or truth or freedom. It is the counterpart of a physical existence insofar as it replaces material limitations (physical structures) with immaterial limitations (metaphysical structures).

Crotchet Castle (1831) is the sixth novel published anonymously by Thomas Love Peacock, written after a decade of rapid social and political reform. In 1826 Lord Brougham helped found the Society for the Diffusion of Useful Knowledge (SDUK). Information was becoming increasingly available to a widening reading public in the form of encyclopaedias such as the *London* and the *Cabinet*; sixpenny treatises on practical and scientific topics promulgated by the Library of Useful Knowledge; John Murray's *Family Library* series (1829–34), which produced cheap versions of nonfiction works; Constable's *Miscellany*, responsible for the mass publication of fiction and works of popular history; and more. London University (later called University College London) was founded in 1826 to make higher education widely available to persons of any creed (and therefore called the 'godless' institution of Gower Street).[24] The Political Economy Club, the Birmingham Political Union and the Ultra Tories were all active organisations in the late 1820s and early 1830s. Whig reformers and radicals sympathetic to working-class education enabled new ideas to be spread on an unprecedented scale and rate. Alan Rauch refers to 'the rapid growth of periodicals, encyclopedias, and societies promoting knowledge' in the early nineteenth century as the 'knowledge industry'.[25]

Crotchet Castle was caught in the middle of this campaign to spread useful knowledge to the masses. As a so-called novel of ideas, it targets not so much the content of a given idea (although ideas about educational reform and political economy are directly satirised), as the irrational tenacity with which a single idea may be held at the exclusion of others. In *Crotchet Castle*, opinions become personal fixations or *crotchets* – 'perverse conceit[s] . . . held by an individual in opposition to common opinion'.[26] Peacock found the reform-era March of Mind disagreeable because it tended to spread singular ideas without assigning them a degree of relative importance within the larger scheme of things. Its 'Whig insistence on educating the mind' and its focus on the 'material condition' of a person instead of 'the whole man' seemed to make – for intellectuals like Peacock – a little knowledge a dangerous thing.[27] *Crotchet Castle* is in some sense an elegiac text that laments the loss of what Matthew Arnold called the 'harmonious expansion of *all* the powers which make the beauty and worth of human nature'.[28] Like Schiller, Coleridge, De Quincey and others, Peacock reinforces the fact that the Greeks 'were wedded to all the delights of art and all the dignity of wisdom, without however, like us, falling a prey to their seduction'.[29] While the ancients preferred intellectual well-roundedness and spontaneity of mind, the era of reform increasingly privileged specialised, disciplinary knowledge.

In a narrative focusing on the increasing proliferation of new ideas, it seems appropriate that the men and women who hold these ideas should be treated as nonentities, vehicles for crotchets. They hardly appear as individuals who assimilate these crotchets into structured personal contexts or linear histories. For the Reverend Dr Folliott (the most likely mouthpiece for Peacock), a parson, gourmand and expert classicist, the possibility of human characterlessness moves gradually into sharper focus and becomes an object of paranoia. As if to alleviate this paranoia, Folliott perpetually refers to his own body, which seems solely responsible for reminding him that he exists. His physicality, appetites, tastes and choice of entrees often interrupt the cerebral dinner conversations he has with his friends. References to his body and habits of consumption assure readers (and himself) that Folliott exists as his own being and has not mysteriously slipped into the identity of one of the other guests. And I would say that the latter is a real danger in *Crotchet Castle*. The reverend clings to his own bodiliness in a diegetic atmosphere in which the characters of individualised, legible, narrativised beings are being buried under free-floating ideas.

Folliott is a relatively well-defined figure in *Crotchet Castle*. Most other men and women in the novel resemble what Douglas Hewitt calls 'types' and Dodson considers faceless allegories: each one is eclipsed by his or her respective crotchet.[30] The eponymous Ebenezer Mac Crotchet (owner of Crotchet Castle) is the one figure in the novel who is not preoccupied by a single idea. The son of a Jewish mother and Scottish father, Mac Crotchet decides 'to obliterate alike the Hebrew and Caledonian vestiges in his name, and sig[n] himself E. M. Crotchet, which by degrees induced the majority of his neighbours to think that his name was Edward Matthew'.[31] This may sound like quixotic self-fashioning, but Crotchet is neither a self nor the vessel of an idea so much as a point of departure. He is important primarily as the owner of the castle where other crotchety figures come to discuss the topics of the day. His friend Folliott, on the other hand, receives the most attention in the novel. Folliott, 'more than any other character, is associated with food and drink', so that 'our sense of his identity comes more from a feeling of his physical presence'.[32] Said differently, his 'central role is to bring the airy nonsense back to reality, the falsely spiritual back to solid truth, and metaphysical nonsense back to pragmatic sense'.[33] According to Richard Kane, 'Dr. Folliott's physical self frequently obstructs the full expression of his spiritual self'. This is meant to be humorous, since 'a person becomes laughable every time he or part of him gives us the impression of being a thing'. Even 'the mind itself' can 'too can easily harden into grooves and inelastic patterns of thought that often become absurd in their incongruity to a mobile and flexible society'.[34] I would add that Folliott is wonderfully paradoxical because he is the foremost proponent of the life of the mind, the free play of the intellect, and yet he is also a glutton who can never quite carry on a conversation without his appetite interrupting it indefinitely.

The parson believes that education is beneficial only to people who are 'naturally' intelligent. It can do nothing for the congenitally dull (the majority of persons) except reinforce their stupidity. He claims that

> as for the human mind, I deny that it is the same in all men. I hold that there is every variety of natural capacity from the idiot to Newton and Shakespeare; the mass of mankind, midway between these extremes, being blockheads of different degrees; education leaving them pretty nearly as it found them, with this single difference, that it gives a fixed direction to their stupidity, a sort of incurable wry neck to the thing they call their understanding. (CC, p. 156)

One reason that a polished classicist like Dr Folliott would hold this opinion is that the education of the masses represented a real political and personal threat to respectable English gentlemen during the reform era. Conservative thinkers like Folliott feared that the diffusers of knowledge conspired 'to teach tradesmen the classics and, worse, foment revolution among the working class, who – newly literate and inquiring – would press for an even wider extension of the franchise than that currently being canvassed in parliament'.[35] But the passage also insists on a certain intellectual essentialism. Folliott argues that there are measurable gradations of intellectual capacities because he wants to believe that physical organisation and the mental aptitudes it entails are reassuringly fixed at birth. In order to reinforce this point, he aligns, metaphorically, the questionable (less quantifiable) idea of mental character with the unquestionable (more quantifiable) reality of the body.

He divides the world into idiots, blockheads and geniuses. Blockheads ('the mass of mankind') are born in varying states of 'stupidity' that education can only harden, giving 'a sort of incurable wry neck to the thing they call their understanding'. (A wry neck is a 'deformity characterized by contortion of the neck and face, and lateral inclination of the head', associated with the bird '*Iynx torquilla*, distinguished by its habit of writhing the neck and head'.)[36] Folliott images the common understanding as a body part bent awry at birth, a physical reality, a 'thing'. Education has no choice but to leave it in its deformed position – making it even it less susceptible to the straightening that knowledge theoretically provides. Interestingly, the metaphor implies that the understandings of the Newtons and Shakespeares of the world are also fixed capacities analogous to things, necks born upright, to whose unalterable rigour and brilliance education gives only 'a fixed direction'. In both cases, Folliott conceives of the human understanding metaphorically as a part of the human anatomy or an object, unchangeable in form and capable only of being fixed in what ever direction it happens to point. He describes what is immaterial and abstract in terms of what is material and concrete.

Folliott clings to bodiliness and body-centred explanations of mental phenomena because the physical and psychological contours of the men and women in *Crotchet Castle* are all but invisible. Peacock provides no physiognomical indices to their characters; they are conspicuously made of discourse. One striking incident in the novel that has received little to no attention is the attempted robbery of the parson by a pair of ruffians, who appear immediately after Folliott experiences a terrifying vision of Mr Eavesdrop. Lady Clarinda first mentions Mr Eavesdrop as 'a sort of bookseller's tool, [who] coins all his acquaintance in reminiscences and sketches of character. I am very shy of him, for fear that he should print me'. Her interlocutor, Captain Fitzchrome, agrees that Eavesdrop is a 'very dangerous' man (*CC*, p. 161). He is dangerous on a basic level because he can print disreputable or skewed portraits of friends and acquaintances to entertain the masses. He is dangerous on a deeper level because the character sketches he writes for the press have as solid a claim to facticity, in the insubstantial world of *Crotchet Castle*, as the supposed personal characters secreted away in the depths of individuals.

In this regard, *Crotchet Castle* both shapes and is shaped by its historical context. The reform era was, after all, a time when newspapers could 'authenticate' the 'existence' of fashionable (and unfashionable) people.[37] It was a time when 'identity [could] only be secured in print', when there was 'no space so deeply interior that it [could] escape the empire of the printed word'.[38] The topos of the feared 'moral anatomist', especially in the capacity of a professional character-sketcher, seems to have flourished if not formed during this period. The author of an 1826 article in the *Literary Chronicle* called 'Character-Painting', for instance, worriedly references a recent publication in two quarto volumes by the British publisher William Miller – *Biographical Sketches of British Characters Recently Deceased, Commencing with the Accession of George the Fourth, with a list of their Engraved Portraits* (1826). The author of 'Character-Painting' expresses his or her 'fear of becoming a subject for the dissecting pen of such a moral anatomist as Mr. Miller'.[39]

Eavesdrop is one such 'moral anatomist as Mr. Miller'. In the context of *Crotchet Castle*, however, his scalpel threatens to reach beyond the characters of individuals and to scratch the very concept of character itself. But to return to the robbery: one night Dr Folliott is walking home alone to his vicarage, when

> [p]resently the image of Mr Eavesdrop, with a printed sketch of the Reverend Doctor F., presented itself before him, and he [that is, Folliott] began mechanically to flourish his bamboo. The movement

was prompted by his good genius, for the uplifted bamboo received the blow of a ponderous cudgel, which was intended for his head. (*CC*, p. 192)

The cudgel belongs to one of two robbers who emerge suddenly in the darkness. Folliott begins thrashing them with his bamboo walking stick. One of the robbers is killed by a ricocheted bullet and the other is wounded. The parson threatens the wounded man mercilessly: 'I will disable you in all your members; I will cotund you . . . I will beat you to a jelly, and I will then roll you into the ditch'. Later he asks the rogue left alive whether he had intended to 'manufacture [Folliott] into a subject, for the benefit of science' – that is, to sell the parson's body to surgeons for dissection and anatomical instruction – and whether the robber was 'marching with a detachment of the march of mind' (*CC*, pp. 192–3). The culprit pleads his innocence to both of these charges. Eventually he escapes, carrying the body of his dead comrade along with him. The next morning, Folliott rejoices that he is not, 'at this moment, lying on the table of some flinty-hearted anatomist, who would have sliced and disjointed me as unscrupulously as I do these remnants of the capon and chine' (*CC*, p. 194).

The attempted robbery is interesting because it is given a significant amount of attention in a novel without much of a plot. Why is it here at all? Is it only a topical allusion to the recent murders of Burke and Hare, whose victims provided the Edinburgh surgeon Robert Knox with dissection material for his anatomy lectures? Or does it dig deeper than the strictly topical? What is strange about the incident is that the character-sketcher Mr Eavesdrop appears in a vision to Folliott immediately before the assault. Why? There is no clear indication that Eavesdrop was present at or responsible for the attempted robbery. Nonetheless, I find it telling that Folliott imagines Eavesdrop, of all figures in the novel, right before he is ambushed by robbers whose employer would likely have 'sliced and disjointed' him 'unscrupulously'. The idea of slicing and disjointing applies not only to the profession of the physical anatomist, but to that of Eavesdrop, the moral anatomist – Eavesdrop slices and dices 'whole' characters to provide popular entertainment. Folliott had earlier accused Eavesdrop of 'publish[ing] a character of your facetious friend, the Reverend Dr. F., wherein you have sketched off me; me, sir, even to my nose and wig. What business have the public with my nose and wig?' When Eavesdrop responds that character-sketching is all in good fun, Folliott is not amused. 'You have dished me up', he complains, 'like a savory omelette, to gratify the appetite of the reading rabble for gossip' (CC, pp. 176–7). This statement reinforces the connection between character-sketchers and anatomists. While Eavesdrop has served Folliott to the public as a 'savory omelette', a hypothetical, 'flinty-hearted anatomist' had nearly sliced him up as 'capon and chine'. Both are invasive acts, treating 'characters' and bodies as commodities sacrificed for the edification of the public. Both character-sketcher and anatomist would 'unscrupulously' murder to dissect, exposing new, potentially uncomfortable truths about inner realities whose survival depends on their not being tampered with.

If the body can be dissected, the 'character' can be vivisected. The parson is threatened with the possibility that the basic elements of his or any character are not safely preserved in or caused by material organisation. Perhaps character itself is nothing more than the epiphenomena of cultural practices like sketches for the press. Folliott *does* believe that the body is unambiguously real. Hence, he feels that to 'disable' and 'cotund' and 'beat' and 'roll' his thieving assailant are the surest means of knocking some sense into him. But although he may have reason to doubt the substantial existence of an internal 'character', he is not prepared to deny that existence altogether simply because it is imperceptible by the senses. He would rather preserve the idea to the last as a familiar source of pride and security. Eavesdrop is especially unsettling to the parson because he holds an unwelcome truth in his hands, not in the form of *a* character of Folliott – an unflattering verbal sketch, a skewed copy of a hidden original – but *the* character of Folliott. The vision of Eavesdrop before the assault hints at a new paradigm according to which the firm principle of character (Hazlitt's 'original bias') is susceptible to being exposed, probed, tampered with and discredited by the agents of the March of Mind. Its unquestionable existence as a metaphysical principle or as a reality grounded in physiological organisation has become – like every other idea – subject to reexamination and reform.

Eavesdrop is not the only one in the novel who raises suspicions that character may be no more than Bentham's 'fictitious entity'. There is also the well-to-do Lady Clarinda, sister of Lord Bossnowl and fiancé to the son of E. M. Crotchet. Her second extended appearance in *Crotchet Castle* occurs in a chapter aptly called 'Characters'. She and her admirer, Captain Fitzchrome, are having a long tête-à-tête on a pleasure-boat while the rest of the passengers dine and talk at a distance. Clarinda describes each passenger to the captain in a series of humorous verbal 'sketches'. Dawson suggests that her cynical characterisations are inspired by *The Satyricon* and *Le Misanthrope*.[40] Dodson compares the 'syntactic economy' of her prose to that of Pope's heroic couplets.[41] But Hoff, I think, provides the most compelling account of her 'descriptive technique', which he argues

> resembles a police line-up. She turns the harsh spotlight of her scrutiny on each character, a light so penetrating that it discovers whatever the character most wishes to hide. Consequently her results are like overexposed photographs. The outlines and contrasts are clear, but the subtle shadings are lost.

For Hoff, Clarinda 'forces a *reductio ad absurdum* upon [her] target[s]'. Her 'spotlight . . . of scrutiny' 'penetrat[es]' whole characters in order to uncover and illuminate one of their parts in isolation.'[42]

Hoff's reading is solid, but problematic to the extent that no *reductio ad absurdum* really needs to be 'force[d]' in a novel like *Crotchet Castle*. The men and women at the party may be considered 'reductions' before the fact. They exist as outlines. The 'subtle shadings' that Hoff claims are 'lost' in the accentuation of their 'outlines and contrasts' were never there in the first place. Hence the typological 'spotlight' does not so much reduce or contract 'whole' characters, as illuminate their nonexistence. When Clarinda tells Fitzchrome that a political economist 'has satisfied me that I am a commodity in the market', her comment is relevant in the context of both economic and ethological discourse (CC, p. 162). Clarinda suspects that her own or any other character has never really existed beyond the circulation of textual commodities. She tells the captain that she plans to turn her verbal character-sketches into a fashionable novel, in which

> you may give yourself any character you like, and the newspapers will print it as if it came from themselves. I have commended you to three of our friends here, as an economist, a transcendentalist, and a classical

scholar; and if you wish to be renowned through the world for these, or any other accomplishments, the newspapers will confirm you in their possession for half-a-guinea a piece. (CC, p. 169)

In this excerpt, Clarinda questions the concept of character as a centred structure according to which being is determined as presence, as an 'original or transcendental signified ... absolutely present outside a system of differences'.[43] Character is playfully imagined as 'absent' in the person and 'present' in an infinite array of cultural artifacts that ostensibly derive from it. The *I* who becomes a commodity in the market and the *selves* whose character the newspapers seem to distort are nothing without the cultural forms that enable their emergence in the first place. Character and consciousness are viewed as synthetic artifacts of culture. Hence Clarinda need not be read as an opportunistic essentialist who would exploit 'real' characters to newspapers for profit. She is not selling lies as truths, so much as decentring Truth. Clarinda suggests that the 'character', say, of Folliott refers not to a real presence in an individual but to a signifier whose signifieds remain in an unlimited state of free play.

Notes

1. Carlyle, ['Signs of the Times'], p. 446.
2. Cronin, *Romantic Victorians*, p. 101.
3. Ibid., p. 104.
4. Ibid., p. 105.
5. Burwick, 'The Anatomy of Revolution', p. 6.
6. Berns and Bradshaw, introduction to *The Ashgate Research Companion to Thomas Lovell Beddoes*, p. 3.
7. All citations of the play are taken from *Death's Jest-Book: The 1829 Text*, ed. Michael Bradshaw (New York: Routledge, 2003); hereafter cited parenthetically in the text as *DJB*.
8. O'Neill, '"The latch-string of a new world's wicket"', p. 36.
9. Burwick, '*Death's Jest-Book* and the Pathological Imagination', p. 105.
10. Leach, 'Between the "Hostile Body"', p. 130.
11. Ibid.
12. 'gingerbread, n.'. Def. 2. *OED Online*. Oxford University Press, December 2014, <http://www.oed.com> (last accessed 22 December 2014).

13. Moylan, 'T. L. Beddoes's Terminable or Interminable End', p. 235.
14. 'homunculus, n.'. *OED Online*. Oxford University Press, December 2014, <http://www.oed.com> (last accessed 22 December 2014). James Allard notes that '"Homunculus" refers to the Jewish mystical notion of "a tiny anthropoid generated during the process of putrefaction of human semen and menstrual blood"' (*Romanticism, Medicine and the Poet's Body*, p. 127).
15. 'mandrake, n.'. Def. 2a. *OED Online*. Oxford University Press, December 2014, <http://www.oed.com> (last accessed 22 December 2014).
16. Burwick, 'The Anatomy of Revolution', p. 5.
17. O'Neill, '"The latch-string of a new world's wicket"', p. 42.
18. Berns, 'Thomas Lovell Beddoes and Johann Friedrich Blumenbach', p. 212.
19. Moylan, 'T. L. Beddoes's Terminable or Interminable End', p. 238.
20. Derrida, *Writing and Difference*, pp. 278–9.
21. Berns, 'Thomas Lovell Beddoes and Johann Friedrich Blumenbach', pp. 206–7.
22. 'unborn, adj.'. Defs 1a, 2 and 3. *OED Online*. Oxford English Dictionary, December 2014, <http://www.oed.com> (last accessed 23 December 2014).
23. Shelley, *Hellas*, pp. 453–4, lines 768–9, 782, 799–802.
24. Ashton, *Victorian Bloomsbury*, p. 21.
25. Rauch, *Useful Knowledge*, p. 23.
26. 'crotchet, n.^{1}'. Def. 9a. *OED Online*. Oxford English Dictionary, December 2014, <http://www.oed.com> (last accessed 23 December 2014).
27. Dodson, introduction to *Nightmare Abbey, The Misfortunes of Elphin and Crotchet Castle*, pp. xvii–xviii.
28. Arnold, *Culture and Anarchy*, p. 62.
29. Schiller, *Letters upon the Aesthetic Education of Man*, p. 98.
30. Hewitt, 'Entertaining Ideas', p. 201; and Dodson, introduction to *Nightmare Abbey, The Misfortunes of Elphin and Crotchet Castle*, p. x.
31. Peacock, *Crotchet Castle*, in *Nightmare Abbey/Crochet Castle*, ed. Raymond Wright (New York: Penguin, 1986), p. 128; hereafter cited parenthetically in the text as *CC*.
32. Hewitt, 'Entertaining Ideas', p. 208.
33. Hoff, 'The Voices of Crotchet Castle', p. 194.
34. Kane, 'Bergsonian Comic Theory', pp. 40, 42.
35. Ashton, *Victorian Bloomsbury*, p. 21.
36. 'wryneck, n.'. Defs 3a and 1a. *OED Online*. Oxford English Dictionary, December 2014, <http://www.oed.com> (last accessed 23 December 2014).

37. Cronin, *Romantic Victorians*, p. 118.
38. Cronin, *Paper Pellets*, p. 112.
39. 'Anon.', 'Character-Painting', p. 430.
40. Dawson, *His Fine Wit*, p. 260.
41. Dodson, introduction to *Nightmare Abbey, The Misfortunes of Elphin and Crotchet Castle*, p. xii.
42. Hoff, 'The Voices of *Crotchet Castle*', pp. 190–1.
43. Derrida, *Writing and Difference*, p. 280.

Afterword: Meta-characterisation – Dickens' *Sketches by Boz* and Carlyle's *Sartor Resartus*

The reform era witnessed an explosion of prose genres, many of which have been classified as sub-genres of the novel: the fashionable or silver fork novel, the Irish novel, the Scottish novel, the marine novel, the Newgate novel, the Chartist novel, the historical novel, prose collections of 'sketches of life and character' and so on. Literary texts produced in this period – especially some of the 'sketches of life and character' sort – tend to receive considerably less critical attention (if any) than the 'great achievements of realistic fiction' beginning with the industrial novel.[1] The reasons for this neglect are beyond the scope of this book. Perhaps a lot of reform-era fiction was generally less admired and/or reviewed in its time; perhaps later audiences found its characters too 'flat' and its plots too loosely arranged and often painfully confusing (as any reader of the average silver fork novel may fairly contest); perhaps the stories it told about contemporary politics or culture or social life were less coherent and amenable to the extraction of neat scholarly arguments.[2] Whatever the reasons for its marginalisation, reform-era fiction reveals much about the politics of character and characterisation. It often portrays characterising acts as naturalised modes of social control. Literary discourse in the reform era features what may be called 'meta-characterisation'. It describes, 'enfleshes', 'rounds' fictional characters with an ironic sense of confidence and authority, drawing attention to characterisation as an arbitrary and political act even as it tries to convince readers that the fictional beings in the text are possible or probable representations of living beings in the world.

The narrative plots in Dickens' *Sketches by Boz* are often hinged by instances of meta-characterisation. *Sketches* began in 1833 with a few essays and stories published in magazines and newspapers. These were increased and collected twice in 1836 (in the 'First Series' and 'Second Series') until they were all gathered and published as *Sketches by Boz* in 1839. *Sketches* is interesting as narrative discourse for several reasons. The obvious one is that it resembles a conventional novel in length and style (the same narrator seems to tell all the stories) but makes no pretensions to being one (there are few recurring characters or later references to earlier plots). Another that its fifty-six prose portraits of London life are divided rather loosely into four groups – 'Seven Sketches from Our Parish', 'Scenes', 'Characters' and 'Tales' – so that, say, a given 'Scene' or 'Character' does not seem structurally very different from a given 'Tale'. Still another is that the characters in *Sketches* acquire meaning more as incitements to virtuosic acts of description, than as 'round' psychological essences or 'flat' functionaries in a plot. Both the (paradigmatic) content and the (syntagmatic) function of who or what is represented give way to representing representation itself as a political and problematic act (just as, as I argued earlier, Scott's and Lamb's texts did). This way of reading *Sketches* somewhat qualifies Lynch's claim that 'the last two decades of the eighteenth century . . . worked to validate and naturalize a concept of character *as* representational'.[3] *Sketches* emphasises the 'instabilities and ironies of representation' despite the increasing insistence, on the part of contemporary readers and writers, that 'round' characters in narrative texts represent 'round' moral-constitutive characters in life.[4] *Sketches* portrays 'representation' as a special (a culturally cherished) kind of 'performance', and as the 'authority vested in personation', Dickens 'cedes to the epistemological and moral ambiguity of role-playing'.[5]

The narrative voice of *Sketches* belongs technically, or at least nominally, to 'Boz'. He can present to the reader as little or as much of his London as he alone sees fit and how he sees fit. In giving his narrator a name, Dickens immediately establishes a sense of distance between his authorial persona (AP) and Boz. This distance affords the AP occasional opportunities to compromise or ironise what Boz has to say about life in London – however often, to whatever extent or by whatever methods the AP feels it useful or necessary. At one point in *Sketches*, Boz observes that '[w]e are very fond of speculating as we walk through a street, on the character . . . of the people who inhabit it'. If these people happen to be unavailable for observation, one need only examine the knockers on their doors:

> The various expressions of the human countenance afford a beautiful and interesting study; but there is something in the physiognomy of street-door knockers, almost as characteristic, and nearly as infallible . . . between the man and his knocker, there will inevitably be a greater or less degree of resemblance and sympathy. (*SB*, p. 58)

According to Boz, a hospitable person tends to have a 'large round' knocker 'with the jolly face of a convivial lion', while a prig is likely to have 'a little pert Egyptian knocker, with a long thin face, a pinched up nose, and a very sharp chin'. '[C]old and formal' people, on the other hand, usually live behind faceless knockers, so as not to create a welcoming impression to potential visitors. Later Boz asserts:

> Some phrenologists affirm, that the agitation of a man's brain by different passions, produces corresponding developments in the form of his skull. Do not let us be understood as pushing our theory to the length of asserting, that any alteration in a man's disposition would produce a visible effect on the feature of his knocker. Our position merely is, that in such a case, the magnetism which must exist between a man and his knocker, would induce the man to remove, and seek some knocker more congenial to his altered feelings . . . This is a new theory, but we venture to launch it, nevertheless, as being quite ingenious and infallible as many thousand of the learned speculations which are daily broached for public good and private fortune-making. (*SB*, pp. 58–69)

These last two excerpts do a good deal of ideological work. One could say that they satirise the efforts of physiognomists and phrenologists to unravel the mysteries of character with scientific exactitude. These 'sciences', Boz seems to argue, are probably not 'infallible' sciences pursued for the 'public good'. In fact, one might just as well study door-knockers as facial expressions or cranial protrusions to learn 'infallible' truths about human characters. This reading of Boz's rhetoric is safe and fair – and yet it begs the question: who is doing the satirising here? Is it Boz? Is Boz, that is, being deliberately tongue-in-cheek? If so, we can presume that he has not actually observed correlations between the faces of real Londoners and their door-knockers; that he is simply imagining what it would be like if there *were* such correlations, and then considering how ridiculous it would be to theorise based on them – with the implication that theorising about character based on facial features and cranial bumps is, at least in some cases, just as ridiculous. According to this reading, Boz takes a creative opportunity to make fun of physiognomy and especially phrenology; and if we are meant to think that the AP also discredits these sciences, then the AP and Boz think alike and are more or less one and the same. But there is also the possibility that Boz is meant to be taken seriously here, that he really believes (as the AP would likely not) that his 'ingenious and infallible' new theory of door-knockers is somehow legitimate. In this case, the text positions the AP somewhere in the background with an opportunity to laugh at the credulity of his narrator. At the very least, it seems evident that some parties are ridiculing phrenology and physiognomy to some extent – either Dickens, the AP and Boz, or just the first two.[6]

In another sketch, Boz remarks of one Mr Carlton that 'it was impossible to look at his face without being forcibly reminded of a chubby street-door knocker, half-lion half-monkey; and the comparison might be extended to his whole character' (SB, p. 326). This sentence achieves humour by hyperbole. It would probably continue to do so even if the word 'impossible' were replaced with 'difficult' and the word 'forcibly' were omitted. But there is more to be said about such witticisms than that, as Richard Kane has observed about Bergsonian comic theory in *Crochet Castle*, 'a person becomes laughable every time he or part of him gives us the impression of being a thing'. The comment about Mr Carlton is more than just another example of Boz being Boz, observing that it is all but impossible *not* to perceive an immediate resemblance between persons and things. To some extent – perhaps just barely enough that the point is not entirely lost in the humour – Dickens implies that certain flâneur-ish minds can and do become 'harden[ed] into grooves and inelastic patterns of thought that often become absurd in their incongruity to a mobile and flexible society'. Part of what Dickens accomplishes through Boz is comparable, in fact, to what Peacock accomplishes through the voices in *Crotchet Castle*. The narrator of *Sketches* may be said to have his own 'crochet' or *idée fixe* in the form of idling about town and estimating characters from appearances – only the ideological apparatus that structures his scopophilic observations gets lost in the humour. Boz is so amusing and informative, that is, and seems to wield such obvious power and authority over the objects of his gaze, that we give his wit the benefit of the doubt at almost every turn.

The question becomes: is Boz more often a mouthpiece for the AP, or a discrete character with fallible opinions whom the AP occasionally makes fun of? I think that on some occasions the AP and Boz are meant to converge in opinion, and that on others they are not. In still others the matter remains unclear. For instance, in one sketch Boz visits Newgate Prison and notices 'casts of the heads and faces of two notorious murderers' in an anteroom. One of these murderers is John Bishop (hanged in 1831), whose head and face 'would have afforded sufficient moral grounds for his instant execution at any time, even had there been no other evidence against him' (*SB*, p. 236). What does Boz mean by 'sufficient moral grounds?' Sufficient to whom? to the credulous public? to prosecuting attorneys? to Dickens? to the AP? to himself? It is hard to estimate how and to what extent the AP is speaking through Boz here. If we assume that the AP is mostly speaking – ironically – with and through Boz, and that the AP, like Boz, is likely to dismiss such evidence of character, say, as Edinburgh phrenologists gathered from the skulls of criminals, then the passage is more or less a complaint that too many rational members of British society are gulled into considering fanciful speculation as hard evidence. If we assume that the AP is not speaking through Boz, on the other hand, then the passage is an additional example of Boz indulging in theories that the AP and all sensible people know are absurd. In the first case, Boz and the AP are united in their ironic fun-making. In the second, Boz is sincere, credulous like a credulous public, and the AP has some fun at Boz's expense.

Sketches does present certain points of convergence between the AP and Boz that are, arguably, relatively clear. I am interested in moments, however, where the two diverge. I suggest that the AP occasionally positions Boz as a smug ethological aficionado for whom a fixed character needs to be reliably evident in all persons by countless means, however absurd. These means include old clothes (as when the second-hand clothes in Monmouth Street shops come to life and tell stories about their previous owners – stories as accurate as 'autobiograph[ies] engrossed on parchment') and immediate appearances (as when Boz sees a stranger in St James's Park whose 'manner and appearance . . . told us . . . his whole life, or rather his whole day, for a man of this sort has no variety') (SB, pp. 99, 252). Many of the fictional men and women in Sketches try to transcend boundaries of class and character only to fail miserably and be returned to their point of origin. It is not necessarily Boz who returns them there, but it is he who implies how pointless their efforts at crossing such boundaries were in the first place. As a narrator, Boz is disagreeably complicit in the circumstances that put men and women 'back in their places'. On a theoretical level he helps to reassert their inscription in and through language, which entraps them again in reified concepts like 'character'.

On one occasion, Boz visits a London lounge near City Road for 'a glass of ale', where he hears a local agitator named Rogers declaiming to a handful of men against the national debt, slavery, pensions, sinecures, standing armies, the window tax and so on, informing his audience that they are all willing slaves to 'an insolent and factious oligarchy'. 'We stand, in these times, upon a calm elevation of intellectual attainment', Rogers exclaims, from which it is clear that the 'domination of cruel laws' need no longer curtail the political enfranchisement of the lower and middle classes. Presumably, Dickens himself witnessed similar speeches. He was living at an inn near the one Boz describes when he wrote this sketch. It is therefore easy to assume that everything Boz says may be safely attributed to the AP. But this sketch – called 'The Parlour Orator' and one of twelve sketches categorised under 'Characters' – is not just about Rogers, but about how Boz unwaveringly dismisses him. Boz pronounces rather arbitrarily that Rogers is an excessive drinker and smoker and should not be taken seriously on any counts. He is 'inflamed' with alcohol more than righteous causes and seems to have no business rallying the greengrocer and broker (who are too ignorant anyway to

Afterword: Meta-characterisation 199

see Rogers for the pretender he is). It is when Rogers asks 'What is a man?' and 'What is an Englishman?' that Boz finally has had enough. Rogers leaves the lounge and Boz thinks to himself:

> If we had followed the established precedent in all such instances, we should have fallen into a fit of musing, without delay. The ancient appearance of the room – the old panelling of the wall – the chimney blackened with smoke and age – would have carried us back a hundred years at least, and we should have gone dreaming on, until the pewter-pot on the table, or the little beer-chiller on the fire, had started into life, and addressed to us a long story of days gone by. But by some means or other, we were not in a romantic humour; and although we tried very hard to invest the furniture with vitality, it remained perfectly unmoved. Being thus reduced to the unpleasant necessity of musing about ordinary matters, our thoughts reverted to the red-faced man, and his oratorical display.

The sketch ends with a small paragraph on the 'numerous race' of 'red-faced' and '[w]eak-pated dolts' like Rogers. Boz explains his motivation for including the story about Rogers in his narrative: 'to hold a pattern . . . up, to know the others by, we took his likeness at once, and put him in there. And that is the reason why we have written this paper' (*SB*, pp. 272–7).

Boz does not tell us exactly why he is out of his familiar 'romantic humour' at this point, and therefore decides not to animate the furniture in the room. Perhaps he has found it more important to justify the inclusion of this 'Character' in his *Sketches* as a means to help the public recognise oratorical charlatans and drunks like Rogers. What I find interesting is how strangely curmudgeonly Boz sounds at the end of 'The Parlour Orator'. His narrative powers are apparently suspended and the 'necessity of musing about ordinary matters' takes precedence. In a sense, 'The Parlour Orator' is about two 'Characters'. The alleged idiocy of Rogers (who sounds more rational than Boz gives him credit for) seems somehow out of proportion – and ultimately gives way to Boz's grumbling typological profiling. This is one of several instances in which the AP appears to increase the distance between himself and his narrator so as to call attention to the eccentricities of the observer as well as the observed. The pragmatic Boz characterises Rogers as one of a type or 'race' easily detectable by the wary eye. The 'metaphysical' questions that Rogers asks about personal and national character ('What is a man?', 'What is an Englishman?') test the patience of the narrator and prompt his defensive attitude. To ask questions about the hegemony of concepts and definitions is to imply the possibility of dismantling them. This is a threat to Boz – although Boz would hardly grant Rogers the intellectual powers equal to such a task.

Boz tells several stories involving men and women who venture beyond acceptable boundaries of class and character, only to be humbled (if not humiliated) by the experience. In one tale, the grocer Joseph Tuggs inherits £20,000 after a 'long-pending lawsuit respecting the validity of a will' (SB, p. 390). His children Simon and Charlotte immediately prefer to be called Cymon and Charlotta, and the family relocates from Gravesend to Ramsgate in the interests of living more genteelly. Their ingenuousness turns out to be easily detectable in Ramsgate. In almost no time, a group of three flattering con-artists swindles the family of out of £1,500 and the story ends. It seems to have something of a moral – that nouveaux riches who are as pretentious as they are ingenuous will eventually pay a price – but the delivery of the moral is by no means heavy-handed. Boz is not especially didactic in tone. He concludes matter-of-factly that 'there are not wanting those who affirm that three designing imposters never found more easy dupes . . . in the Tuggs's at Ramsgate' (SB, p. 408). This statement is interesting because of its implied impartiality or aloofness. Boz is careful not to include himself among those who make 'affirm[ations]' about the Tuggs family – at least not by way of a stated opinion or moral and the end of his tale. His own opinions are more hidden, couched in physical descriptions and ethological extrapolations. When Charlotte Tuggs insists that her father 'leave off all his vulgar habits' now that he has come into money, Joseph Tuggs responds 'complacently' that he will 'take care of all that', though Boz notes wryly that he 'was at that very moment eating pickled salmon with a pocket-knife', suggesting that Joseph Tuggs will take care of nothing of the sort (SB, p. 390). At another point in the sketch, Boz observes that young Simon Tuggs

> was as differently formed in body, as he was differently constituted in mind, from the remainder of his family. There was that elongation in his thoughtful face, and that tendency to weakness in his interesting legs,

which tells so forcibly of a great mind and romantic disposition. The slightest traits of character in such a being, possess no mean interest to speculative minds. (*SB*, p. 388)

Here the narrator suggests that he has condescended to 'speculat[e]' about Simon merely as an object of ethological 'interest', not one of moral judgement. Simon cuts an 'interesting' figure that 'tells so forcibly of a great mind and romantic disposition' to any informed observer. But the phrase 'great mind' becomes retroactively ironised by later events and by association with the phrase 'romantic disposition'. It is his 'romantic disposition', in fact, that induces Simon to fall for a married woman (whom he venerates with effusions of sensibility) and to implicate his own family in a near-scandal that costs them £1,500.

The story of 'Horatio Sparkins' is a more pronounced cautionary tale against pretension. First, there is the businessman Mr Malderton, whom a

> few successful speculations had raised . . . from a situation of comparative poverty, to a state of affluence. As frequently happens in such cases, the ideas of himself and his family became elevated to an extraordinary pitch and their means increased; they affected fashion, taste, and many other fooleries, in imitation of their betters, and had a very decided and becoming horror of any thing which could possibly be considered *low*. (*SB*, p. 411)

This insistence on genteel taste and behaviour (combined with ignorance) induces the Maldertons to take a great interest in Horatio Sparkins, a young man whose hair, dress, dancing and general grace convince everyone that he is nobly born. Like the 'Parlour Orator' before him, Sparkins waxes metaphysical, but in a leisurely, romantic, Byronic fashion:

> 'And after all, sir, what is man?' said the metaphysical Sparkins – 'I say, what is man?'
> 'Ah! very true', said Mr Malderton – 'very true'.
> 'We know that we live and breathe', continued Horatio; 'that we have wants and wishes, desires and appetites – '
> 'Certainly', said Mr Frederick Malderton, looking very profound.

'I say, we know that we exist', repeated Horatio, raising his voice, 'but there we stop; there is an end to our knowledge; there is the summit of our attainments; there is the termination of our ends. What more do we know?' (*SB*, pp. 415–16)

His eloquence aside, the family is soon disenchanted when the

> mysterious, philosophical, romantic, metaphysical Sparkins – he who, to the interesting Teresa [Malderton], seemed like the imbodied idea of . . . young dukes and poetical exquisites . . . was suddenly converted into Mr Samuel Smith, the assistant at a 'cheap shop;' the junior partner in a slippery firm of some three weeks' existence. (*SB*, p. 425)

It appears that 'Sparkins' has all along been Smith, and letting everyone (especially the Maldertons) believe he is a gentleman. After this and numerous similar tales in *Sketches*, the reader may pause to wonder why Boz is so concerned with these various 'transgressions' of character and station. One can argue that gentle satires on affected parvenus, romantics and would-be nobles are part and parcel to the genre of the 'sketch' in an era of increasing social mobility. While this is a logical explanation, it is not an entirely satisfactory one. Boz singles himself out as a 'speculative min[d]' who can observe the 'slightest traces of character' in appearances and extrapolate these traces accurately – in spite of the fact that his extrapolations usually sound ludicrous. Even when he blatantly exaggerates, he manages to secure our trust that he somehow sees comprehensively and with a certain urbane wisdom tutored by experience. This is partly because his superior ethological judgement is thrown into relief by the comparatively blind judgement of the men and women in *Sketches* who are easily deluded by appearances. It is not, however, necessary to assume that the AP (or Dickens, for that matter) considers Boz as infallible a judge of character as Boz considers himself. The 'metaphysical' questions posed by Rogers the Orator and Horatio Sparkins, however silly and romantic Boz renders them in context, may be said to threaten his own firm assumption that character is almost always knowable, calculable and describable down to the very last detail and by whatever means present themselves. Boz maintains a firm grip on the characters of the men and women whose stories he tells, and ridicules their efforts to elude these characters. It may indeed be that in many cases he serves as an unequivocal mouthpiece for the AP, but in others it seems more than likely that the AP is as critical and merciless a flâneur to Boz, as Boz is to the 'characters' he sees-invents in *Sketches*.

Thomas Carlyle's *Sartor Resartus* was published serially in *Fraser's Magazine* beginning in 1833 – the year in which the stories gathered in *Sketches* started to appear in newspapers and magazines. Both of these 'liminal' texts are spoken by a dramatic narrator whose efforts to reveal eternal truths about personal character are at once legitimated and compromised in context. The narrator of *Sketches* is the scopophilic and omnipresent idler-about-town, Boz, who speculates on the characters of Londoners based often on their appearance alone. He extrapolates the unseen from the seen, and with an authority that no one doubts less than he. The narrator of *Sartor Resartus* is similarly occupied – though far more tentative in his conclusions. Quite unlike Boz, he struggles to understand the first principles or conditions by which a knowledge of character is possible. Boz would rather observe, and entertain the reader with his observations, than understand how or to what extent he can actually know what he claims to know. We can therefore think of *Sketches* as narrativised practical ethology, and of *Sartor Resartus* as narrativised theoretical ethology.

The narrator of *Sartor Resartus* is an unnamed British editor whose major aim is to understand and impart to British audiences the life and thought of the German philosopher Diogenes Teufelsdröckh, author of a tome entitled 'Clothes, their Origin and Influence'. *Sartor Resartus* is ostensibly about clothing; the obsession of silver fork novels with the minute details of aristocratic clothing worn in Regency Britain helped motivate Carlyle to write it. The basic argument of Teufelsdröckh's 'Clothes, their Origin and Influence' – assuming one can encapsulate what the Editor explains piecemeal by enigmatic wordplay – is that clothing is important insofar as it separates humankind from animals, and codifies the various levels and gradations of social hierarchy, but more so as a conduit to the divine Nature of the being it covers. Clothing 'is not there on its own account', the Editor observes; 'strictly taken, [it] is not there at all: Matter exists only spiritually, and to represent some Idea, and *body* it forth'.⁷ Garments must be viewed not only with the physical but with the spiritual eye. The spiritual eye can perceive, in and through clothing as if it were suddenly transparent, the noumenal reality of which, according to Teufelsdröckh, clothing partakes. Hence clothing is a 'mystic grove-encircled shrine for the Holy in man', a dynamic symbol that partakes of the divine reality it symbolises (*SR*, p. 32). The broader aim of *Sartor Resartus* has less to do with clothing per se than with popularising German Idealist philosophy for nineteenth-century British audiences, audiences used to the utilitarianism inspired by British empiricism and its legacies. In a word, there is phenomenal knowledge and there is noumenal knowledge; the understanding supplies one with phenomenal knowledge, while reason, intuition and imaginative insight supply one with noumenal knowledge. A knowledge of the origin and influence of 'clothing' can teach us to perceive the world through both the understanding and reason – provided that we assume 'clothing' to mean one of countless divine hieroglyphs of which the universe is made and by which it is bodied forth.

The prevailing tension that drives *Sartor Resartus* (the same as that which drives *Sketches*) may be illustrated with the following two criticisms of the novel:

> For Carlyle, character is self-generated: it reflects each person's unique and essential nature; more important, it can reveal the divinity that is inherent in each individual if the individual has the will to make his or her spirituality manifest.⁸

> [T]he most significant way in which Carlyle's fiction differs from the tradition of the realistic novel is found in its attitude to character and to ordinary human experience. The author of *Sartor* is uninterested in either, and gives no evidence of the human sympathy that seems an essential feature of the realistic novel.⁹

These two passages seem to clash on a fundamental level. Surely an author for whom character 'reflects each person's unique and essential nature' and 'can reveal the divinity that is inherent in each individual' must also consider it an object of interest. One can reconcile these critical statements in the following way. Perhaps the first excerpt refers to character in a strictly metaphysical sense and

Afterword: Meta-characterisation

the second refers to it in a strictly aesthetic sense, so that character is important in *Sartor Resartus* as an idea, as an object of noumenal knowledge, but not as an aesthetic device that secures sympathies between readers and fictional beings – the Editor, Heuschrecke and/or Teufelsdröckh. In this reading, Carlyle does not need to create realistic literary 'characters' to make readers interested in the abstraction 'character'. But I would suggest that *Sartor Resartus* demands that these two senses of the word not be considered separately. They function dynamically in endless dialectic. The enigmatic or elusive characters in the novel serve as evidence that 'character' in an abstract sense can never be real or knowable; in turn, the conceptual incoherence of character is revealed in the fictional beings who would instantiate it. Thus the text reveals the aporia at which all discussions of character must ultimately halt: character is always transparent and hidden, knowable and unknowable, revealed perpetually and perpetually deferred. It is one of the most mischievous of Bacon's Idols of the Marketplace, in that it constantly promises and fails to make an abstraction the object of everyday observation.

A complete understanding of 'Clothes, their Origin and Influence' is impossible, according to the Editor, without an understanding of its author:

> no Life-Philosophy (*Lebensphilosophie*), such as this of Clothes pretends to be, which originates equally in the Character (*Gemüth*), and equally speaks thereto, can attain its significance till the Character itself is known and seen; 'till the Author's View of the World (*Weltansicht*), and how he actively and passively came by such view, are clear: in short till a Biography of him has been philosophico-poetically written, and philosophico-poetically read. (*SR*, p. 58)

The Editor comments on and quotes from 'Clothes, their Origin and influence', which, like all texts, proceeds from and illuminates the 'Character' of its author – 'character' in the sense of worldview or *Weltansicht*. The text and the character of its author cannot be separated. To assist the Editor in his efforts, therefore, Herr Hofrath Heuschrecke, German friend to Teufelsdröckh, is said to have provided the Editor with certain documents relative to the biography of the philosopher. '[O]n the first perusal' of these documents, the

Editor observes that 'it became apparent that . . . an almost unexampled personal Character, that, namely, of Professor Teufelsdröckh the Discloser', was in fact 'disclosed' (*SR*, p. 8). We learn, among other facts, that Teufelsdröckh did not know his biological parents and that he was raised by a schoolmaster and his wife (at whose house a stranger had left him one night); that his countrymen perceived him as a sort of dishevelled wanderer and eccentric; and that he was awarded a nominal professorship in Germany (his title was 'Professor of Things in General'), but never taught.

No matter how many biographical facts he amasses, the Editor portrays the character of Teufelsdröckh – and character itself – simultaneously as i) knowable objects and as ii) epiphenomena of language-play whose meaning is infinitely deferred. In a remarkably luminous passage, the Editor writes that

> In an atmosphere of Poverty and manifold Chagrin, the Humour of that young Soul, what character is in him, first decisively reveals itself; and, like strong sunshine in weeping skies, gives out variety of colours, some of which are prismatic. (*SR*, p. 84)

The apposition in this statement equates 'the Humour of that young Soul' with 'what character is in him' (by 'humour' the Editor probably means the '[u]sual or permanent mental disposition; constitutional or habitual tendency; temperament' – although the four bodily fluids or humours may be implied).[10] If the soul is the immaterial foundation or principle of a person, his or her character is its constitutive 'Humour' or bent (a far cry from character as *Weltansicht*). That bent reveals itself to the Editor on practical and metaphorical levels of refraction. On a practical level, Teufelsdröckh's character is refracted through 'an atmosphere of Poverty and manifold Chagrin'. In other words, his moral-constitutive character is tested and formed through adverse circumstances. On a metaphorical level, the 'Soul' is compared to the sun and 'character' to a sunbeam. But we are not meant to see this sunbeam – character – except as its spectral components are refracted through atmospheric moisture ('weeping skies') in the form of a rainbow ('variety of colours'). Both levels of refraction work together to suggest an initial definition: 'character is the humour of the soul, refracted by circumstance and viewed prismatically'. Moreover, the phrase 'what character is in him' implies that, as a young man, Teufelsdröckh does not yet contain or possess the character he ultimately will. At a later stage in his investigation, the Editor will indeed decide that the 'character' of Teufelsdröckh 'has now taken its ultimate bent' ('bent' in the sense of 'inclination or tendency; disposition; propensity, bias'),[11] 'and no new revolution, of importance, is to be looked for' (*SR*, p. 154). So character develops in leaps and strides up to a certain point of maturity, after which any developmental modifications are minor and of little 'importance'. We are now in a position to expand our definition: 'character is the humour of the soul, refracted by circumstance and viewed prismatically, whose developmental modifications become relatively immaterial after a certain point of maturity'. This definition, as it happens, becomes even more complicated when we consider that, on the metaphorical level, only 'some' of the colours of character are 'prismatic'. This may mean that some aspects of character can be shaped by circumstances, while others may remain permanently unaffected. Or, if we take 'prismatic' in the sense of '[b]rightly coloured, colourful; brilliant', then the phrase may mean that some aspects of Teufelsdröckh's character are simply more splendid than others.[12]

Although the biographical documents are meant to provide 'glimpses into the internal world of Teufelsdröckh' that render his 'Character . . . less enigmatic', the Editor never seems to have a clear sense of who (or what) that 'Character' is (*SR*, p. 155). The reason may lie either in his own ignorance or in the documents themselves (or some combination of both). The Philosophy of Clothes insists that hidden realities like character are indeed apprehensible through reason and imagination and intuition – which supply noumenal knowledge. The understanding, on the other hand, contains impressions derived from sense-experience and supplies only knowledge of appearances. So either Teufelsdröckh was wrong about the rational/imaginative/intuitive accessibility of character, or the Editor has relied too heavily on his understanding to gain access to Teufelsdröckh's character. Although *Sartor Resartus* provides no easy way out of these uncertainties, it does invite readers to sympathise with the British Editor. The actual auto/biographical documents that Herr Heuschrecke provides to assist the Editor in his task are all but impenetrable. They consist of six 'considerable PAPER-BAGS' inscribed 'with the symbols of the Six southern Zodiacal Signs, beginning at Libra' – 'unimaginable Documents', a 'universal medley of high and low, of hot, cold, moist and dry' (a dispersion of the humours), 'printed and written Chaos' (*SR*, pp. 60–2). Teufelsdröckh has composed a few notes on 'his own personal history', but only 'at rare intervals, and then in the most enigmatic manner'. Some of these notes contain

> Dreams, authentic or not, while the circumjacent waking Actions are omitted. Anecdotes, oftenest without date of place or time, fly loosely on separate slips, like Sibylline leaves. Interspersed also are long purely Autobiographical delineations; yet without connection, without recognizable coherence. (*SR*, p. 60)

There are also 'fragments of all sorts; scraps of regular Memoir, College Exercises, Programs, Professional Testimoniums, Milkscores, torn Billets ... all blown together as if by merest chance'. Ultimately, these documents are neither '[b]iography or autobiography'. At best they may yield 'some sketchy, shadowy, fugitive likeness [of Teufelsdröckh] by unheard-of efforts, partly of intellect partly of imagination, on the side of Editor and of Reader'. Nor are these documents any help in understanding the doctrine of clothing itself. The whole set of paper bags is an 'airy Limbo which[,] by intermixture[,] will [only] farther volatilize and discompose' the Philosophy of Clothes as the Editor has come to understand it (*SR*, pp. 84, 61). Here the metaphor is a chemical one. If one mixes the records of Character (auto/biographical documents) with Character's most powerful source/product/text (the Philosophy of Clothes), then the latter is bound to be 'volatise[d]' – 'render[ed] volatile ... cause[d] to evaporate or disperse in vapour'.[13] Earlier, the character of Teufelsdröckh was described metaphorically as a sunbeam refracted through moist skies in the form of a rainbow. Here, his life-writings and semi-biographical scraps are described in terms of chemicals. In this light it comes as little surprise that the Editor finds Teufelsdröckh 'not so much a Man as a Thing', whose history resembles that of 'mountain rocks and antediluvian ruins' – inanimate objects 'created by unknown agencies' and 'in a state of gradual decay, [which] for the present reflect light and resist pressure; that is, are visible and tangible objects in this phantasm world, where so much other than mystery is' (*SR*, p. 14).

Either the Editor cannot see far or consistently beyond the limitations of his understanding, or there is nothing to see – no numinous character to be 'disclosed'. He seems close to an intuitive sense of the 'Character' of Teufelsdröckh when he perceives it imaginatively – comparing the philosopher to old 'mountain rocks and antediluvian ruins' 'created by unknown agencies' and 'in a state of gradual decay'. This description recalls the old leech-gatherer in Wordsworth's 'Resolution and Independence', 'not all alive nor dead', whom Wordsworth compares to a 'huge Stone' '[c]couched on the bald top of an eminence' that 'seems a thing endued with sense'.[14] On more than a few occasions, the Editor calls the biographical documents 'sibylline leaves', referencing the leaves hung in the cave of the Sibyl (in *Aeneid* 3) and inscribed with prophetic signs and symbols, to which the Sibyl does not restore order when winds scatter them. *Sibylline Leaves* is also the title Coleridge gave to his 1817 collection of poems originally scattered in many different publications. When the Editor calls the auto/biographical texts 'sibylline leaves', he associates the apprehension of the 'unexampled personal Character' of Teufelsdröckh with the accurate reading of prophecy. The gods or fates become the 'unknown agencies' that created the philosopher in some ancient past.

Carlyle is clearly romanticising Teufelsdröckh as a sort of marginalised and misunderstood philosopher-king who should have but never did lead his people to intellectual clarity. He resembles a combination of Prometheus, Christ, Satan, Socrates and many more. On some level, Carlyle may have considered him the proper object of hero-worship who carries an antidote to British utilitarianism, but he nonetheless caters to the incredulity of his readers by providing them with a relatable British Editor – a man who obviously doubts (as many of them probably did) whether Teufelsdröckh and his creed can have anything substantive to offer a nation far more concerned with practical policies of social and political reform than with cleansing the doors of perception. Importantly, in terms of character discourse, Teufelsdröckh is another Bernard Blackmantle, Lord Ruthven, Junius, Gil-Martin, L. E. L. He eludes definition; his features, behaviours, compositions, all the observable phenomena of his existence, decidedly resist legibility. He will not be taxonomised or typologised as Comte, Mill and Martineau thought was necessary to an informed awareness of social organisation. He also stands in marked contrast to the unfortunate Londoners in *Sketches* whose old clothes serve Boz as clear records of their characters – as legible and intimately revealing as 'autobiograph[ies] engrossed on parchment'.

The literary authors discussed at length in this book – Scott, Lamb, Hazlitt, Hartley Coleridge, Landon, Peacock, Beddoes and the early Dickens and Carlyle – all betray a certain scepticism regarding the uses and abuses of characterisation and character discourse. Each one questions the value and legitimacy of what Emerson calls 'a Familiar or Genius, by whose impulses the man is guided but whose counsels he cannot impart'. This Emersonian image of character is actually well suited to the concept of character as received in reform-era literary texts, since it splits the conscious mind from that hidden congenital bias, that permanent sphere of (moral and nonmoral) thought and action, that *qualitas occulta*, to which conventional wisdom has always insisted it was inexplicably tied. Emerson images this bias as a kind of ever-present-but-ever-inaccessible agent driving minds and bodies along. The texts studied in this book imagine the dissolution of the ligatures with which that familiar agent is thought to bind a consciousness for life in a sort of master–slave relationship. They can be viewed as proto-postmodern texts – laced with a species of Nietzschean doubt before Nietzsche. Whether they suspect character discourse as inhibiting purer ideas of human freedom, holding back truer forms of development, hiding the ideological threads with which consciousness is woven or curtailing imaginative energies, reform-era texts engage character discourse in part to interrogate its currency and authority – to render that 'Familiar' more unfamiliar than it had always been thought to be.

The phrase 'character discourse' is vital here to the extent that character was viewed by reform-era authors as a product of discourse rather than as a real thing inside human bodies. Although post-reform-era novelists such as Henry James, George Eliot and Thomas Hardy may not have agreed on precisely what character was – Eliot stressing its 'vulnerability' and Hardy its role as 'ethos', 'daimon', 'fate' in an Emersonian sense – all three writers agreed that it was a reality both determined and determining: a product of 'heredity and environment' that 'in turn interacts with environment to work out the individual's destiny'.[15] Or to re-quote Janice Carlisle: character for the Victorians 'implies a shared understanding of what constitutes individuals without specifying how they are so constituted'. In any case, character was for these authors a decided 'something' that demanded discursive articulation in a world – the novel genre – in which (as Lukács has famously claimed) the gods of the epic were dead. What I hope to have shown is that some reform-era authors tended not to take character so readily for granted as a relatively knowable substance or first principle either in persons or in texts. Whether the famous claim by Novalis that 'character is fate' means that individual character is predetermined by fate, or that it single-handedly decides the fate of an individual, or that it cooperates with external circumstances to decide the fate of an individual to a lesser or greater degree depending on that individual's 'strength' or 'energy' or 'decision' of character (what Hegel called character's 'executive aspect') – many reform-era authors viewed the concept both as a problem to be solved and as a construct all too easily exploited for ideological ends. It was not always an Emersonian daemon to be understood, or even to be crushed. It was also a word. A word whose highly problematic referent was dramatically at odds with its excessive cultural currency.

Notes

1. Walder, introduction to *Sketches by Boz*, p. xvi. All passages from *Sketches by Boz* (hereafter cited as *SB* parenthetically within the text) are taken from this edition.
2. A notable exception is Edward Copeland's pioneering study of silver fork novels in their political context. Copeland argues that these novels 'supported the liberalizing Whig Party policies of social and political reform that led to the Reform Bill', by means of an attempt to reconcile 'liberal impulse and aristocratic constraint' (*The Silver Fork Novel*, pp. 3, 30).
3. Lynch, *Economy of Character*, p. 3.
4. Parker, *Literary Magazines and British Romanticism*, p. 11.
5. Manning, *Poetics of Character*, p. 39.

6. Elsewhere Boz boasts to have 'claim[ed] . . . credit as a physiognomist' on at least a few occasions, and is surprised when one of his speculations falls short of the mark (*SB*, p. 111). Should we infer that Dickens also wants to claim credit as a physiognomist? In what loose or strict sense of the word? Perhaps Dickens approves of most definitive statements about character that are carefully drawn from intuition and observation, but only up to the point that these conclusions are taken to an anatomic level – up to the point that internal organs and facial muscles are somehow part of the physiognomic 'equation'. I would suggest that *Sketches* problematises all characterising acts whether or not one supplements intuition, observation and experience with pseudo-scientific theories.
7. Carlyle, *Sartor Resartus*, ed. Kerry McSweeney and Peter Sabor (Oxford: Oxford University Press, 1999), p. 56. All passages from the novel (hereafter cited as *SR* parenthetically within the text) are taken from this edition.
8. Carlisle, *John Stuart Mill and the Writing of Character*, p. 6.
9. McSweeney and Sabor, introduction to *Sartor Resartus*, p. xviii.
10. 'humour, n.'. Def. 7a. *OED Online*. Oxford University Press, February 2015, <http://www.oed.com> (last accessed 16 February 2015).
11. 'bent, n.²'. Def. 6b. *OED Online*. Oxford University Press, February 2015, <http://www.oed.com> (last accessed 16 February 2015).
12. 'prismatic, adj. and n.'. Def. 2b. *OED Online*. Oxford University Press, February 2015, <http://www.oed.com> (last accessed 16 February 2015).
13. 'volatilize, v.'. Def. 1a. *OED Online*. Oxford University Press, February 2015, <http://www.oed.com> (last accessed 16 February 2015).
14. Wordsworth, 'Resolution and Independence', p. 262, lines 71, 64–5, 68.
15. King, *Tragedy in the Victorian Novel*, p. 27; Bloom, introduction to *Thomas Hardy: Modern Critical Views*, p. 10; and King, *Tragedy in the Victorian Novel*, p. 26.

Bibliography

Ahnert, Thomas and Susan Manning (eds), introduction to *Character, Self, and Sociability in the Scottish Enlightenment* (New York: Palgrave Macmillan, 2011), pp. 1–30.
Allard, James, *Romanticism, Medicine and the Poet's Body* (Burlington, VT: Ashgate, 2007).
Anon., 'I. – Essays on Phrenology; Or an Inquiry into the Utility of the System of Drs Gall and Spurzheim', *Blackwood's Edinburgh Magazine* 10: 58 (1821), pp. 682–91.
—, 'Aboriginal Character', *Chambers's Edinburgh Journal* 5 (1832), p. 39.
—, 'Anti-Phrenologia; A Plain Statement of Objections against the System of Drs Gall and Spurzheim', Sec. I, *Blackwood's Edinburgh Magazine* 13: 72 (1823), pp. 100–8.
—, 'Anti-Phrenologia; A Plain Statement of Objections against the System of Drs Gall and Spurzheim', Sec. II, *Blackwood's Edinburgh Magazine* 13: 73 (1823), pp. 199–206.
—, 'Art. I. 1. *An Enquiry into the Probability and Rationality of Mr. Hunter's Theory of Life. . . . 8. A Letter to the Rev. Thomas Rennell. From a Graduate in Medicine. 1819*', *The Quarterly Review* 22: 43 (1819), pp. 1–34.
—, 'Art. VIII. – *Political Essays, with Sketches of Public Characters*. By William Hazlitt', *The Quarterly Review* 22: 43 (1819), pp. 158–63.
—, 'Art. VIII. *Reflections on Gall and Spurzheim's System of Physiognomy and Phrenology*. Addressed to the Court of Assistants of the Royal College of Surgeons, in London, in June 1821. By John Abernethy, F. R. S.', *Eclectic Review* 17 (1822), pp. 551–60.
—, 'Art. XI. 1. *A New View of Society . . . Employment of the Poor*. By Robert Owen, of New Lanark', *The Edinburgh Review* 32: 64 (1819), pp. 453–77.
—, 'Art. XXIII. – *Fisher's Drawing-Room Scrap-Book, for 1838: with Poetic Illustrations*. By. L. E. L. London: Fisher', in *The Monthly Review: From September to December Inclusive* (London: E. Henderson, 1837), p. 452.

—, 'Character, – Principle, – with Other Grave Matters', *Edinburgh Magazine and Literary Miscellany* (1821), pp. 209–12.
—, 'Character-Painting', *The Literary Chronicle* 373 (1826), pp. 429–30.
—, 'On the Knowledge of Character', *The Oriental Herald and Journal of General Literature* 6: 20 (1825), pp. 225–33.
—, 'The Female Character', *The Mirror of Literature, Amusement, and Instruction* 2: 50 (1823), pp. 313–16.
—, '*The Gem, A Literary Annual.* Edited by Thomas Hood, Esq., Author of "Whims and Oddities". London. J. Marshall', *The London Literary Gazette* 613 (1828), pp. 661–3.
—, 'The Pleasure of Being without a Character', *Chambers's Edinburgh Journal* 257 (1836), p. 391.
—, 'Value of a Good Character', *Penny Magazine of the Society for the Diffusion of Useful Knowledge* 8: 468 (1839), p. 280.
Aristotle, *Nicomachean Ethics, Books II–IV*, trans. C. C. W. Taylor (Oxford: Oxford University Press, 2006).
Arnold, Matthew, *Culture and Anarchy*, in Stefan Collini (ed.), *Culture and Anarchy and Other Writings* (Cambridge: Cambridge University Press, 1993), pp. 53–211.
Ashton, Rosemary, *Victorian Bloomsbury* (New Haven, CT: Yale University Press, 2012).
B., J. R., 'On the System of Gall and Spurzheim', *The Newcastle Magazine* 3: 1 (1824), pp. 11–18.
B., T. W., 'Decision of Character', *The Imperial Magazine* 5: 53 (1823), pp. 412–13.
Baiesi, Serena, *Letitia Elizabeth Landon and Metrical Romance: The Adventures of a 'Literary Genius'* (Bern, Switzerland: Peter Lang, 2009).
Ball, Terence, 'The Formation of Character: Mill's "Ethology" Reconsidered', *Polity* 33: 1 (2000), pp. 25–48.
Ballard, Joseph, *England in 1815, As Seen by a Young Boston Merchant, Being the Reflections and Comments of Joseph Ballard on a Trip through Great Britain in the Year of Waterloo* (Boston, MA: Houghton Mifflin, 1913).
Barmby, Catherine, 'Phrenology', *Co-Operative Magazine and Monthly Herald* 1: 9 (1826), pp. 278–81.
Bauer, Josephine, 'Some Verse Fragments and Prose "Characters" by Samuel Butler not Included in the "Complete Works"', *Modern Philology* 45: 3 (1948), pp. 160–8.
Beddoes, Thomas Lovell, *Death's Jest-Book: The 1829 Text*, ed. Michael Bradshaw (New York: Routledge, 2003).

Behrendt, Stephen, 'Mary Shelley, *Frankenstein*, and the Woman Writer's Fate', in Paula Feldman and Theresa Kelley (eds), *Romantic Women Writers: Voices and Countervoices* (Hanover, NH: University Press of New England, 1995), pp. 69–87.

Bender, John, *Imagining the Penitentiary: Fiction and the Architecture of Mind in Eighteenth-Century England* (Chicago: University of Chicago Press, 1987).

Bentham, Jeremy, *An Introduction to the Principles of Morals and Legislation*, revised edn (Mineola, NY: Dover, 2007).

Berns, Ute, 'Thomas Lovell Beddoes and Johann Friedrich Blumenbach', in Christoph Bode and Sebastian Domsch (eds), *British and European Romanticisms: Selected Papers from the Munich Conference of the German Society for English Romanticism* (Trier, Germany: WVT, 2007), pp. 203–13.

Berns, Ute and Michael Bradshaw, introduction to *The Ashgate Research Companion to Thomas Lovell Beddoes* (Burlington, VT: Ashgate, 2007), pp. 1–31.

Bloom, Harold, introduction to *Thomas Hardy: Modern Critical Views* (New York: Chelsea House, 1987), pp. 1–22.

Boyce, Benjamin, *The Polemic Character, 1640–1661* (Lincoln: University of Nebraska Press, 1955).

Brandt, Richard, 'Traits of Character: A Conceptual Analysis', *American Philosophical Quarterly* 7: 1 (1970), pp. 23–37.

Brewer, David, *The Afterlife of Character, 1726–1825* (Philadelphia: University of Pennsylvania Press, 2005).

Bricke, John, 'Hume's Conception of Character', *Southwestern Journal of Philosophy* 5: 1 (1974), pp. 107–13.

—, 'Hume's Theories of Dispositional Properties', *American Philosophical Quarterly* 10: 1 (1973), pp. 15–23.

Bromwich, David, *Hazlitt: The Mind of a Critic* (New York: Oxford University Press, 1983).

Burke, Edmund, *A Philosophical Enquiry into the Origin of Our Ideas of the Sublime and Beautiful*, ed. Adam Phillips (Oxford: Oxford University Press, 1990).

—, *Reflections on the Revolution in France*, ed. L. G. Mitchell (Oxford: Oxford University Press, 2009).

Burroughs, Catherine B., *Closet Stages: Joanna Baillie and the Theater Theory of British Romantic Writers* (Philadelphia: University of Pennsylvania Press, 1997).

Burwick, Frederick, 'The Anatomy of Revolution: Beddoes and Büchner', *Pacific Coast Philology* 6 (1971), pp. 5–12.

—, 'Death's Jest-Book and the Pathological Imagination', in Ute Berns and Michael Bradshaw (eds), *The Ashgate Research Companion to Thomas Lovell Beddoes* (Burlington, VT: Ashgate, 2007), pp. 97–121.

—, 'Schelling and Hazlitt on Disinterestedness and Freedom', in Tom Paulin and Duncan Wu (eds), *Metaphysical Hazlitt* (New York: Routledge, 2005), pp. 137–50.

Butler, Marilyn, *Romantics, Rebels and Reactionaries: English Literature and its Background, 1760–1830* (Oxford: Oxford University Press, 1982).

Butler, Samuel, *Characters and Passages from Note-Books*, ed. A. R. Waller (Cambridge: Cambridge University Press, 1908).

Byron, Lord George Gordon, *Lord Byron: The Complete Poetical Works*, 7 vols, ed. Jerome McGann (Oxford: Oxford University Press, 1980–93).

C., A. B., 'The Character, Nature, and Power of Man', *The Mirror of Literature, Amusement, and Instruction* 8: 209 (1826), pp. 83–5.

Canuel, Mark, *The Shadow of Death: Literature, Romanticism, and the Subject of Punishment* (Princeton: Princeton University Press, 2007).

Carlile, Richard, 'Dr. Spurzheim and Phrenology', *The Prompter* 31 (1831), pp. 497–500.

—, 'Organization-Intellect', *The Republican* 8: 3 (1823), pp. 79–83.

Carlisle, Janice, *John Stuart Mill and the Writing of Character* (Athens: University of Georgia Press, 1991).

Carlson, Julie, *England's First Family of Writers: Mary Wollstonecraft, William Godwin, Mary Shelley* (Baltimore: Johns Hopkins University Press, 2007).

Carlyle, Thomas, 'Art. VII.-1. *Anticipation; or, an Hundred Years Hence . . . The Last Days; Or, Discourses on These Our Times &c., &c.* By the Rev. Edward Irving. 8vo. London, 1829 ['Signs of the Times']', *The Edinburgh Review* 49: 98 (1829), pp. 439–59.

—, *Sartor Resartus*, ed. Kerry McSweeney and Peter Sabor (Oxford: Oxford University Press, 1999).

Cavell, Stanley, *Emerson's Transcendental Etudes* (Stanford: Stanford University Press, 2003).

Chapman, Robert Willan, 'On the Phenomena of Intelligence as Dependent upon Organization', *The Newcastle Magazine* 10: 2 (1831), pp. 58–61.

Chas., R—r, 'On the Formation of Moral Character', *Co-operative Magazine and Monthly Herald* 2: 2 (1827), pp. 60–74.

Clare, John, 'An Invite to Eternity', in Eric Robinson and David Powell (eds), *The Later Poems of John Clare, 1837–1864*, vol. 2 (Oxford: Clarendon Press, 1984), pp. 348–9.

Coleridge, (David) Hartley, *Poems by Hartley Coleridge. With a Memoir of his Life by his Brother. In Two Volumes*, 2nd edn, ed. Derwent Coleridge (London: Edward Moxon, 1851).
Coleridge, S. T., *General Introduction; Or, Preliminary Treatise on Method* (London: B. Fellowes, 1818). A-29 fC693T c.1. David M. Rubenstein Rare Book and Manuscript Library Materials. Duke University Libraries.
Combe, George, *A System of Phrenology*, 3rd edn (Edinburgh: John Anderson, 1830).
—, *The Constitution of Man Considered in Relation to External Objects* (Boston, MA: Marsh, Capen, Lyon, and Webb, 1841).
Comte, Auguste, *The Positive Philosophy of Auguste Comte. Freely Translated and Condensed. By Harriet Martineau. In Two Volumes*, 3rd edn, vol. 1 (London: Kegan Paul, Trench, Trübner, 1893).
Cooper, Andrew, *Doubt and Identity in Romantic Poetry* (New Haven, CT: Yale University Press, 1988).
Cooter, Roger, *The Cultural Meaning of Popular Science: Phrenology and the Organization of Consent in Nineteenth-Century Britain* (Cambridge: Cambridge University Press, 1984).
Copeland, Edward, *The Silver Fork Novel: Fashionable Fiction in the Age of Reform* (Cambridge: Cambridge University Press, 2012).
Craciun, Adriana, *Fatal Women of Romanticism* (Cambridge: Cambridge University Press, 2003).
Craig, William, '*The Mirror*, No. 31 (May 11, 1779)', in Cheryl L. Nixon (ed.), *Novel Definitions: An Anthology of Commentary on the Novel, 1688–1815* (Peterborough, ON: Broadview Press, 2009), pp. 194–7.
Cronin, Richard, *Paper Pellets: British Literary Culture after Waterloo* (Oxford: Oxford University Press, 2010).
—, *Romantic Victorians: English Literature, 1824–1840* (Basingstoke: Palgrave, 2002).
Daiches, David, 'Scott's *Waverley*: The Presence of the Author', in Ian Campbell (ed.), *Nineteenth-Century Scottish Fiction: Critical Essays* (New York: Harper and Row, 1979), pp. 6–17.
Darden, Lindley, 'Character: Historical Perspectives', in Evelyn Fox Keller and Elisabeth Lloyd (eds), *Keywords in Evolutionary Biology* (Cambridge, MA: Harvard University Press, 1992), pp. 41–4.
Dart, Gregory, *Metropolitan Art and Literature, 1810–1840: Cockney Adventures* (Cambridge: Cambridge University Press, 2012).
Dawson, Carl, *His Fine Wit: A Study of Thomas Love Peacock* (Berkeley: University of California Press, 1970).
De Bolla, Peter, *The Discourse of the Sublime: Readings in History, Aesthetics and the Subject* (Oxford: Basil Blackwell, 1989).

De Quincey, Thomas, 'Letters to a Young Man Whose Education Has Been Neglected. By the Author of the Confessions of an English Opium Eater. No. III. *On Languages*', *The London Magazine. January to June, 1823* (London: Taylor and Hessey, 1823), pp. 325–35.

—, 'Postscript [to *On Murder Considered As One of the Fine Arts*]', in Robert Morrison (ed.), *On Murder* (Oxford: Oxford University Press, 2009), pp. 95–141.

Derrida, Jacques, *Writing and Difference*, trans. Alan Bass (Chicago: University of Chicago Press, 1978).

Dick, Alex J., 'Walter Scott and the Financial Crash of 1825: Fiction, Speculation, and the Standard of Value', *Romanticism, Forgery and the Credit Crisis*, Romantic Circles, February 2012 <https://www.rc.umd.edu/praxis/forgery/HTML/praxis.2011.dick.html> (last accessed 17 February 2017).

Dickens, Charles, *Hard Times*, ed. Fred Kaplan (New York: Norton, 2017).

—, *Sketches by Boz*, ed. Dennis Walder (New York: Penguin, 1995).

Diderot, Denis, 'Rameau's Nephew', in *Rameau's Nephew and D'Alambert's Dream*, trans. Leonard Tancock (New York: Penguin, 1966), pp. 33–130.

Dix, Robin, 'Wordsworth and Lucretius: The Psychological Impact of Creech's Translation', *English Language Notes* 39 (2002), pp. 25–33.

Dodson, Charles, introduction to *Nightmare Abbey, The Misfortunes of Elphin and Crotchet Castle* (New York: Holt, Rinehart, and Winston, 1971), pp. vii–xxviii.

Donne, John, 'The Extasie', in John Shawcross (ed.), *The Complete Poetry of John Donne* (New York: Anchor, 1967), pp. 130–2.

Duncan, Ian, 'Fanaticism and Civil Society: Hogg's *Justified Sinner*', *Novel* 42: 2 (2009), pp. 343–8.

—, introduction to Evan Gottlieb and Ian Duncan (eds), *Approaches to Teaching Scott's Waverley Novels* (New York: MLA, 2009), pp. 19–25.

Eliot, George, *Middlemarch*, ed. Bert Hornback (New York: Norton, 2000).

Emerson, Ralph Waldo, 'Character', in *Essays: First and Second Series*, vol. 2 (Boston, MA: Houghton Mifflin, 1883), pp. 87–113.

Erickson, Lee, *The Economy of Literary Form: English Literature and the Industrialization of Publishing, 1800–1850* (Baltimore: Johns Hopkins University Press, 1996).

Esterhammer, Angela, 'The Scandal of Sincerity: Wordsworth, Byron, Landon', in Timothy Milnes and Kerry Sinanan (eds), *Romanticism, Sincerity, and Authenticity* (New York: Palgrave Macmillan, 2010), pp. 101–19.

—, 'Spontaneity, Immediacy, and Improvisation in Romantic Poetry', in Charles Mahoney (ed.), *A Companion to Romantic Poetry* (Malden, MA: Wiley-Blackwell, 2010), pp. 321–36.

Fahenstock, Jeanne, 'The Heroine of Irregular Features: Physiognomy and Conventions of Heroine Description', *Victorian Studies* 24: 3 (1981), pp. 325–50.

Fang, Karen, *Romantic Writing and the Empire of Signs* (Charlottesville: University of Virginia Press, 2010).

Ferguson, Stuart, 'The Imaginative Construction of Historical Character: What Georg Lukács and Walter Scott Could Tell Contemporary Novelists', *Scottish Studies Review* 6: 2 (2005), pp. 32–48.

Feuer, L. S., 'John Stuart Mill as a Sociologist: The Unwritten Ethology', in John Robson and Michael Lane (eds), *James and John Stuart Mill: Papers on the Centenary Conference* (Toronto: University of Toronto Press, 1976), pp. 86–110.

Forbes, Deborah, *Sincerity's Shadow* (Cambridge, MA: Harvard University Press, 2004).

Foucault, Michel, *Discipline and Punish*, 2nd edn, trans. Alan Sheridan (New York: Vintage Books, 1995).

—, 'Nietzsche, Genealogy, History', trans. Donald F. Bouchard and Sherry Simon, in Donald F. Bouchard (ed.), *Language, Counter-Memory, Practice: Selected Essays and Interviews* (Ithaca: Cornell University Press, 1977), pp. 139–64.

Freeman, Lisa A., *Character's Theater: Genre and Identity on the Eighteenth-Century English Stage* (Philadelphia: University of Pennsylvania Press, 2001).

Freud, Sigmund, *Beyond the Pleasure Principle*, trans. James Strachey (New York: Norton, 1961).

Frow, John, *Character and Person* (Oxford: Oxford University Press, 2014).

Gallagher, Catherine, 'Counterhistory and Anecdote', in Stephen Greenblatt and Catherine Gallagher (eds), *Practicing New Historicism* (Chicago: University of Chicago Press, 2000), pp. 49–74.

—, *Nobody's Story: The Vanishing Acts of Women Writers in the Marketplace, 1670–1820* (Berkeley: University of California Press, 1995).

Garcha, Amanpal, *From Sketch to Novel: The Development of Victorian Fiction* (Baltimore: Johns Hopkins University Press, 2009).

Gee, Lisa, *Bricks without Mortar: The Selected Poems of Hartley Coleridge* (London: Picador, 2000).

Godwin, William, *An Enquiry concerning Political Justice*, ed. Mark Philp (Oxford: Oxford University Press, 2013).

—, *St. Leon: A Tale of the Sixteenth Century*, ed. William Brewer (Peterborough, ON: Broadview Press, 2006).

Grainger, Margaret (ed.), introduction to *The Natural History Prose Writings of John Clare* (Oxford: Clarendon Press, 1983), pp. xxxiii–l.

Griggs, Earl Leslie, *Hartley Coleridge: His Life and Work* (London: University of London Press, 1929).

—, 'Hartley Coleridge on His Father', *PMLA* 46: 4 (1931), pp. 1246–52.

H., 'On Keeping, or Costume in Character', *The New Monthly Magazine and Literary Journal* 10: 37 (1824), pp. 162–7.

H., R., 'On the Dangerous Influence of Injustice in the Formation of the Character of Children', *The New British Lady's Magazine* 1: 6 (1818), pp. 260–2.

Haefner, Joel, '"The soul speaking in the face": Hazlitt's Concept of Character', *Studies in English Literature* 24: 4 (1984), pp. 655–70.

Hall, Joseph, *Characters of Virtues and Vices. In Two Books*, in Josiah Pratt (ed.), *Practical Works*, vol. 7 of *The Works of . . . Joseph Hall . . . with Some Account of His Life and Sufferings, Written by Himself . . . in Ten Volumes* (London: Williams and Smith; A. Burditt; Byfield and Son; T. Conder; J. Hatchard; Mathews and Leigh; J. Nunn; F. C. and J. Rivington; L. B. Seeley; Vernor, Hood, and Sharpe; J. Walker; and J. White, 1808), pp. 81–115.

Hall, Robert, 'Effects of Infidelity on Character and Conduct', *The Saturday Magazine* 19: 15 (1839), p. 151.

Hartman, Herbert, *Hartley Coleridge: Poet's Son and Poet* (London: Oxford University Press, 1931).

Hazlitt, William, *The Complete Works of William Hazlitt*, 21 vols, ed. P. P. Howe (New York: J. M. Dent, 1933).

—, *An Essay on the Principles of Human Action and Some Remarks on the Systems of Hartley and Helvetius*, ed. John Nabholtz (Gainesville, FL: Scholars' Facsimiles and Reprints, 1969).

—, 'On Prejudice', in *Sketches and Essays By William Hazlitt. Now First Collected by His Son* (London: John Templeman, 1839), pp. 83–104.

—, *The Selected Writings of William Hazlitt*, 9 vols, ed. Duncan Wu (London: Pickering and Chatto, 1998).

Healey, Nicola, *Dorothy Wordsworth and Hartley Coleridge: The Poetics of Relationship* (New York: Palgrave Macmillan, 2012).

—, '"A living spectre of my Father dead": Hartley Coleridge, Samuel Taylor Coleridge, and Literary Representation', *The Coleridge Bulletin*, New Series 33 (2009), pp. 96–105.

—, 'The Reception of Hartley Coleridge's Poetry, from 1833 to the Present', *Romanticism* 16: 1 (2010), pp. 25–42.

Hegel, Georg Wilhelm Friedrich, *Philosophy of Fine Art*, vol. 2, trans. F. P. B. Osmaston (London: G. Bell and Sons, 1920).
—, *Phenomenology of Spirit*, trans. A. V. Miller (Oxford: Clarendon Press, 1997).
Hewitt, Douglas, 'Entertaining Ideas: A Critique of Peacock's *Crotchet Castle*', *Essays in Criticism* 20 (1970), pp. 200–12.
Higgins, David, *Romantic Culture and the Literary Magazine: Biography, Celebrity and Politics* (London: Routledge, 2005).
Hodgetts, Lucy, 'William Hone and the Reading Public', *Victorian Network* 4: 1 (2012), pp. 8–26.
Hoff, Peter, 'The Voices of *Crotchet Castle*', *The Journal of Narrative Technique* 2 (1972), pp. 186–98.
Hogg, James, *The Private Memoirs and Confessions of a Justified Sinner*, ed. Ian Duncan (Oxford: Oxford University Press, 2010).
—, *The Spy: A Periodical Paper of Literary Amusement and Instruction*, ed. Gillian Hughes (Edinburgh: Edinburgh University Press, 2000).
Hook, Theodore, *Sayings and Doings. A Series of Sketches from Life. In Three Volumes*, vol. 1 (London: Henry Colburn, 1824).
Howe, P. P., *The Life of William Hazlitt* (New York: George H. Doran, 1922).
Hume, David, *An Inquiry Concerning Human Understanding*, ed. Charles Hendel (Upper Saddle River, NJ: Prentice Hall, 1995).
—, 'The Sceptic', in *Essays and Treatises on Several Subjects, in Two Volumes. Volume I. Containing Essays, Moral, Political, and Literary. A New Edition* (London: T. Cadell, 1777).
Hunter, Ian, 'Reading Character', *Southern Review* 16: 2 (1983), pp. 226–43.
Jacobson, Howard, 'Lucretian Encomia in Wordsworth's *Prelude*', *American Notes and Queries* 24: 1/2 (1985), pp. 12–13.
Jacyna, L. S., 'Immanence or Transcendence: Theories of Life and Organization in Britain, 1790–1835', *Isis* 74: 3 (1983), pp. 310–29.
Jarrold, Thomas, 'Of the Influence of Early Impressions on the Future Character', *Monthly Magazine* 59: 408 (1825), pp. 193–6.
—, 'Of the Influence of Early Impressions on the Future Character [*cont.*],' *Monthly Magazine* 59: 409 (1825), pp. 301–5.
Johnston, Kenneth, *Unusual Suspects: Pitt's Reign of Alarm and the Lost Generation of the 1790s* (Oxford: Oxford University Press, 2013).
Jones, John, 'Keats and "The Feel of Not to Feel It"', in D. W. Jefferson (ed.), *The Morality of Art: Essays Presented to G. Wilson Knight by His Colleagues and Friends* (London: Routledge and Kegan Paul, 1969), pp. 185–94.

Kane, Richard, 'Bergsonian Comic Theory and *Crotchet Castle*', *Pennsylvania English* 12: 2 (1986), pp. 39–43.
Keach, William, *Shelley's Style* (New York: Methuen, 1984).
Keanie, Andrew, 'Hartley Coleridge and His Art of Dovetailing Miscellaneous Particulars', *The Coleridge Bulletin, New Series* 33 (2009), pp. 106–13.
—, *Hartley Coleridge: A Reassessment of His Life and Work* (New York: Palgrave Macmillan, 2008).
—, 'Hartley Coleridge: Son of the Mariner, King of Ejuxria', *The Coleridge Bulletin, New Series* 28 (2006), pp. 54–62.
Keats, John, *John Keats: Complete Poems*, ed. Jack Stillinger (Cambridge, MA: Harvard University Press, 1982).
—, *Letters of John Keats*, ed. Robert Gittings (London: Oxford University Press, 1970).
Kelley, Paul, 'Wordsworth and Lucretius' *De Rerum Natura*', *Notes and Queries* 228 (1983), pp. 219–22.
Khalip, Jacques, *Anonymous Life: Romanticism and Dispossession* (Stanford: Stanford University Press, 2009).
Kinnaird, John, *Hazlitt: Critic of Power* (New York: Columbia University Press, 1978).
Klancher, Jon, *Transfiguring the Arts and Sciences: Knowledge and Cultural Institutions in the Romantic Age* (Cambridge: Cambridge University Press, 2013).
Knight, Joseph E., 'Hazlitt's Use of the Character Tradition, His Philosophy, and His Aesthetics in *The Spirit of the Age*', PhD dissertation, University of Oregon, 1972.
Kupperman, Joel, *Character* (New York: Oxford, 1991).
La Bruyère, Jean de, *The Works of Monsieur De La Bruyere. Volume II. Containing the Characters, or Manners of the Present Age, with a Key of the Persons Characterized, under Feigned Names*, 6th edn (London: A. Bettersworth, W. Taylor and Jo Batley, 1723).
Lahey, Gerald, Appendix A.1, 'A Word concerning the Imagery of the *Liber Amoris*', in Gerald Lahey (ed.), *Liber Amoris; Or, the New Pygmalion*, by William Hazlitt (New York: New York University Press, 1980), pp. 263–4.
Lamb, Charles, *Elia and the Last Essays of Elia*, vol. 2 of E. V. Lucas (ed.), *The Works of Charles and Mary Lamb*, 7 vols (London: Methuen, 1903; rpt, New York: AMS Press, 1968).
Lambert, Cornelia, '"Living Machines": Performance and Pedagogy at Robert Owen's Institute for the Formation of Character, New Lanark, 1816–1828', *Journal of the History of Childhood and Youth* 4: 3 (2011), pp. 419–33.

Landon, Letitia, *Critical Writings by Letitia Elizabeth Landon*, ed. F. J. Sypher (Delmar, NY: Scholars' Facsimiles and Reprints, 1996).
—, *Ethel Churchill*, ed. by F. J. Sypher (Delmar, NY: Scholars' Facsimiles and Reprints, 1992).
—, *Fisher's Drawing Room Scrap-Book, 1833* (London: H. Fisher, R. Fisher and P. Jackson, 1833 [1832]).
—, *Fisher's Drawing Room Scrap-Book, 1838* (London, Paris, and New York: Fisher, Son, 1837).
—, *Francesca Carrara*, ed. F. J. Sypher (Delmar, NY: Scholars' Facsimiles and Reprints, 1999).
—, *Letters: by Letitia Elizabeth Landon*, ed. F. J. Sypher (Ann Arbor: Scholars' Facsimiles and Reprints, 2001).
—, 'No. 8. – Isabel Vere', in Laman Blanchard (ed.), *Life and Literary Remains of L. E. L.*, vol. 2 (London: Henry Colburn, 1841), pp. 114–15.
—, *Poetical Works of Letitia Elizabeth Landon, 'L.E.L.'*, ed. F. J. Sypher (Delmar, NY: Scholars' Facsimiles and Reprints, 1990).
—, preface to *The Venetian Bracelet, The Lost Pleiad, The History of the Lyre, and Other Poems*, in *The Complete Works of L. E. Landon*, vol. 2 (Boston, MA: Phillips, Sampson, 1854), p. 102.
—, *Romance and Reality*, ed. F. J. Sypher (Delmar, NY: Scholars' Facsimiles and Reprints, 1998).
King, Jeannette, *Tragedy in the Victorian Novel* (Cambridge: Cambridge University Press, 1978).
Leach, Nat, 'Between the "Hostile Body" and the "Hieroglyphic Human Soul": The Ethics of Beddoes's "Mental Theatre"', in Ute Berns and Michael Bradshaw (eds), *The Ashgate Companion to Thomas Lovell Beddoes* (Burlington, VT: Ashgate, 2007), pp. 123–34.
Leary, David, 'The Fate and Influence of John Stuart Mill's Proposed Science of Ethology', *Journal of the History of Ideas* 43: 1 (1982), pp. 153–62.
Leighton, Angela, *Victorian Women Poets: Writing against the Heart* (Charlottesville: University Press of Virginia, 1992).
Levine, George, *The Realistic Imagination: English Fiction from Frankenstein to Lady Chatterley* (Chicago: University of Chicago Press, 1981).
Locke, John, *Some Thoughts concerning Education*, in Ruth W. Grant and Nathan Tarcov (eds), *Some Thoughts concerning Education and Of the Conduct of the Understanding* (Indianapolis: Hackett, 1996), pp. 1–161.
Lootens, Tricia, 'Receiving the Legend, Rethinking the Writer: Letitia Landon and the Poetess Tradition', in Harriet Kramer Linkin and Stephen Behrendt

(eds), *Romanticism and Women Poets: Opening the Doors of Reception* (Lexington: University Press of Kentucky, 1999), pp. 242–59.

Lucretius, *The Nature of Things*, trans. A. E. Stallings (New York: Penguin, 2007).

Lynch, Deidre, 'Cult of Jane Austen', in Janet Todd (ed.), *Jane Austen in Context* (Cambridge: Cambridge University Press, 2005), pp. 111–20.

—, *The Economy of Character: Novels, Market Culture, and the Business of Inner Meaning* (Chicago: University of Chicago Press, 1998).

—, 'Sequels', in Janet Todd (ed.), *Jane Austen in Context* (Cambridge: Cambridge University Press, 2005), pp. 160–8.

— (ed.), 'Sharing with Our Neighbours', introduction to *Janeites: Austen's Disciples and Devotees* (Princeton: Princeton University Press, 2000), pp. 1–24.

Manning, Susan, *Poetics of Character: Transatlantic Encounters, 1799–1900* (Cambridge: Cambridge University Press, 2013).

Martin, Raymond and John Barresi, *Naturalization of the Soul: Self and Personal Identity in the Eighteenth Century* (London: Routledge, 2000).

Martineau, Harriet, *How to Observe. Morals and Manners* (New York: Harper, 1838).

McCalman, Iain (ed.), introduction to *An Oxford Companion to the Romantic Age: British Culture, 1776–1832* (Oxford: Oxford University Press, 1999), pp. 1–11.

McGann, Jerome and Daniel Riess (eds). introduction to *Letitia Elizabeth Landon: Selected Writings* (Orchard Park, NY: Broadview Press, 1997), pp. 11–31.

McIntyre, Jane, 'Character: A Humean Account', *History of Philosophy Quarterly* 7: 2 (1990), pp. 193–206.

McSweeney, Kerry and Peter Sabor (eds), introduction to *Sartor Resartus* (Oxford: Oxford University Press, 1999), pp. vii–xxiii.

Mee, Jon, '"Reciprocal expressions of kindness": Robert Merry, Della Cruscanism and the Limits of Sociability', in Gillian Russell and Cara Tuite (eds), *Romantic Sociability: Social Networks and Literary Culture in Britain, 1770–1840* (Cambridge: Cambridge University Press, 2002), pp. 104–22.

Mellor, Anne, *Romanticism and Gender* (New York: Routledge, 1993).

Mill, John Stuart, *On Liberty*, 2nd edn (London: John W. Parker and Son, 1859).

—, *A System of Logic, Ratiocinative and Inductive; Being a Connected View of the Principles of Evidence and the Methods of Scientific Investigation* (New York: Harper and Brothers, 1858).

Moylan, Christopher, 'T. L. Beddoes's Terminable or Interminable End', in Ute Berns and Michael Bradshaw (eds), *The Ashgate Research Companion to Thomas Lovell Beddoes* (Burlington, VT: Ashgate, 2007), pp. 229–39.

Mulvihill, James, 'Character and Culture in Hazlitt's *Spirit of the Age*', *Nineteenth-Century Literature* 45: 3 (1990), pp. 281–99.

Murphy, Peter T., 'Impersonation and Authorship in Romantic Britain', *ELH* 59: 3 (1992), pp. 625–49.

N., N., 'Further Thoughts on the Formation of Character', *The Athenaeum* 5: 26 (1809), pp. 97–101.

Nemoianu, Virgil, *The Taming of Romanticism: European Literature and the Age of Biedermeier* (Cambridge, MA: Harvard University Press, 1984).

Newlyn, Lucy, 'The Little Actor and His Mock apparel', *The Wordsworth Circle* 14: 1 (1983), pp. 30–9.

Nietzsche, Friedrich, 'On Truth and Lies in a Nonmoral Sense', trans. Daniel Breazeale, in Daniel Breazeale (ed.), *Philosophy and Truth: Selections from Nietzsche's Notebooks of the early 1870s* (Atlantic Highlands, NJ: Humanities Press, 1979), pp. 79–97.

Nussbaum, Felicity, *The Autobiographical Subject: Gender and Ideology in Eighteenth-Century England* (Baltimore: Johns Hopkins University Press, 1989).

O'Neill, Michael, '"Beautiful but ideal": Intertextual Relations between Letitia Elizabeth Landon and Percy Bysshe Shelley', in Beth Lau (ed.), *Fellow Romantics: Male and Female British Writers, 1790–1835* (Burlington, VT: Ashgate, 2009), pp. 211–30.

—, '"The latch-string of a new world's wicket": Poetry and Agency in *Death's Jest-Book; or, The Fool's Tragedy*', in Ute Berns and Michael Bradshaw (eds), *The Ashgate Research Companion to Thomas Love Beddoes* (Burlington, VT: Ashgate, 2007), pp. 33–48.

Owen, Robert, 'Address Delivered to the Inhabitants of New Lanark, 1816, on Opening the Institution for the Formation of Character, on the 1st of January, 1816', in Gregory Claeys (ed.), *Early Writings*, vol. 1 of *Selected Works of Robert Owen*, 4 vols (London: Pickering and Chatto, 1993), pp. 120–42.

—, *The Book of the New Moral World, Containing the Rational System of Society, Founded on Demonstrable Facts, Developing the Constitution and Laws of Human Nature and of Society*, vol. 3 of Gregory Claeys (ed.), *Selected Works of Robert Owen*, 4 vols (London: Pickering and Chatto, 1993).

—, 'A New View of Society; Or, Essays on the Principle of the Formation of the Human Character, and the Application of the Principle to

Practice', in Gregory Claeys (ed.), *Early Writings*, vol. 1 of *Selected Works of Robert Owen*, 4 vols (London: Pickering and Chatto, 1993), pp. 23–100.

Paine, Thomas, *Rights of Man: Being an Answer to Mr. Burke's Attack on the French Revolution*, ed. Moncure Daniel Conway (New York: G. P. Putnam's Sons, 1894).

Park, Roy, *Hazlitt and the Spirit of the Age: Abstraction and Critical Theory* (Oxford: Clarendon Press, 1971).

Parker, Mark, *Literary Magazines and British Romanticism* (Cambridge: Cambridge University Press, 2000).

Pascoe, Judith, *Romantic Theatricality: Gender, Poetry, and Spectatorship* (Ithaca: Cornell University Press, 1997).

Peacock, Thomas Love, *Crotchet Castle*, in Raymond Wright (ed.), *Nightmare Abbey/Crochet Castle* (New York: Penguin, 1986), pp. 125–259.

Philanthropos, 'The Character of a Common Brewer', *The Republican* 8: 16 (1823), pp. 504–6.

Piper, Andrew, *Dreaming in Books: The Making of the Bibliographic Imagination in the Romantic Age* (Chicago: University of Chicago Press, 2009).

Pitson, A. E., *Hume's Philosophy of the Self* (London: Routledge, 2002).

Plotz, Judith, 'The *Annus Mirabilis* and the Lost Boy: Hartley's Case', *Studies in Romanticism* 33: 2 (1994), pp. 181–200.

—, 'Childhood Lost, Childhood Regained: Hartley Coleridge's Fable of Defeat', *Children's Literature* 14 (1986), pp. 133–48.

—, *Romanticism and the Vocation of Childhood* (New York: Palgrave, 2001).

Polidori, John William, *The Vampyre: A Tale*, in D. L. Macdonald and Kathleen Scherf (eds), *The Vampyre: A Tale and Ernestus Berchtold; Or, The Modern Oedipus* (Peterborough, ON: Broadview Press, 2008), pp. 37–60.

Pomeroy, Mary Joseph, *The Poetry of Hartley Coleridge* (Washington, DC: Catholic University of America, 1927).

Porter, James, 'Love of Life: Lucretius to Freud', in Shadi Bartsch and Thomas Bartscherer (eds), *Erotikon: Essays on Eros, Ancient and Modern* (Chicago: University of Chicago Press, 2005), pp. 113–41.

Postman, Neil, *The End of Education: Redefining the Value of School* (New York: Alfred A. Knopf, 1995).

Raleigh, John Henry, '"Waverley" as History; Or 'Tis One Hundred and Fifty-Six Years Since', *NOVEL* 4: 1 (1970), pp. 14–29.

Rauch, Alan, *Useful Knowledge: The Victorians, Morality, and the March of Intellect* (Durham, NC: Duke University Press, 2001).

Reeves, James (ed.), 'Hartley Coleridge', in *Five Late Romantic Poets* (London: Heinemann, 1974), pp. 140–4.
Rennell, Thomas, *Remarks on Scepticism, Especially As It Is Connected with the Subjects of Organization and Life. Being an Answer to the Views of M. Bichat, Sir T. C. Morgan, and Mr. Lawrence, upon Those Points*, 2nd edn (London: F. C. and J. Rivington, 1819).
Richardson, Alan, *Literature, Education, and Romanticism: Reading as Social Practice, 1780–1832* (Cambridge: Cambridge University Press, 1994).
—, *A Mental Theater: Poetic Drama and Consciousness in the Romantic Age* (University Park, PA: Penn State University Press, 1988).
Richardson, Thomas C., 'Character and Craft in Lockhart's *Adam Blair*', in Ian Campbell (ed.), *Nineteenth-Century Scottish Fiction: Critical Essays* (New York: Harper and Row, 1979), pp. 51–67.
Riess, Daniel, 'Laetitia Landon and the Dawn of English Post-Romanticism', *Studies in English Literature* 36: 4 (1996), pp. 807–27.
Rorty, Amélie Oksenberg, 'A Literary Postscript: Characters, Persons, Selves, Individuals', in Amélie Oksenberg Rorty (ed.), *The Identities of Persons* (Berkeley: University of California Press, 1976), pp. 301–23.
Rousseau, Jean-Jacques, *Émile: or on Education: Includes Émile and Sophie; or, The Solitaries*, trans. Christopher Kelly and Allan Bloom, vol. 13 of Roger D. Masters and Christopher Kelley (eds), *The Collected Writings of Rousseau*, 14 vols (Hanover, NH: Dartmouth College Press, 2010).
Russell, John, *Essays, and Sketches of Life and Character. By a Gentleman Who Has Left His Lodgings* (London: Longman, Hurst, Rees, Orme, and Brown, 1820).
Rzekpa, Charles, *The Self as Mind: Vision and Identity in Wordsworth, Coleridge, and Keats* (Cambridge, MA: Harvard University Press, 1986).
Savarese, John, 'Reading One's Own Mind: Hazlitt, Cognition, Fiction', *European Romantic Review* 24: 4 (2013), pp. 437–52.
Schechtman, Marya, *The Constitution of Selves* (Ithaca: Cornell University Press, 1996).
Schelling, F. W. J., *Philosophical Investigations into the Essence of Human Freedom*, trans. Jeff Love and Johannes Schmidt (Albany: State University of New York Press, 2006).
Schiller, Friedrich, *Letters upon the Aesthetic Education of Man*, trans. Elizabeth Wilkinson and L. A. Willoughby, in Walter Hinderer and Daniel Dahlstrom (eds), *Essays*, vol. 17 of Volkmar Sander (ed.), *The German Library* (New York: Continuum, 1993), pp. 86–178.
Schoenfield, Mark, *British Periodicals and Romantic Identity* (New York: Palgrave Macmillan, 2009).

Scott, Walter, *Old Mortality*, ed. Jane Stevenson and Peter Davidson (Oxford: Oxford University Press, 2009).
—, 'Tales of My Landlord, 1817', in Ioan Williams (ed.), *Sir Walter Scott on Novelists and Fiction* (New York: Barnes and Noble, 1968), pp. 237–59.
Seigel, Jerrold, 'Necessity, Freedom, and Character Formation from the Eighteenth Century to the Nineteenth', in Thomas Ahnert and Susan Manning (eds), *Character, Self, and Sociability in the Scottish Enlightenment* (New York: Palgrave Macmillan, 2011), pp. 249–66.
Semple, Janet, *Bentham's Prison: A Study of the Panopticon Penitentiary* (Oxford: Clarendon Press, 1993).
Shelley, Percy Bysshe, *Hellas*, in Donald Reiman and Neil Fraistat (eds), *Shelley's Poetry and Prose*, 2nd edn (New York: Norton, 2002), pp. 427–64.
—, *St. Irvyne; Or, The Rosicrucian: A Romance*, in Stephen Behrendt (ed.), *Zastrozzi, A Romance and St. Irvyne; Or, The Rosicrucian: A Romance* (Peterborough, ON: Broadview Press, 2002), pp. 157–252.
Siskin, Clifford, 'The Historicity of Romantic Discourse', in Michael McKeon (ed.), *Theory of the Novel: A Historical Approach* (Baltimore: Johns Hopkins University Press, 2000), pp. 566–86.
Smeed, J. W., *The Theophrastan 'Character'* (Oxford: Clarendon Press, 1985).
Smith, Kevin, 'Typologies, Taxonomies, and the Benefits of Policy Classification', *Policy Studies Journal* 30: 3 (2002), pp. 379–95.
Spiegelman, Willard, 'Some Lucretian Elements in Wordsworth', *Comparative Literature* 37 (1985), pp. 27–49.
Spurzheim, Johann Gaspar, *Phrenology, in Connection with the Study of Physiognomy. Part I. Characters. With Thirty–Four Plates* (London: Treuttel, Wurtz and Richter, 1826).
—, *The Physiognomical System of Drs. Gall and Spurzheim; Founded on an Anatomical and Physiological Examination of the Nervous System in General, and of the Brain in Particular; and Indicating the Dispositions and Manifestations of the Mind*, 2nd edn (London: Baldwin, Cradock and Joy, 1815).
St Clair, William, *The Godwins and the Shelleys: The Biography of a Family* (Baltimore: Johns Hopkins University Press, 1989).
Stapleton, Laurence, *The Elected Circle: Studies in the Art of Prose* (Princeton: Princeton University Press, 1973).
Stephenson, Glennis, *Letitia Landon: The Woman Behind L. E. L.* (Manchester: Manchester University Press, 1995).
Stevenson, Jane and Peter Davidson (eds), *Old Mortality*, by Walter Scott (Oxford: Oxford University Press, 2009).

Stewart, David, *Romantic Magazines and Metropolitan Literary Culture* (New York: Palgrave Macmillan, 2011).
Story, Patrick, 'Emblems of Identity: The Spirit of the Age', *The Wordsworth Circle* 10: 1 (1979), pp. 81–90.
Strawson, Galen, 'The Impossibility of Ultimate Moral Responsibility', in Derk Pereboom (ed.), *Free Will*, 2nd edn (Indianapolis: Hackett, 2009), pp. 298–306.
Swinburne, Algernon Charles, *Algernon Charles Swinburne: Major Poems and Selected Prose*, ed. Jerome McGann and Charles Sligh (New Haven, CT: Yale University Press, 2004).
Taylor, Anya, '"A Father's Tale": Coleridge Foretells the Life of Hartley', *Studies in Romanticism* 30: 1 (1991), pp. 37–56.
Taylor, Charles, *Sources of the Self: The Making of the Modern Identity* (Cambridge, MA: Harvard University Press, 1989).
Trilling, Lionel, *Sincerity and Authenticity* (Cambridge, MA: Harvard University Press, 1972).
Tucker, Herbert. 'House Arrest: The Domestication of English Poetry in the 1820s', *New Literary History*, 5: 3 (1994), pp. 521–48.
Tucker, James, 'On the Formation of Character', *The Magazine of Useful Knowledge and Co-operative Miscellany* 3 (1830), pp. 44–5.
van Wyhe, John, 'The Authority of Human Nature: The "Schädellehre" of Franz Joseph Gall', *The British Journal for the History of Science* 35: 1 (2002), pp. 17–42.
Walder, Dennis, introduction to *Sketches by Boz* (New York: Penguin, 1995), pp. ix–xxxiv.
Watt, Julie, 'We Did Not Think That He Could Die: Letitia Elizabeth Landon and the Afterlife of Scott's Heroines', *Scottish Literary Review* 7: 2 (2015), pp. 119–34.
Watts, Alaric A. (ed.), *Scenes of Life and Shades of Character, in Two Volumes* (London: Henry Colburn and Richard Bentley, 1831).
Westmacott, Charles, *The English Spy, An Original Work, Characteristic, Satirical, and Humorous, Comprising Scenes and Sketches in Every Rank of Society, Being Portraits of the Illustrious, Eminent, Eccentric and Notorious, Drawn from the Life by Bernard Blackmantle, the Illustrations Designed by Robert Cruikshank*, vol. 1 (London: Methuen, 1907).
Whale, John, *Imagination under Pressure, 1789–1832: Aesthetics, Politics and Utility* (Cambridge: Cambridge University Press, 2000).
Wilson, Cheryl, *Fashioning the Silver Fork Novel* (London: Pickering and Chatto, 2012).
Wilson, James, *On Character* (Washington, DC: The AEI Press, 1995).

Wollstonecraft, Mary, *The Wrongs of Woman, Or Maria*, in Michelle Faubert (ed.), *Mary, A Fiction and The Wrongs of Woman, or Maria* (Peterborough, ON: Broadview Press, 2012), pp. 149–288.
Wordsworth, William, *Lyrical Ballads and Other Poems*, ed. Martin Scofield (Ware: Wordsworth Editions Limited, 2003).
—, 'Resolution and Independence', in Stephen Gill (ed.), *William Wordsworth: The Major Works* (Oxford: Oxford University Press, 2000), pp. 260–4.
Wu, Duncan, (ed.), *The Selected Writings of William Hazlitt*, 9 vols (London: Pickering and Chatto, 1998).
—, *William Hazlitt: The First Modern Man* (Oxford: Oxford University Press, 2008).
Yousef, Nancy, *Isolated Cases: The Anxieties of Autonomy in Enlightenment Philosophy and Romantic Literature* (Ithaca: Cornell University Press, 2004).

Index

Note: 'n' indicates chapter notes; **bold** indicates tables; *italics* indicate figures.

Abernethy, John, 15
abstraction, 98, 100, 103–4, 112–13, 114n17, 204–5
Ahnert, Thomas, 19, 29
Allard, James, 191n14
anatomists, 171–2, 182, 186–8
annuals, literary, 3, 148, 159, 168n18
Aristotle, *Nichomachean Ethics*, 31
Arnold, Matthew, 183
art, 91, 97–8, 103, 112
atheism, 121–2, 125–6, 139n22
Athenaeum, The, 9, 36, 86–7
audience *see* readership
Austen, Jane, 5, 7, 16, 24n8, 147
authenticity *see* 'real' characters

Baiesi, Serena, 167n13
Ball, Terence, 40
Ballard, Joseph, *England in 1815*, 44
Barbauld, Anna, 102
Barmby, Catherine, 47–9
Beddoes, Thomas, 172
Beddoes, Thomas Lovell, 171–82, 210
  The Brides' Tragedy, 172–3

Death's Jest-Book, 171–82, 191n14
Bender, John, 20
Bentham, Jeremy, 27, 35, 40, 46, 118, 167, 188
  'Of Circumstances Influencing Sensibility', 40–2, **41**
Bentley's Miscellany, 9
Berns, Ute, 172, 179, 180
'bias' of character, 11, 14–15, 36, 76, 90–1, 93, 107–8, 113, 188, 210
Blackwood's Edinburgh Magazine, 9, 13, 16, 19, 38, 42, 46, 62, 65
Blanchard, Laman, *Life and Literary Remains of L. E. L.*, 57
body, human, 130, 157, 171–2, 185, 210
Bourne, J. G. H., 173, 179
Boyce, Benjamin, 100, 115n22
Bradshaw, Michael, 172
Brewer, David, 4–7, 24n8, 57
Bricke, John, 30
Bromwich, David, 109, 114n14
Brummell, Beau, 148
Burke, Edmund, 64, 143–4, *144*
Burwick, Frederick, 105, 172, 179

Butler, Marilyn, 16
Butler, Samuel, *Characters*, 31, 32, 33
Byron, Lord George Gordon, 9, 16, 70–1

Canuel, Mark, 51n3
capital, character as, 37
Carlile, Richard, 47, 51
Carlisle, Janice, 204, 211
Carlson, Julie, 145
Carlyle, Thomas, 3, 171, 203–10
  Sartor Resartus, 3, 203–10
Chambers's Edinburgh Journal, 69
Chambers's Edinburgh Magazine, 34
Chapman, Robert Willan, 51
'character', as term, 9–11
'character sketches' (Theophrastan tradition), 3, 10–13, 16–17, 31–4, 58–61, 69, 77, 80–1, 84, 100–4, 186–9, 193
characterisation, 4, 15–16, 18–21, 73–81, 193, 210; *see also* meta-characterisation
characterlessness, 3, 70–1, 87, 118, 123, 137, 166–7, 183
character-reading, 34, 38, 62–4, 96–7
childhood, 2, 44–5, 82–4, 117–20, 129, 137
  infancy, 126–7, 129, 141n28
  unborn children, 126, 179–81
Christianity, 47, 50, 158
  and the poetry of Hartley Coleridge, 119, 121–5, 128–32, 136–7, 139n17, 139n22
Clare, John, 'An Invite to Eternity', 117
class, social, 8–9, 198, 200–2
classicism, 183
classification *see* taxonomy; typology and 'types'

clothing, 203–8, 210
Colburn, Henry, 9, 57
Coleridge, Derwent, 120, 123
Coleridge, Hartley, 22, 117–37, 138nn11–12, 139n17, 139n22, 141n28, 141nn37–8, 210
  'A Schoolfellow's Tribute to the Memory of the Rev. Owen Lloyd', 134
  'Fear', 139n22
  'I Have Written My Name on Water. The Proposed Inscription on the Tomb of John Keats', 135–6, 142n40
  'Leonard and Susan', 133
  'Lines Written by H.C. in the Fly-Leaf of a Copy of Lucretius Presented by Him to Mr. Wordsworth', 123–6
  'Prometheus. A Fragment', 134
  Sonnet 'V. May, 1840', 132–3
  Sonnet 'X', 126
  Sonnet 'XI', 139n22
  Sonnet 'XII', 134
  Sonnet 'LIII. Prayer', 131–2
  Sonnet 'LIV', 127
  'The Birth-Day: To James Brancker, Esq.', 126
  'The Forsaken to the Faithless', 133–4
  'The Sabbath-Day's Child', 126–7
  'To a Deaf and Dumb Little Girl', 137
  'To a Posthumous Infant', 126–7
  'Twins', 127
  'Why Is There War on Earth?', 130–1
Coleridge, Samuel Taylor, 11, 32, 49, 92, 117–19, 122, 138n11, 145, 209
Combe, George, 12, 45–7, 63

Comte, Auguste, *Positive Philosophy of Auguste Comte*, 15, 17, 42
concepts of 'character', 150, 174, 190, 198, 200, 205
consciousness, 13, 24n26, 87, 118–19, 180–1
consistency *see* inconsistency
constancy, 147–8, 152
constitutive character ('essence'), 10, 62, 94, 106, 118, 125, 130, 135–6, 173, 175, 194; *see also* traits, character
Cooper, Samuel, 97–8
Co-Operative Magazine, The, 37, 47
Cooter, Roger, 54n75
Copeland, Edward, 8, 211n2
Craciun, Adriana, 139n22, 157
Craig, William, 31–2
craniology, 46–7, 67, 95, 197
Cromwell, Oliver, 97–8
Cronin, Richard, 8, 9, 13, 42, 57, 62, 65, 77, 115n42, 146–7, 150, 168n18, 171

Dacre, Charlotte, 145
Darden, Lindley, 53n57
Darnfield, Henry, 58
Dart, Gregory, 16, 94–5, 110, 116n42
Davidson, Peter, 78
Davy, Humphry, 145
Dawson, Carl, 189
De Quincey, Thomas, 13–14, 62, 70
de Staël, Madame, 168n24
death, 122–30, 134–7, 138n10
'decided' character, 10, 37, 150, 151
Della Cruscan poetry, 94–5, 101
Derrida, Jacques, 180
determinism, 40, 45, 90, 105, 106, 123, 172, 180, 211

development, character, 56–8, 107, 127–8
Dick, Alex, 74
Dickens, Charles, 27, 58, 81, 210
Sketches by Boz, 16, 58, 60, 193–203, 210, 212n6
Diderot, Denis, 28, 68
Rameau's Nephew, 151–3
discourse, character, 3, 19–20, 56, 62, 69–70, 209–11
'disposition' of character, 27–30, 51n3
Dodson, Charles, 183, 189
door-knockers, 195–6
Duncan, Ian, 64–5, 73

Earle, John, *Microcosmographie*, 31
Eclectic Review, The, 47
Edgeworth, Maria, 171
Edinburgh Magazine and Literary Miscellany, The, 35, 36
Edinburgh Phrenological Society, 46
Edinburgh Review, The, 68
education, 36–8, 44–5, 105, 182–6; *see also* knowledge
Eliot, George, 89, 128, 210–11
Elliotson, John, 15
Emerson, Ralph Waldo, 166, 210–11
encyclopaedias, 11–14, 50, 55n96, 91–2, 94, 107, 182
Enlightenment, 2, 6, 28–30, 151
Epicureanism, 124–5
Erickson, Lee, 8
espionage, 63–5
'essense' of a person *see* constitutive character
Esterhammer, Angela, 153–4
ethics, 30, 154–5
ethology, 3, 17–18, 33, 34–51, **41**, 56, 62, 75, 89–104, 146–8, 198
popular ethologies (essays), 35–6

Examiner, The, 102, 158
'executive' aspect of character, 68, 172, 211

faces and features *see* physiognomy
fatalism, 17, 54n75, 102, 153
female characters, 57–8, 61–2, 113, 116n42, 150–1
  constancy in love, 147–8
  'feminine Romanticism', 120, 139n22
Ferguson, Stuart, 75
'fictitious entity', character as, 27, 35, 118, 167, 188
Fielding, Henry, 6
Fisher's Drawing Room Scrap-Book, 158–62
fixed character, 89–90, 112, 198
Foucault, Michel, *Discipline and Punish*, 1, 4
fragmentation of character, 92–4
Fraser's Magazine, 9, 15, 57, 203
freedom, 45, 90, 105–7, 109, 118, 172, 210
Freeman, Lisa, 5–7, 10–11, 53n40
French Revolution, 8, 143–5
Freud, Sigmund, 122–3, 127–8
Frow, John, 6, 11, 90

Gall, Franz Joseph, 17, 46–7, 51
Gallagher, Catherine, 4, 5, 7
Garcha, Amanpal, 58–9, 77
Gaskell, Elizabeth, 58
Gee, Lisa, 119
Gem, A Literary Annual, The, 141n38
generalisations, 39, 75, 97, 102–4, 109
Gillray, James, 'A Uniform Whig' (print), 143–4, *144*

Godwin, William, *Enquiry concerning Political Justice*, 1–3, 18, 48, 145–6
Gothic novels, 63, 85–6
Griggs, Leslie, 138n12, 139n17
growth of character, 29, 107, 127–8

habits, 2, 29–30, 105
Haefner, Joel, 68, 113n4
Hall, Joseph, *Character of Virtues and Vices*, 31, 32, 80
handwriting, 38, 53n46
Hardy, Thomas, 105, 210–11
Hartman, Herbert, 129, 138n12
Haydon, Benjamin Robert, 110
Hazlitt, William, 11–14, 18, 31, 33, 89–113, 114n8, 119, 162, 210
  An Essay on the Principles of Human Action, 91–3, 103, 105
  Liber Amoris, 33, 90, 108–12, 116n42, 147
  Political Essays, with Sketches of Public Characters, 103
  Table-Talk, 33
  The Round Table, 101–2
  The Spirit of the Age, 92, 94–5, 100
  'Character of John Bull', 94
  'Madame Pasta and Mademoiselle Mars', 93–4
  'On a Portrait of a Lady by Vandyke', 93
  'On Clerical Character', 101
  'On Dr Spurzheim's Theory', 96, 107
  'On Effeminacy of Character', 101
  'On Familiar Style', 102
  'On Genius and Common Sense', 97–8
  'On Gusto', 70

'On Personal Character', 33, 104–5, 107
'On Reason and Imagination', 103
'On Self-Love and Benevolence', 91
'On the Elgin Marbles', 112
'On the Knowledge of Character', 33, 38, 104–5, 110
'On the Literary Character', 101
'On the Living Poets', 94
'Paragraphs on Prejudice', 104
'The Same Subject Continued', 102
Healey, Nicola, 119–21, 138nn10–11
Hegel, Georg Wilhelm Friedrich, 68, 172, 211
Hewitt, Douglas, 183
hierarchy of knowledge, 11–13, 15, 107–8
Higgins, David, 15, 57
historical characters, 75–9
Hoff, Peter, 189
Hogg, James, 19, 38, 53n46, 63–5
Hone, William, *Every-Day Book*, 67
Hood, Thomas, 31
Hook, Theodore, *Sayings and Doings, a Series of Sketches from Life*, 60
human nature, 39, 42, 63, 75–6, 154, 174, 183
Hume, David, 2, 18, 27–34, 39, 64, 157
humour, 196–7
humours, 206–7
Hunt, Leight, 31
Hunter, John, 15, 49

identity, 9–10, 25n31, 28, 91–2
ideology, 47, 90, 159–60, 167, 174, 195–7, 210–11

Idler, The, 31
imagination, 83, 87, 97, 102–3, 107–9, 112, 133–5, 156–7
'imaginative expansion' of texts, 5–6, 24n8
immanentism, 15, 49–51, 56, 171–2, 188
Imperial Magazine, The, 37
improvisation, 153–4
inconsistency, 44–5, 77, 85, 143–52
Institute for the Formation of Character, 45

Jacyna, L. S., 49
James, Henry, 210
Jarrold, Thomas, 'Of the Influence of Early Impressions on the Future Character', 36–7, 83, 89
Johnston, Kenneth, 145
'Junius', 70–1

Kane, Richard, 184, 196
Kant, Immanuel, 28, 32, 68, 151
Keach, William, 159
Keanie, Andrew, 120, 129, 136, 138n11
Keats, John, 70, 135–6, 163–4
  Endymion, 101
  'In drear nighted December', 117, 121, 135, 142n39
  'Ode to a Nightingale', 163–4
Kelsall, Thomas Forbes, 173, 179
Klancher, Jon, 49
Knight, Joseph E., 100, 113n6
knowledge, 12–13, 204–7, 211
  hierarchical system of, 11–13, 15, 107–8
  mass dissemination of, 182–6
  see also education
Korzybski, Alfred, 114n17

La Bruyère, Jean de, *Caractères*, 31, 32
Lahey, Gerald, 112
Lamb, Charles, 31, 33, 80–7, 119, 141n38, 210
   Elia essays, 33, 80–7
   The Last Essays of Elia, 84–6
   'A Bachelor's Complaint of the Behaviour of Married People', 84
   'Barrenness of the Imaginative Faculty in the Productions of Modern Art', 86–7
   'Imperfect Sympathies', 81–2
   'New Year's Eve', 82–3
   'Poor Relations', 80–1
   'Sanity of True Genius', 85–7
   'The Two Races of Men', 81
Lambert, Cornelia, 34
Landon, Letitia, 21–22, 139n22, 143, 146–67, 167n13, 168n18, 168n24, 169n37, 210
   Ethel Churchill, 151
   Francesca Carrara, 156–9
   'poetic illustrations' in *Fisher's Drawing Room Scrap-Book*, 158–66
   The Improvisatrice, 151, 168n24
   Romance and Reality, 143, 147–8, 151, 156, 158, 165
   The Venetian Bracelet, The Lost Pleiad, The History of the Lyre, and Other Poems, 154–5
   'The Dream', 159
   'The Female Portrait Gallery', 57–8, 62, 77
   'Glengariffe', 162–4
   'Linmouth', 161–2
   'The Lost Pleiad', 159
   'No. 8. – Isabel Vere', 158
   'On the Ancient and Modern Influence of Poetry', 154
   'Roland's Tower', 157
   'Rydal Water and Grasmere Lake, the Residence of Wordsworth', 162–6
   'A Summer Evening's Tale', 155–6
Lawrence, William, 15, 49, 55n96, 91
Leach, Nat, 173
Leary, David, 53n54
Leighton, Angela, 168n18
literary annuals, 3, 148, 159, 168n18
Literary Chronicle, The, 186
Literary Gazette, The, 9, 135, 141n38
Literary Souvenir, The, 60
Lloyd, Charles, 145
Lloyd, Rev. Owen, 134
Locke, John, *Some Thoughts concerning Education*, 89
Lockhart, J. G., 62
London Magazine, The, 13–14, 33, 62, 80
Lootens, Tricia, 150–1
love, 127, 147–8, 150, 152, 158–9
Lucretius, 122–5, 129–33, 136
   The Nature of Things, 125–6, 130–1, 133, 136, 141n35
Lukács, George, 75, 211
Lynch, Deidre, 4–7, 19, 194

McGann, Jerome, 7, 168n18, 172
McIntyre, Jane, 30, 39
Mackintosh, James, 145
Maclise, Daniel, 15–16
McSweeney, Kerry, 204
magazines, 3, 9, 13–16, 35, 57, 62; *see also* periodicals
Maginn, William, 'Gallery of Illustrious Literary Characters', 15, 57–8
Manning, Peter, 172

Manning, Susan, 6, 29, 37, 76, 90, 146
March of Mind, 175, 183, 188
Martineau, Harriet, 15, 17
 How to Observe. Morals and Manners, 42–4
materialism, 28–9, 68, 121–2, 125, 130–6, 157
maturity, 2, 30, 207
Mee, Jon, 95
Mellor, Anne, 120, 150, 157
Merry, Robert, 95
meta-characterisation, 23, 193–211
metaphysics, 10, 21, 23, 42, 90–2, 107, 172, 175–82, 188
Metropolitan, The, 9
Mill, John Stuart, 35, 38–40, 42, 48, 53n54, 75–6, 90
 On Liberty, 76
 System of Logic, 17–18, 39, 97
Miller, William, 186
mimicry, 64, 159–61
mind, human, 12, 14, 67, 90, 99, 105, 108, 141n35, 157, 184, 210
Minerva Press, 85–7
Mirror, The, 31, 45, 147
Mitford, Mary, *Our Village*, 58
money, paper, 68
Monthly Magazine, The, 83
Moore, Thomas, 94–5
'moral' character, 28–9, 32, 62, 68, 76–9, 83, 94, 106, 117–18, 130, 151, 197
More, Hannah, 102
Morgan, T. C., 15, 50
Moylan, Christopher, 175, 179
Mulvihill, James, 114n8

Napier, Macvey, 62
Napoleonic Wars, 7–8, 32–4, 63, 145
nations, 15, 43–4

Native Americans, 34
'natural' character, 28–9, 68–9, 86, 151
nature, 15, 42, 118, 122, 131, 160–5
nature, human, 39, 42, 63, 75–6, 154, 174, 183
necessity, internal and external, 105–7, 109
Nemoianu, Virgil, 7, 151
neoclassicism, 134
neo-Platonism, 22, 121, 149, 157–9
New British Lady's Magazine, The, 44
New Monthly Magazine, The, 13, 85, 154
Newcastle Magazine, The, 12, 63
Newlyn, Lucy, 138n12
newspapers, 23, 186, 189–90, 194, 203
Nietzsche, Friedrich, 99–100, 112, 210
Novalis, *Heinrich von Ofterdingen*, 1, 4, 211
novels, 4–9, 16, 19–20, 29–32, 59, 62–3, 73–9, 85, 193; *see also* Gothic novels; silver fork novels

O'Neill, Michael, 169n37, 173, 179–80
Opie, Amelia Alderson, 145
organic existence, 122–3, 126–9, 135–7
organisms, 3, 15, 49–50, 53n57, 89, 128, 173
Oriental Herald and Journal of General Literature, The, 33, 34
Overbury, Thomas, *Characters*, 31
Owen, Robert, 15, 44–5, 47–8, 118
Owenism, 44–5, 54n75, 56, 150

Paine, Tom, *Rights of Man*, 69
pantheism, 118, 120–2, 130, 132, 136, 140n23
paranoia, 171–90
Parker, Mark, 9
Pascoe, Judith, 169n30
passion, 30–2, 39, 50
Peacock, Thomas Love, 9, 11–12, 182–90, 210
  Crotchet Castle, 182–90, 196–7
periodicals, 9, 13–16, 18, 35, 42, 59, 65; *see also* magazines
'personal' aspect of character, 11, 51, 68, 104, 172
'personalities' (gossip texts), 18, 32, 35, 42
personality, 11, 42, 121, 139n22; *see also* traits, character
phrenology, 3, 12–14, 17, 45–9, 54n75, 56, 63, 67, 95–7, 107, 195–7
physiognomy, 11, 17, 19, 21, 38–9, 44–6, 50, 64–5, 68, 93–8, 101–2, 112, 195–6, 212n6
physiology, 23, 30, 38, 49, 91, 171–3, 188
Piper, Andrew, 38
Pitson, A. E., *Hume's Philosophy of the Self*, 9–10
Plotz, Judith, 119, 127, 129, 137, 138nn10–12
poetry, 8–9, 153–7
Polidori, John William, *The Vampyre*, 70
Pomeroy, Mary Joseph, 139n17
Pope, Alexander, *Epistle to a Lady: Of the Characters of Women*, 31
Porter, James, 122, 129
'portrait-characters' (texts), 32–3, 78, 100, 109

'portraits' (texts), 3, 32–3, 35, 57–8, 66, 78, 109, 118; *see also* 'character sketches'
positivism, 18, 29, 42
'possession' of character, 3, 19, 48
Postman, Neil, 112, 114n17
predictability of character, 1–2, 67, 119, 146, 151
privacy/privation, 124, 137
'private' character, 18–19
Procter, Bryan Waller, 173, 179
psychological 'laws', 18, 86–7, 90, 105
Public Advertiser, The, 70
'public' character, 18–19
Public Characters of 1798, 33
publishing, 8–9, 11

Quarterly Review, The, 55n96, 74–5, 103

Rambler, The, 31
Rauch, Alan, 182
readership, 4–7, 15–16, 19, 146–7, 160
'real' characters, 5, 7, 46, 58–9, 77, 83–4, 146–7, 165, 190, 205
realism, 5, 20–1, 56, 73–9, 193, 205
rebirth, 176–81
Rees's *Cyclopædia* (Rev. Abraham Rees), 50, 55n96, 91, 107
Reeves, James, 139n17, 139n22
reform era, 3–4, 7–11, 20, 186, 193, 210
Regency period, 8, 21, 49, 148, 203
regression, 123, 127–30, 133, 136, 146
representation, 6–7, 20–1, 29, 32, 58, 77, 193–4; *see also* typology and 'types'

Republican, The, 34
reputation, 63, 69
Reynolds, Joshua, 103
Richardson, Alan, 29, 114n8
Riess, Daniel, 7, 157, 168n18
Rorty, Amélie Oksenberg, 95
'round' characters, 5, 23, 58, 193–4
Rousseau, Jean-Jacques, *Émile*, 89
Rowan, Archibald Hamilton, 145
Rowton, Frederic, 164
Russell, John, *Essays, and Sketches of Life and Character*, 16, 59–60

Sabor, Peter, 204
Saumarez, Richard, 15
Savarese, John, 103
Schechtman, Marya, 10
Schelling, Friedrich, *Philosophical Investigations into the Essence of Human Freedom*, 105–6
Schoenfield, Mark, 18, 33, 63, 65
science and the 'sciences', 3–4, 11–13, 15–17, 34, 195; *see also* ethology; phrenology
Scott, Walter, 16, 57–8, 73–87, 118, 141n38, 210
  Tales of My Landlord (and *Old Mortality*), 73–4, 77–80
  Waverley, 73–4, 77
Scottish Enlightenment, 29–31
Seigel, Jerrold, 28, 44–5
self, 19–20, 24n26, 25n31, 28, 48, 117, 121, 130–1, 172
Shakespeare, William, 70, 85–7
Shelley, Mary, 13, 16, 110–11
Shelley, Percy Bysshe, 63, 158–60, 169n37, 171
  Hellas, 181
  Posthumous Poems, 181
  Queen Mab, The Daemon of the World, 158

'Hymn to Intellectual Beauty', 158
silver fork novels, 22, 147, 193, 203, 211n2
Siskin, Clifford, 56
'sketches' *see* 'character sketches'
sleep, 133–5
Smeed, J. W., 31
Smith, Kevin, 64
Society for the Diffusion of Useful Knowledge, 182
sociology, 17, 42–3, 53n57, 56
soul, human, 39, 63, 122–5, 128–35, 141n35, 171–2, 177, 206–7
Southey, Robert, 45, 91, 145
Spectator, The, 31
Spenser, Edmund, 85–7
Spiegelman, Willard, 141n37
spirit, 106, 141n35
Spirit of the Age, The, 33
Spurzheim, Johann Gaspar, *Phrenology, in Connection with the Study of Physiognomy*, 17, 45–6, 95
Spy, The, 63–4
Stephenson, Glennis, 150, 169n42
Stevenson, Jane, 78
Stewart, Dugald, 75–6
Story, Patrick, 100
Swinburne, Algernon Charles, 122–3, 134

Tatler, The, 31
taxonomy, 15–16, 20, 39, 42, 60–1; *see also* typology and 'types'
Taylor, Charles, 25n31
temperament, 29, 90–1, 112, 156, 182, 206
temporality, 56–9
Thackeray, William Makepeace, *Paris Sketchbook*, 58

Theophrastus, *Characters*, 31–4; see also 'character sketches' (Theophrastan tradition)
tone, 68, 83
traits, character, 10, 17–19, 30, 37, 61, 80, 99–100
'transcendence' of character, 118, 121, 130, 133, 138n11, 176, 198
transcendentalism, 49–51, 56, 171, 189–90
Trilling, Lionel, 48
truth, 100, 145–6
Tucker, Herbert, 7
typologies and 'types', 10–11, 16–17, 31–4, 39, 53n54, 60–1, 78, 80–1, 84, 98, 100–4, 109

utilitarianism, 27, 29, 154, 204, 209

vampires, 70
Victorian era, 7–8, 210–11
vitalism, 49, 171
voice, narrative, 150, 156, 159, 165–6, 194, 197

Walker, Sarah, 18–19, 33, 109–13, 116n42
Watt, Julie, 57–8, 167n13

Watts, Alaric, *Scenes of Life and Shades of Character*, 16, 60–2
Westmacott, Charles, *The English Spy*, 65–7
Westminster Review, The, 9
Whale, John, 104
Whigs, 8, 143, *144*, 182–3, 211n2
Wilson, James, 52n38
Winter's Wreath, The, 141n38
Wodrow, Robert, *History of the Sufferings of the Church of Scotland*, 78–9
Wolfson, Susan, 172
Wollstonecraft, Mary, 58, 145
wombs, 126–7, 129, 179–81
women, 4, 33, 57, 62, 96
  writers, 22, 148
  see also female characters
Wordsworth, William, 16, 101, 118, 120, 122, 130, 138n11, 141n37, 145, 157, 160–7
  'Lines Written a Few Miles above Tintern Abbey', 162, 164
  Recluse, 164
  'Resolution and Independence', 209
  'The Tables Turned', 161–2
Wu, Duncan, 115n23